Hidden in the Enemy's Sight

Resisting the Third Reich from Within

To Gerrie Morriss

[signature]

August 20 2009

Hidden in the Enemy's Sight

Resisting the Third Reich from Within

Jan Kamieński

Foreword by the Right Honourable Edward R. Schreyer

DUNDURN PRESS

TORONTO

Editor: Michael Carroll
Copy-editor: Shannon Whibbs
Map: Eric Leinberger
Design: Erin Mallory
Printer: Webcom

Library and Archives Canada Cataloguing in Publication

Kamieński, Jan, 1923–
    Hidden in the enemy's sight : resisting the Third Reich from within / by
Jan Kamieński.

ISBN 978-1-55002-854-6

    1. World War, 1939–1945--Underground movements--Poland--Biography.
I. Title.

D802.P6K266 2008   940.53'37092   C2008-903973-4

1 2 3 4 5   12 11 10 09 08

We acknowledge the support of the **Canada Council for the Arts** and the **Ontario Arts Council** for our publishing program. We also acknowledge the financial support of the **Government of Canada** through the **Book Publishing Industry Development Program** and **The Association for the Export of Canadian Books**, and the **Government of Ontario** through the **Ontario Book Publishers Tax Credit** program, and the **Ontario Media Development Corporation**.

Care has been taken to trace the ownership of copyright material used in this book. The author and the publisher welcome any information enabling them to rectify any references or credits in subsequent editions.

J. Kirk Howard, President

Printed and bound in Canada.
www.dundurn.com

Dundurn Press	Gazelle Book Services Limited	Dundurn Press
3 Church Street, Suite 500	White Cross Mills	2250 Military Road
Toronto, Ontario, Canada	High Town, Lancaster, England	Tonawanda, NY
M5E 1M2	LA1 4XS	U.S.A. 14150

To the memory of my parents,
Lucjan Dołęga-Kamieński and Linda Kamieńska (née Harder)

CONTENTS

FOREWORD

All wars are ugly. All wars are bloody. Almost all wars are unnecessary. Yet we remember them in many ways by raising monuments in memory of the millions who fell in battle for a plethora of causes: a ruler's vanity, a desire to play Caesar or Napoleon, political ideology, and an always-present and burning desire for everlasting fame. And so war writing deals with the history of armed conflicts, their causes, courses, and results. Sometimes these works are fictional, at other times strongly realistic as witnessed "in situ," yet they all reveal war's impact in the pathos, drama, and misery that always follows the initial heroic posturing and jingoistic declarations. These are creations of compelling realism. Jan Kamieński's book is different. Both clear-headed and penetrating in its summary of futile diplomacy and treaties, it leads the reader toward the fatal year of 1939 and the German invasion of Poland. It is convincingly descriptive of the conditions endured by the Polish civilian population in those September 1939 weeks of despair as a young teenage refugee flees eastward from his Poznań home, away from the German Blitzkrieg's deadly ravages. He also uses compelling word imagery to describe the three days and nights of stark horror in January/February 1945 — this time in reverse, reverse of bloody 1939 — as it was now the German refugees fleeing westward from the approaching Red Army.

Between these two epic disasters are six years of a bloodbath in which 40 million or more of humanity perished — some under military firepower and targeted bombing (Dresden, to mention but one). Others died as innocent victims of bestiality and torture. For most, it was at best a miserable existence under the Nazi state's and Communist Party's control. These conditions, too, are well described in this book.

Apart from Jan Kamieński's ability to formulate human feelings and articulate events at the political-state level, there is another major element in this book. It is the surprise, the intrigue, the "stranger than fiction" reality of his having served for much of that period as a very young "Resistance agent" — in enemy territory. Being under constant threat of detection and arrest must surely have been terrifying for an eighteen-year-old. But the author hardly dwells on this. Living in Dresden, he was witness to the three consecutive air raids on that city, carried out by the Royal Air Force and the United States Army Air Forces on February 13 and 14, 1945. He describes the horror of that time in intensely moving, evocative words of an eyewitness present at that catastrophe. He approaches his subject from several angles, freely applying a writer's skill and an even-handed philosophical detachment to write with such insight.

This book is a treat as a memoir, a synopsis of the European diplomacy's madness, German militarism, and Nazi politics in that era sixty-five years ago. With this book of memories you can begin to understand those times — and sympathize with those caught up in the vortex of misery. The author paints a written portrayal of a remarkable journey.

The Right Honourable Edward R. Schreyer
P.C., C.C., C.M.M., O.M., C.D.

ACKNOWLEDGEMENTS

Thanks to my daughter, Barbara Kamieńska, who was an indefatigable assistant in helping me get the whole story down and putting it in sequence. My thanks also to my wife, Nadya Kamieńska, for tirelessly transposing rough texts into readability. And last but not least, thanks to my granddaughter, Alyssa Thiel, for diligently putting in order and scanning photos and other visual material.

Part 1

IN POLAND

0 100 miles

0 100 kilometres

PRE-WAR STATE BOUNDARY
OF POLAND 1939

Baltic Sea

LITHUANIA

Königsberg
(Kaliningrad)

Danzig
(Gdańsk)

EAST PRUSSIA

SOVIET
UNION

Neman

Berlin

Oder

ANNEXED BY
GERMAN REICH

Vistula

Poznań

Września

Kutno

Koło

Łódź

Warsaw

Bug

SOVIET
OCCUPIED

Elbe

Kamenz

Görlitz

Warta

Lublin

Dresden

Bad Schandau

Breslau
(Wrocław)

GENERAL
GOUVERNEMENT

GERMANY

Kraków

Jarosław

Auschwitz (Oświęcim)

Dniester

Danube

SLOVAKIA

HUNGARY

ROMANIA

1 BEGINNINGS

The past is but the beginning of a beginning, says H.G. Wells, and now that I'm well into the fourscore of my life's years, I'm looking at my past to try to figure out where that beginning actually began. Not in childhood, I'm sure, since those are mostly years of being prepared — and preparing ourselves — for the future. Sometimes that transition period goes by smoothly. At other times, we're thrust into adulthood by sudden, extraneous events that we never expected to happen.

My own childhood was, overall, pleasant. In itself, this was unremarkable, considering that I was an only child and therefore treated with great gentleness. To be frank, I was quite spoiled. I'll skip those years, even though that period and the surroundings in which I grew up shaped my easy and uncomplicated transition into adolescence.

It was an environment in which music was of primary importance. My father was a composer, a renowned researcher and collector of Polish musical folklore, a professor of musicology and, later, also dean of the Faculty of Philosophy (Humanities) at the University of Poznań. My mother was a concert singer and voice teacher. Of course, they took an active part in the city's cultural life, and our home naturally attracted not only other musicians, but also writers, artists, and even politicians, who attended the literary and musical evenings which my mother regularly hosted on Thursdays. This was the milieu in which I grew up, one that in my formative years shaped my attitude toward the world around me.

We travelled regularly. Even now, in my old age, I still carry with me memories of playing on the Adriatic beach of Dubrovnik as a six-year-old, visiting the Schönbrunn Palace near Vienna at the age of eight, and being frightened by the ghostly interior of enormous castle ruins high up on a plateau above the Danube, dominating the city of Bratislava.

Around the age of ten, I already knew that my life would follow a certain course laid out partly by custom and partly by family tradition. After finishing high school, I would pass a final, rigorous exam called *matura*, register in the Cadet School and, from there, progress to an Officers' School, where I could decide which branch of service I preferred (or so we were told). Having attained a junior rank of sub-lieutenant, I would be released into civilian life but, of course, remain in the reserves. This status would allow me to enter university and study my favourite subject, history, with an eventual academic career in mind. Clearly, none of the above came to pass.

I was still in my mid-teens when a classmate of mine, a boy named Henryk Komorowski (or was it Komierowski?), told me about a politically motivated youth group he belonged to and asked if I'd like to come to one of the group's meetings — not really to join — but just to listen to the discussion. By then I had already become interested in politics by listening to the radio and reading newspapers. I'd followed the Italian invasion into Ethiopia, as well as the murderous Spanish Civil War, and had become acutely aware of the danger threatening Poland from Hitler's Germany. My country's domestic politics also held a certain allure for me. Sometime in May 1938, Henryk and I walked into a small room in the basement of a large residential building on Łąkowa Street, located in Poznań's lower middle-class district. The room was crowded, even though there were only six of us. Our host was a young man named Zenek, a student at the Polytechnic, who was also the group's leader and main speaker. I was introduced, shook hands with everyone, and then sat down in a corner to listen to the proceedings.

It was all quite simple. Zenek spoke of domestic politics and how they affected Poland's stand in international affairs. Obviously, I cannot quote verbatim everything the small group was told, but I remember clearly the general tenor of his comments and speculative musings. After Germany's march into Austria earlier that year, he told us, the Sudeten Germans were becoming restive and demanding separation from Czechoslovakia in order to join Hitler's Germany. This could lead to further territorial demands by Hitler and possibly end in armed conflict, which would also affect Poland, one way or another. He did not talk about party doctrine, though it eventually became clear to me that if he had spoken of it, it would have been slightly right wing and heavily Catholic in its leanings. Later meetings that I attended, by then a member of the group, revealed to me that the political movement we were being drawn into was the *Stronnictwo Narodowe* (National Party), opposed to the existing Warsaw regime and firmly anti-German.

But all that theorizing and politicking soon began to bore me. I wanted something more exciting than mere talk. The excitement came soon enough, toward the end of September and at the beginning of October

With my parents in May 1929. The picture was taken by my Uncle Czesław, who was visiting Poznań from Canada.

1938, when Zenek's prediction about the Sudetenland's annexation by Germany came true. Poland got her slice of the pie by reoccupying the ethnically Polish Cieszyn Silesia territories, which Czechoslovakia had grabbed from her while Poland was desperately fighting the Soviet invasion of 1920. Now, even before Polish troops had recovered that territory, an information office was opened in downtown Poznań, presumably to boost public opinion of the government's decision to forestall a German military move into the area in question. Inspired by patriotic enthusiasm, a classmate and I, both only fifteen years old, attempted to join the armed forces and take part in the military operation — but we were most politely told to be good boys and go back to school.

Much of Europe at this time was bound together by a web of military agreements and guarantees of mutual help. A French-Polish alliance dated back to 1921. Poland and Romania had signed similar agreements in 1921 and 1926, and a British guarantee of military assistance to Poland was ratified on March 31, 1939. Non-aggression pacts between Poland and its immediate neighbours, the Soviet Union and Germany, had been signed in 1932 and 1934 respectively, but when Hitler declared the latter "null and void" in March 1939, most of Poland's 36 million citizens naively believed in the power and ability of its other alliances to defeat the Wehrmacht. We were soon to find out that these alliances were no more than pieces of paper, but in the spring of 1939 we still marched proudly, singing patriotic songs and waving our red-and-white flag to cheer our allies' embassies and consulates. Our spirit and eagerness to fight for our country was strong and unswerving. Young and impatient, we hardly paid attention to news that a current French slogan, *"Mourir pour Dantzig? Jamais!"* ("Die for Danzig? Never!") was making the rounds on the streets of Paris and throughout France. Hitler's abrogation of the Polish-German non-aggression pact intensified the already-existing tensions between the two countries, and now Germany began to make territorial demands on its neighbour. Quite naturally, the Polish government rejected them, and our armed forces were put on alert. A beautiful but uneasy summer followed, and Zenek disappeared from view. I assumed (correctly, as it turned out) that, as a reservist, he'd been called back to serve in his unit.

I spent two weeks of my summer holidays in Turew (which I called Turwia), an estate where I had enjoyed many happy summers. It belonged to a very distant relative of our family by marriage, Mme. Thecla Chłapowska, whom I called "Aunt Uja," and consisted of a manor, surrounded by a huge park, and 37,000 *morg* (ca. 50,000 acres) of beautiful and fertile land. After returning to Poznań, I travelled with my parents to Borsk, a small summer resort situated between the shore of the large Lake Wdzydze and a magnificent pine forest and located in the so-called Polish Corridor, an area that separated Germany from Eastern Prussia. The resort, with its half-dozen small cottages and a larger building containing a common dining room and the owner's quarters, belonged to Kazimierz Jasnoch, a well-known portrait artist whose wife, Halszka, was a singer and one of my mother's voice students.

By mid-August, Nazi Germany and the Soviet Union were negotiating a non-aggression pact, and rumours of an impending war grew day by day. At the dinner table, the mood among the few holidayers present swung between pensiveness and devil-may-care fearlessness, even though odd things were going on. Small, obviously civilian aircraft kept flying regularly and frequently from west to east and back again, sometimes also circling over us. Some resort guests said, "Oh, yes, they're our Polish planes patrolling the sky!" To which Mr. Jasnoch, who knew about such things from his military past, which included an uprising against the Germans in 1918, would say, "Don't fool yourselves, those are German reconnaissance planes spying and taking pictures of roads and bridges." They'd say, "Oh, that's nonsense," and the common feeling was that should the war break out, we'd give the Germans a thrashing they'd never forget. Mobilization was in full swing.

The German-Soviet Non-Aggression Pact was signed on August 23, creating general unease, but the radio and printed press were cautiously optimistic. My mother kept saying, "We don't use peas for bullets!" It was that "we" that revealed to me the kind of allegiance that she, German-born and -educated, felt to our country, which she now saw as her own. I don't think my father was quite that optimistic about a war's outcome.

We returned to Poznań toward the end of August. The tension had become insufferable. The LOPP (League for Protection Against Air and Poison Gas Warfare) was handing out gas masks. Military barracks stood empty, and troops had left for their positions. Ominously, on August 29, it was announced that all schools, which traditionally opened their doors around September 3, would remain closed for an indefinite period of time. Along with this announcement, the morning dailies printed firm assurances of our country's capability to withstand any enemies. In my memory, I can still hear the government's enthusiatic slogan — *SILNI! ZWARCI! GOTOWI!* — a firm statement about our being STRONG! UNITED! READY! After our defeat, this slogan became a typically Polish sardonic judgment of the tragic past. So we didn't go to school and for a day or so played soccer, blissfully ignorant of the tomorrow.

2 BOMBING AND EVACUATION

The war broke out on September 1. I was alone in the apartment, sitting near a window of the music room and reading that morning's edition of the *Kurier Poznański*, which carried a hastily-put-together report that the Huns had crossed the Polish border at five o'clock that morning as well as a terse message by the President of the Republic, calling on all citizens to stand firm in their country's defence.

I had barely finished reading when, at precisely noon, I heard what sounded like a fast-approaching aircraft formation. Although I couldn't see anything through the window, I felt the air inside the room vibrating. The sound became a roar, and suddenly, there was a long, high-pitched whistle followed by a thunderous, split-second explosion that shook everything around me. I found myself in the centre of complete pandemonium. Paintings were falling off the walls, the Biedermeier sofa and its complement of chairs bounced around as if dancing some crazy gavotte, the Bechstein grand piano slid past me on two of its casters — the third one having collapsed — and the chandelier, wrenched from its ceiling anchor, crashed in a cloud of dust onto a small, elegant table with its inlaid chessboard, its cut glass pieces tinkling in mad disharmony as they rained onto the impossibly buckled carpet. Shaken by the tremors, the support propping up the lid of the grand piano slipped, and the lid slammed down, making all the strings cry out like a great, tragic choir. As if in accompaniment, a resounding crash, followed by clanging and clinking, came from the dining room.

Our housekeeper, Zosia, who had been out shopping, was the first to return home. Confronted by the unbelievable damage, she let out a wail of despair. But, having been raised on a farm, and being therefore a sane and practical person, she quickly overcame her shock and headed for a closet to get a broom. Somewhat later, my mother came home, already expecting a heartbreak, since she'd seen the front door leaning crazily off its hinges. She stood mute and motionless in the dining room, crying silently as she gazed at the toppled-over credenza, out of which her beloved Sèvres, Meissen, Rosenthal, and Limoges china had spilled. Shards lay strewn all over the floor, on chairs and the dining table, which, miraculously, was still standing. Amazingly, the pendulum of the old wall clock was still swinging as usual.

As I saw the tears flowing down her face, I felt utterly helpless. Zosia, usually so garrulous, was now silent, too. And I, having never before seen

My mother, Linda Kamieńska (née Harder), at her desk in 1935. This is where I was sitting, reading the newspaper, when the first bombs fell.

my mother cry, and in the helplessness and bewilderment of my sixteen years, did the only thing I knew I could do: I went up to her and kissed her hand. She put her arms around me and held me to herself, as if shielding me from something that neither of us knew or recognized. Had we been able to see into the future, we would have realized that this day was a momentous turning point marking the irrevocable end of a quiet life and ushering in years of unimaginable horrors.

But, at that moment, in my youthful inability to cope with my mother's emotional state as she grieved at the loss of the things she so deeply cherished, I did not realize that I should stay and somehow support her. As gently as I could, I detached myself from her embrace. Suddenly, as if awakening from a torpor, she raised a fist toward the ceiling and cried out in Polish, "*Zbrodniarze! Mordercy!*" ("Criminals! Murderers!") Later, together with Zosia, she went about cleaning up the damage — in silent fury.

Meanwhile, I stood around helplessly, before following a childish notion to have a look at the results of the cataclysm. I walked carefully down the partly cracked back stairs and found a bomb crater practically in the centre of the courtyard. It was perhaps a metre and a half deep, and about the same at entry point. Compared with bomb craters I was fated to see in the future (and once even fall into), this was a mere hole in the ground. But the bomb had apparently hit at such an angle that the pressure of the blast was directed at the wall of our building, causing a deep crack that extended upward to the third floor, one below ours. The sand and soil sent up by the explosion went through the blown-out windows into kitchens, pantries, and all other rooms facing the courtyard. There were no casualties in our building.

Amazingly, the central phone exchange was still functioning. My father, obviously shaken, phoned us from the university in the middle of a seminar and was told by my mother, in a voice broken by sobs, about the past hour's disaster. He assured her that he would get home by whatever means possible, maybe by streetcar, some of which, amazingly, appeared to be still in service. I recall running to the tram stop two blocks away from our apartment and waiting for him. As he stepped off the streetcar, I saw that he was holding a handkerchief to his face, apparently fearing poison gas. I was able to calm his misgivings, and on our way home I told him about the bomb that had dropped into our courtyard and of the damage it had done to the building and the apartments, among them ours. He was enraged when he saw the results of the bombing raid, but managed nonetheless to calm my mother's despair and even Zosia's silent anger. I recall hearing the wail of an ambulance along our street. About two hours after the first raid, there was a second one, with indiscriminate bombing of residential districts. No industrial areas were hit, so this was clearly intended simply to strike the population. On this day and in the weeks to follow, similar attacks wrought appalling destruction on cities and towns throughout Poland.

Later, in a small family conclave, and with Zosia's participation, my father told us that for quite a while he'd been privy to a plan under which Poznań University's teaching staff and administration, as well as its archives and other valuable possessions, would be evacuated and relocated in the event of war — which they hoped would be brief. The destination was Jarosław, a town about six hundred kilometres to the southeast. Departure was set for September 3, which allowed a whole day and two nights to assemble the rolling stock and get it ready for the exodus. The boarding of the train was set for late September 2. Zosia stubbornly refused to leave, saying that she preferred to stay put in the damaged apartment rather than face an uncertain future away from what she considered home.

My mother, still in a state of shock at the disastrous turn in our lives, and now beset by panic, suggested we spend the coming night in the safety of the massive stone building in which several university departments were located, among them my father's Institute of Musicology. He fully agreed with her, but Zosia balked once again, preferring to stay in the apartment, regardless of its partly demolished condition. But she helped us to pack some necessities — and inevitable unnecessities — along with valuables into two well-sized travelling trunks. She even somehow managed to flag down a passing car carrying no passengers and promised the driver good money to take us to our temporary refuge. I remember my father handing the man a fistful of banknotes before we, eyes filled with tears, bade our farewells to an equally tearful Zosia. As we left, she made the sign of the cross over us.

It was a short drive from our home to the Collegium Maius. Poznań University's Institute of Musicology was located in an enormous, oppressive-looking, Romanesque-style castle erected between the years 1905 and 1908 and dedicated amidst much pomp in 1910. It was intended to provide suitable accommodation for the Kaiser of Germany and King of Prussia should he visit Poznań and western Poland, which had been under Prussian occupation since 1795. Built with thousands of huge granite stones, six stories high, and with a colossal tower dominating the city's silhouette, it stands to this day on many acres of ground. After the 1918 collapse of the German-Prussian monarchy and the return of Poland's sovereignty, the newly founded Poznań University had taken possession of this graceless monument of Teutonic might and turned it into a seat of learning. My father's institute, with its lecture halls, was on the second floor, but its extensive library was in the cavernous basement, together with the libraries of other departments. In addition to shelves and reading tables and as behooved the quiet gentility of this scientific milieu, the library was furnished with comfortable club chairs and a large sofa.

None of us slept well. With worries to be voiced and plans to be made for the journey, our night's rest could only be described as fitful. In the morning, the problem of getting ourselves and our luggage to the Poznań West railway station was solved by sheer luck. Professor Zakrzewski, whose Department of Numismatics was located next to my father's institute, was fortunate in capturing one of the few taxis carrying a "free" sign on its roof and invited us to share it with him. I remember the three of us having breakfast in the station's still-functional restaurant, then spending a lot of time getting space in the train reserved for us, talking to many other professors and their families, and later lunching with them. We learned that most of the trains consisted of boxcars with blanket-covered straw on the floor. A great number of Polish Railways passenger coaches were either stuck in foreign countries such as France, Spain, or Switzerland, or had been taken by the Germans as "enemy property" while crossing German territory on their way back to Poland.

We had an early supper and bought plenty of food supplies in the restaurant before moving on to the boxcar to which we'd been assigned.

All I recall of boarding the train is losing sight of my parents in the melee of people shoving, pushing, prodding, and crying out the names of errant family members. Fortunately, I'd remembered the number of our wagon, where I found my mother already inside and my father pushing one of our two trunks in through the big, open door. I scrambled into the wagon to help him. In all this chaos, a rumour about gunfire being heard in the city began to spread among those waiting on the platform. No one seemed to know the source of this hearsay, but it caused a touch of panic among the evacuees, who assumed (wrongly, as it turned out) that the Wehrmacht had already entered Poznań. However, these fears dissipated the moment the signal sounded to board the train.

Trying to sleep on the straw-covered wagon floor wasn't any easier than attempting it in the basement library of the university's immense edifice. There were other evacuees in our wagon, altogether probably a dozen people, all adults of various ages, somehow or other attached to the university. Oddly enough, there were also two or three cavalry soldiers heading east toward besieged Warsaw, toting with them a small terrier named "Adolf." To this day I wonder how all of us were able to find room to lie down or sit on the wagon's floor, or how we overcame the lack of hygienic facilities, but somehow we did.

It was still dark when we left Poznań the next morning. No one seemed to have gotten any sleep. We all spoke in low voices, as if not wishing to be heard. But no matter. The train crept slowly ahead, and it was daybreak when we neared a tiny village called Siedlec. Suddenly, the reality of war came at me for the second time. While it had scared and bewildered me to hear an exploding bomb and to see our furniture do a dance on a shaking floor, it was sheer terror that now came upon me as I heard the sound of aircraft closing in lightning-fast … and then the wild staccato of what sounded like hail on the wagon's strong corrugated-steel roof, but were in fact bullets from a plane's machine gun, strafing the length of the train and causing someone in our wagon to cry out, "Jesus!" But it wasn't Jesus up there. It was one of Hitler's executioners having a grand time! In the wagon, women were crying. My mother was cowering in a corner with my father holding her fast, and I sat on the floor, numb with fright and by now thoroughly disabused of my boyish notion that war was a splendid adventure. Luckily for us, the low-calibre bullets could not penetrate the wagon's sturdy roof. The strafing attack was over in seconds and the train never even stopped.

We had, of course, no source of news, only the immediate memory of the strafing attack, but we kept our spirits up with the certainty that the invincible French army and British navy would quickly do away with the German Nazi regime. What we were living through, we thought, was just a nasty episode, one we'd soon be able to forget.

Yet, this had been only a baptism by fire. The nightmarish journey continued with trains like ours alternately moving and stopping under almost constant attack by the Luftwaffe's low-flying fighter planes, while Stuka dive bombers demolished railway tracks and stations. Soon the calibre of strafing bullets became heavier and began to pierce the wagons' roofs. In our wagon a young woman was killed and a man injured — the first time I'd seen injury and death. It happened so fast that no one else seemed to know what had occurred. It took my mother a few seconds to realize the horror of it. When she did, it was only to curl against my father and stare, her mouth open in a silent scream.

Later on, when the train had stopped to take on water for the locomotive, we once again heard the sound of aircraft. Some of the more agile passengers jumped out through the big sliding door and dove under the wagon, expecting yet another strafing attack. It was just as well that I stayed with my parents. This attack did not hit the train, but concentrated on the road running parallel to the rail track, probably between forty and sixty metres away. Everyone's terrified attention was centred on the massacre outside. The Luftwaffe was not selective in their choice of targets — the road was crowded with refugees fleeing the German juggernaut. Dead horses and cattle and, yes, human bodies too, lay on and near that road. We passed burning farmhouses, barns, and freshly harvested, stooked grain. There were people trundling with carts loaded with bedding, and carrying children, their aged mothers, and invalids unable to walk. Black smoke and the smell of death pervaded everything.

The man injured in the previous strafing had died. Under existing circumstances, his body and that of the young woman couldn't be buried, so, for the time being, they were placed in one corner of the boxcar. Later, when the train stopped near a small village to take on water, they were left for the locals to bury. The hot September days made this measure exceptionally urgent. The first two weeks of the war were sunny and dry, perfect weather for the invaders to carry out their work of death and destruction. Inside the boxcar, the heat was stifling, even at night, and the large door had to be kept open at all times. This not only let in some fresh air, but gave us a view of the countless fires that seeemed to cover the entire countryside as far as the horizon, and whose smoke blotted out a starry sky.

Ours was not the only train evacuating the Poznań University personnel. Another train, put together from rolling stock as old and timeworn as ours, preceded or followed us if a parallel track was available. Both trains moved slowly, with interminable stops for reasons mostly unknown. But move they did, always by short crawls forward, then resting as if to come up for breath before wheezing ahead to the next halt. Unable to travel more than a few kilometres a day, we soon began to wonder when, if ever, we would arrive in Jarosław.

Near the town of Września, the train stopped because the main track had been bombed farther up along the line and was being urgently repaired. Some evacuees had left the train and stood around, stretching their legs and chatting. Only moments later, hearing the approach of fighter aircraft, they dove to safety under the wagons. There was no time for my parents and me to do so — we merely huddled together inside the wagon, which, luckily, wasn't

My father, Professor Lucjan Kamieński, in full professorial garb around 1930.

28

hit. The machine guns worked for less than a minute before the planes turned and flew away. But once the shooting was over and the Luftwaffe had disappeared from view, I and a couple of others went off to see what the Germans had done. My parents wanted me to stay, but my curiosity won out.

The Messerschmitts had done their work in a wide stretch between the refugee-packed road and the railway track. Among others, this area accommodated a field of September-ripened corn, and I decided to take a few stalks back to my parents. I walked into that thick, unharvested growth, but a few steps in, I saw that the stalks were crazily bent, broken down and spattered with some dark red stains. Then I saw a gaily-patterned piece of fabric covering part of a bare leg and, farther on, people lying down — women, men, children — all very quiet and motionless in grotesque poses, with those dark red stains on and around them. By now, no one had to tell me what all this meant. These people, clearly refugees, had sought shelter, assuming that the dense growth of the cornfield would shield them from the view of the enemy above.

I stumbled back to our wagon and told my parents about what I had seen. But once the story was told, I vomited and then got a case of jitters that lasted quite a long time. It was as if I'd survived a bad accident, followed by a few minutes of strange calm, and then by an overwhelming physical reaction. I still hesitate to think back to that day and that incident.

There seemed to be no end to my juvenile foolishness. A day after that ghastly cornfield experience, the train stopped again, this time to take on coal near the small town of Koło. The train stood in the shadow of a huge, obviously newly constructed grain silo, next to a fairly large expanse of grass richly dotted with masses of dandelions and all sorts of other wildflowers. To me, the journey seemed endless, and I decided to leave the train once again, this time to enjoy some solitude. As I left my parents, I promised to stay close enough to the train that I could instantly return when the whistle signalled the resumption of our journey. In a rucksack strapped to my back, I carried a few books and some apples we'd bought somewhere along the way. I was out of the silo's shade, and as I lay there enjoying the warmth, sunshine, and the buzzing of insects, the war seemed, for a while, to be no more than a hideous nightmare.

Unfortunately, the respite was all too short. It can't have been more than a minute later that the war again announced itself with the ever-so-familiar, quickly rising sound of an aircraft approaching from the south. There was no way for me to run; it was all happening lightning-quick. Face down and with the rucksack still on my back, I intuitively covered my head with my arms and almost kissed the ground just a split second before the plane released a bomb that exploded in the soft soil at the base of the silo. Clumps of earth and turf dropped on and around me, and I felt the rucksack pushing me violently to the side. By the whine of its engine, I knew that the plane was accelerating and peeling off to fly away — by now, I'd already heard and seen this a few times. I lay motionless until the sound abated and only then opened my eyes. Getting to my feet, I looked

over toward the train, probably around fifty yards yards away, and saw the evacuees standing there, and my parents in the open door of our wagon. My mother's face was marked with an expression of utter panic, and the sight of her in such distress made me feel so guilty that I hastily gathered a few wildflowers to take to her with my apologies for leaving her and my father. She forgave me, but my father gave me a well-deserved talking-to about my childish stupidity. Never had he been that angry with me, and

At age six or seven I pose proudly in a military-style uniform that my mother had sewn for me.

his lecture was so strong that I said, "Tato, I swear that I'll never be so foolish again." How could I know that the next day my oath would lose its meaning?

It was September 9, the seventh day of our journey. The train ahead of ours was to stay overnight on a siding, and we were to follow its example. By now it was known that the Luftwaffe did not operate during the night, and we were assured of getting a quiet night's sleep. It was odd, though somehow not surprising that, given the tight quarters of the boxcar, there was virtually no personal accord between the passengers. Not even the natural closeness of the academic community seemed to foster any social contact between us evacuees. To be sure, words were exchanged when absolutely necessary, and I'm certain we all shared fears about the danger we were in. But these emotions seemed to be kept inside, as if venting them was something to be ashamed of. Most of the passengers in our wagon were single, with only one couple and, of course, the three of us constituting a family. But even we kept to ourselves most of the time.

3 AN ABRUPT HALT

Next morning, the early sunrise woke everyone up, as did the train's usual sluggish forward motion. After a quick morning bite, my father and I talked about the previous day's excitement and the measure of my luck in having the rucksack strapped to my back. The exploding bomb had sent not only clumps of soil and turf my way, but also a jagged piece of concrete from the foundation of the silo, with a small bit of rusty steel stuck in it. The rucksack — torn open by this missile, which made a mess of the apples and also mangled a couple of my books — had saved my life.

A little later the train preceding us began to move ahead, and ours eventually followed. But after covering more than thirty or so kilometres, the train ahead of us came to a stop and, of course, so did we. It appeared that some vital part of the lead train's ancient locomotive had given up the ghost, and a substitute had to be machined and installed before the evacuation trains could move again. We stood a mere couple of kilometres from the town of Kutno, where, no doubt, the aged part could be repaired. How long would that take? No one knew, but we were told it could be a whole day. The evacuation of the Poznań University's personnel was halted, with everyone hoping the stop would only be temporary. But, as it happened, we and many other passengers were getting short of food supplies. A prolonged stay close to the town would allow us to get the victuals we needed. My father and I left my mother in charge of our belongings, and two of the three soldiers travelling with us stayed behind to keep an eye on everyone's possessions. We walked leisurely, for the first time since we had left Poznań the week before. The one soldier walking with us said that he was going to buy some vodka for himself and his comrades. I also remember him remarking on the strange, unwarlike quiet, and the noticable absence of the Luftwaffe and of any, even distant, artillery fire. "Maybe it's Sunday, or the war's over …?" he joked as we neared the town's market square. He was right about it being a Sunday. There was a large crowd of people in the square, some dressed festively, and I recall my father wondering whether stores would be open on such a holy day. It was at that point that all the calm and sanctity of the day ceased. I remember only the deafening howl of aircraft motors, brief machine-gun fire, and, simultaneously, the flash of an explosion, hot and blinding for a millionth of a second, and then — nothing. No progressive memory, no images, but later tiny flickers of consciousness as my father dragged me into a wide doorway and later put me on the back of a small military vehicle that took me to a hospital. I was placed on the floor, on a layer of straw between two beds.

It seemed to me that my hands felt the straw, but I was still too much in shock for my mind to function properly. I vaguely recall being asked if I wanted to confess and replying with a "no." I don't remember actually seeing a chaplain or the doctors, who surely must have been looking me over and stemming the flow of blood, which (I was told afterwards) was worrisome. At some point I was given liquid food by a nurse. Still in a state of confusion, I said that I could feed myself. No, I couldn't, the nurse insisted — I was unable to see. I drifted off again, and when I surfaced two days later, I saw milky, foggy shapes moving before my open eyes. I suppose I got restless, because a nurse bent over me and asked what the matter was. When I told her about my eyesight, she called a doctor, who told me that the explosion had probably blinded me only temporarily and that there was a good chance of recovery. In this, he was right, because my sight gradually came back, although it was never quite as perfect as it had been before. I also learned that my heavy loss of blood was the result of a shrapnel wound I had received during the Luftwaffe attack. But even though the bleeding had been stemmed, it was impossible under the existing circumstances to remove the bomb fragment lodged high up in my inner left thigh, practically in the groin. The hospital was overcrowded with civilian casualties, all of whom urgently needed medical attention, whereas I could presumably have the shrapnel removed at some later date. I had been unbelievably lucky; the sister of Felicja Niemczewska, my father's assistant, had been standing only six or seven feet away from me at the time of the attack and was killed outright.

Meanwhile, heavy fighting began in the Kutno region, a battle in which both sides achieved some successes but also suffered enormous losses. German artillery used heavy guns to fire at Kutno, including the hospital, even though there was a huge red cross displayed on its roof. The hospital received hits that resulted in a dozen or so dead and a great many wounded. Miraculously, the ward I was on was not affected.

On an outing with my father and some of his students in July 1939. Less than two months later, Teresa Niemczewska, the young woman wearing the kerchief (second from right), was killed during the attack in Kutno, only a few feet from where I was standing.

The furious battle, involving several divisions on each side, went on for two or three days, and the hospital became filled far beyond its modest capacity. Wounded soldiers, both Polish and German, were brought in from the field of battle and laid down in the hallways. The Germans, wounded and left behind when their units were forced to retreat, had become prisoners of war. They looked frightened, but they were treated with as much care as their Polish enemies.

On the drizzly morning of September 16, a group of German officers conducted an inspection of the hospital and ordered all the Polish patients, even the most gravely injured and those practically dying, to be moved out in order to make room for German casualties still to come. This was to be accomplished within three or four hours — and it was done, despite the obviously immense difficulties. There were probably anywhere between 100 and 150 Polish wounded, among them also a lot of civilians like me, waiting outside the hospital and covered with whatever could be found to protect them from the cold rain. I remember half lying on the building's stairs, wearing a heavy soldier's coat that had some bullet holes and blood spatters on its left sleeve. I was sure it had come off a dead man.

It cannot have been easy to find new accommodations on such short notice, but nonetheless, we soon found ourselves placed in three different locations that had been quickly turned into temporary hospitals. Some of us were taken to a church, where the pews had been shoved aside to make room for straw on which to lay the wounded. Another group was directed to an abandoned brewery, and I was fortunate enough to end up in a former, and now empty, orphanage. I was put into a room together with a handful of young officers and three or four enlisted men. Most of us lay on real beds — under the circumstances an unheard-of luxury — but were treated no differently than those who lay on straw or other improvised arrangements.

My bed was between that of cavalry Lieutenant Madaliński, who had received a shot in the jaw and had his knee crushed when his horse was shot under him and fell on its side, and that of infantry Captain Lutostański, whose arm had been ripped off at the elbow by an exploding

German anti-tank grenade. Our room was located next to an improvised operating theatre, and we were frequently treated to the sight of wounded men being wheeled in, still in one piece, and later being wheeled out minus a limb, which was later carried out in a shallow wash basin by a male nurse or attendant.

Two doctors took care of the patients. One, whose name I don't recall, appeared to be in charge of less urgent cases, but always assisted in surgery performed by the other, Dr. Pawłowski. It is the latter whom I will never forget as a shining example of physical and mental endurance and devotion to his calling. On one occasion, he operated for over thirty long hours, taking only five-minute breaks for strong coffee and equally strong Egyptian cigarettes. He saved many lives when other physicians might have given up.

One of the enlisted men in our room was a young Jewish soldier, delivered to the hospital with a large piece of shrapnel lodged in his stomach. He had been operated on, but it was clear that his case was hopeless. He lay on his cot, moaning ever so softly, maybe aware that he was about to die. A day or so later, the chaplain who sporadically appeared in that makeshift hospital to look after the patients' spiritual needs, paid us a visit. He was a youngish, rotund, and pink-faced man with the gruff manners one occasionally encounters among small-town clergy. Noticing the quietly suffering young soldier, he became interested. Told that the man was at death's door and that his moans might in fact be prayers, the priest nodded, draped his stole over his shoulders, and walked over to where the man lay on a cot. We watched as he bent over the dying soldier and began telling him that he was going to be baptized in the Christian faith. Moments later, we heard the dying man give out a deep groan, and say "*Nie ... nie ...*" ("No ... no ..."), repeating the word several times. Unmoved, the priest was now whispering something into the soldier's ear, but a sub-lieutenant named Podoski shouted: "Stop that, man! He doesn't want you to baptize him!" and someone else cried out, "Can't you see he's saying 'no' with his dying breath?" or words to that effect. Protests came now from all sides, culminating in a collective demand for the priest to go away and not show his face again. This was *vox populi* at its most forceful.

The chaplain shrugged and left the room. The Jewish soldier died shortly afterwards, in his own faith.

Going back to the day I was wounded, I must complete the picture: I was only vaguely aware of events between the moment of the bomb explosion and my gradual coming-to in the hospital. The principal figure in this picture was, of course, my father. It was he who had dragged me from the square into the doorway and then used his respected position as a university professor and faculty dean to persuade a junior officer to drive both of us to the town's hospital. As my father also told me, it helped that the officer belonged to a Poznań-based infantry regiment and knew my father's name quite well. Once I was safely delivered to the hospital, my father waited until the doctors had stabilized my condition and only then returned to the train to, in his gentlest way, tell my mother what had happened. Evidently, in time, she managed to take it quite well, although she never really got over it, not even after I had fully recovered. In order to stay near me, my parents had to leave the train and find accommodations as quickly as possible. They rented a room in the vicarage of the village of Grochowo, a couple of kilometres away; the parish priest was something of a boor, but a music lover, and they were able to get along with him quite well. Throughout my stay in the hospital and later in the orphanage, my father visited me at least once a week, sometimes even twice, but the constant autumn rains that were beginning just then made the roads quite impassable for my mother, whose warm clothes and suitable footwear had to be left on the train along with all the other luggage. Tragically for my parents, the train had resumed its journey just as they were looking for a place to stay. I remember my mother only shrugging when we later talked about her clothes being worn by some unknown woman. But when her thoughts inevitably went back to the subject of our family silver and my father's manuscripts, she became very still.

News of the Soviet invasion of Poland's eastern territories on September 17 reached us around September 25. It was initially received in stunned silence followed by a gradual realization of the extent of our country's tragic defeat. That Poland, whose almost thousand-year history rested on its vaunted indomitability, should fall was unimaginable. Gradually, as the wounded soldiers and officers around me began to grasp the full import of this development, tearful oaths of revenge and blasphemous cries questioning God's idea of justice filled the air. Having grown up in a rather genteel family environment, I had never had occasion to experience such an outburst of hate-filled invective and helpless fury as now pervaded this makeshift hospital room.

"We've been made to believe in cavalry instead of tanks!" cried out sub-Lieutenant Podoski, himself an infantryman, and others joined in to lay the blame for our defeat on Poland's government and the obsolete armament policies of our military authorities. One young officer cadet stood in the middle of the room, venting loud accusations against the supreme chief of our armed forces, Marshal Śmigły-Rydz, whom I still remember as a tireless propagator of Poland's invincibility.

From the bed on my left, Lieutenant Madaliński spoke in a voice broken by sobs and muffled by the blood-soaked bandage covering his wounded jaw. "This is the Fourth Partition!" he cried, referring to three previous partitions of Poland in 1772, 1793, and 1795. Russia and Germany (then Prussia) had divided our hapless country between them— with Austria's participation in 1793 — and now Poland, which had been restored to nationhood only twenty-one years before, was once again to suffer the yoke of occupation.

On my right, one-armed Captain Lutostański tried to inject a note of optimism, however slight, into the discussion. "As long as the Germans don't hand us over to their Russian friends," he said, "we'll still have a chance." Such hope was, of course, totally unwarranted.

Gradually the hubbub abated and a heavy silence fell over the room. I turned to Lieutenant Madaliński. "And now what?" I asked. "Are we going home?" He sat on the side of his bed, leaning sideways, and shrugged lightly. "*Niewola*," (captivity) he said.

I lay quietly, numb with disbelief and overwhelmed by frustration. I was sixteen, a young man with an already manly voice and a marksmanship badge and — dear God! — unable to go into battle and do my part! I wished that I could have been one of those soldiers who had fought for Poland. Although wounded and still incapable of even shuffling without help, I decided then and there that I would somehow find a way to play a role in helping my country. The strong emotions I experienced that day stayed with me, and when I left that company of soldiers a few weeks later, I was bereft of my shiny ideas, but not without hope for the future.

4 THE GERMAN OCCUPATION

As soon as I was able to move, my parents and I returned to Poznań. Now that the German invasion was over and the tracks had been repaired, the return trip took only a few hours. But when we stepped out of the railway station, we found ourselves in an unknown world. The city had been renamed and was now "Posen." While the old, familiar horse-drawn cabs still stood waiting for customers in the centre of the big square, the facade of the station had been adorned with the Reich's flags and Party swastika banners, which fluttered in the breeze. People in strange ochre or black uniforms were milling around the station's entrance, saluting and addressing one another in sharp, barking tones.

We had no luggage beyond what my mother carried in her purse and my father had in his various pockets. I had a cane to help me hobble along. We hired a cab, and once we were settled inside it, my father asked the coachman how things were in town. All the old man would say was that he didn't want to talk about it. When my father gave him our address, Ulica Słowackiego 29, the man replied that the names of all streets had been Germanized and that our street, which had been named after a Polish poet and playwright, was now called Robert-Koch-Strasse, in honour of a German physician and bacteriologist.

We arrived home to find that the worst damage to our building had been more or less repaired. Inside the apartment, faithful Zosia had managed to clean up most of the destruction and had even been able, all by herself, to board up the windows blown out by the pressure of the explosion.

A day or two after our return to the city, my father and I went out to pay a brief visit to the centre of town. What we saw confirmed the impression we'd had from the cab. Martial music blared from loudspeakers installed in public places, and the swastika flag flew from virtually every building and lamppost. Banks, businesses and institutions now bore German signage only, since every Polish- or Jewish-owned business had been seized and put under German ownership. Almost every German, even the youngest, seemed to be wearing one of the many different Nazi uniforms. We returned home in silence — a discussion of what we'd seen was not necessary.

Warsaw had fallen on September 28, although fighting continued in some parts of the country until October 5. While we had suffered the brutalities of the German blitzkrieg ("lightning war"), our allies, France and England, had been engaged in a new form of warfare called "*Sitzkrieg*" ("sitting war"). Consequently, Poland as a political entity had once again ceased to exist.

Ulica Słowackiego 29 (29 Słowackiego Street), where we lived from 1935 on. The building belonged to the university and was occupied exclusively by professors and their families. Our apartment was on the fourth floor.

The Nazis declared its western territories (Pomerania, Poznań Province, and Upper Silesia) to be "Ancient German Lands" and annexed them outright, simply incorporating them into the Third Reich. The eastern part of the country fell to Stalin. The territory in between, consisting of about 150,000 square kilometres and including the cities of Warsaw, Kraków, and Lublin, became a German-administered protectorate known as the General Gouvernement, an area that during the entire war was the site of some of the most appalling human suffering the world has ever seen. While Jews from all over Europe were crowded into ghettos and then deported to the Germans' mass extermination camps, Poles expelled from the western provinces were "resettled" here to serve as a huge reservoir of expendable slave labour for the German master race. According to the Nazis' long-range plans, once the war was over and the need for slave labour no longer existed, all non-German elements here would be obliterated. The chief administrator of this arena of mass murder was Hans Frank, the merciless killer of Poles and Jews alike, who prided himself on his ruthlessness and efficiency in carrying out Hitler's orders. "Once we have won the war," he is quoted as saying, "then for all I care you can make mincemeat out of the Poles and the Ukrainians and anything else hanging around here." Frank was sentenced to death at Nuremberg and hanged on October 16, 1946, along with the likes of Ribbentrop, Kaltenbrunner, and other Nazi butchers.

The annexed region of Western Poland looked back on a long history of Teutonic brutality. Under German Chancellor Otto von Bismarck, these territories, with an indigenous Polish population of 3.5 million, had been subject to ruthless Germanization. In the Reichstag, Bismarck openly advocated the *Ausrottung* (extermination) of all things Polish. Schoolchildren were literally beaten bloody for praying in Polish. German authorities evicted Polish landowners or forced them to sell their possessions, and drove farmers off their land, which was then given to German settlers. An additional ruling allowed some Poles to remain on their properties temporarily, but forbade them to erect any new residential buildings. To get around this edict, a quick-minded peasant by the name of Michał Drzymała bought a circus caravan, drove it onto his land, and made it his family's home. This solution caught the mirthful attention of the international press, much to the fury of Prussian authorities, who saw their policies exposed for what they were.

A story from that time, apocryphal or not, exemplifies the hatred that Poles felt toward the German occupiers. Visiting a Polish home in the late 1880s, a German was astonished to see pictures of Bismarck and Kościuszko, a Polish national hero, hanging side by side on the wall. "How is it possible," the visitor asked, "that you have a picture of someone you so deeply hate right next to one of your national hero?" To this, the man answered, "Because the more I look at Bismarck, the more Polish I feel."

Now, under Hitler, the occupiers had moved swiftly to Germanize their annexed territories. Arthur Greiser, an ardent Nazi whose hatred of Poles and all that was Polish knew no bounds, was Hitler's natural choice as *Gauleiter* (governor and Nazi Party leader) of Western Poland, an area known to the Germans as the Wartheland. From his headquarters in Poznań, he eagerly put Hitler's policies into action, ruthlessly eradicating Polish culture and creating an all-encompassing reign of terror. After the war, he pleaded innocence, blaming Hitler and Himmler, both already dead, for the monstrosity of his own rule, but was sentenced to death, carried in a cage through the streets of Poznań, and publicly hanged on the slopes of the Citadel.

In Poznań, about 100,000 Polish families were evicted from their homes. Given only ten minutes to pack one small suitcase per person, they were sent to transit camps and, from there, transported east in cattle cars to the General Gouvernement. Their vacant homes were given, fully furnished and with all their former owners' belongings, to German officials and German immigrants from such places as Estonia, Latvia, and lands in southeastern Europe. Some Poles were allowed to stay, mostly to do menial work the Germans were loath to perform.

We were fortunate. Most of our apartment was requisitioned as Wehrmacht officers' quarters, with one room left for my parents and me and Zosia allotted her own little accommodation. The German officers who took up residence in the remaining rooms were, to my surprise, not at all unpleasant toward us, and their presence seemed to shield us from being kicked out of the apartment.

Their occupancy brought with it an additional advantage — a steady supply of firewood. Although the tiled woodstoves found in every apartment of our building had been restored to good working order after the September bombing, the scarcity of heating fuel as well as the exceptional severity of the winter of 1939–40 made keeping warm difficult. Burning furniture was obviously unthinkable, and it was our indomitable Zosia who got together with some of the enterprising local wizards of a budding black market and provided us and other residents with scrap lumber and even with the odd lump of coal. But since that only partially solved the problem, we kept warm by wearing several layers of clothing or simply staying in bed. Once, when we had completely run out of any kind of fuel, we resorted to burning, a few at a time, the fifty or so copies we possessed of a book my father had written concerning the Polish origins of Kashubian folk music in the German-claimed, so-called "Polish Corridor." Now with firewood compliments of the Wehrmacht, our lives — at least as far as heating was concerned — could return almost to normalcy.

Our home became subject to a number of brutal house searches, during which ancestral portraits were cut to ribbons and valuable books and documents in my father's library either destroyed or stolen. On one occasion, though, one of the officers billeted in our apartment delivered a severe dressing-down to a couple of Gestapo bullies who wanted to enter our home, for whatever purpose they had in mind. How strange — or maybe not strange at all — that I should remember that officer's name and rank. His name was Hühne, he held the rank of major, and the space that the military housing authority had assigned him happened to be the room in which my parents' musical and/or literary evenings had formerly been held. Most of the furniture had been pushed against the walls to make room for a chaise longue, which served as a makeshift bed. But it was our Bechstein grand piano that, after some repairs, still dominated the room with its massive presence.

Major Hühne was a great lover of music, and often asked my father to play for him, preferably works of the German Romantics. He loved the music of Liszt, Schumann, Schubert, and — yes! — even that of Chopin, which was forbidden by the Nazis. On one such occasion, the major reached into his briefcase and produced a bottle of liqueur, so that he and my father might drink to the memory of some great musical genius of the past. My father brought the glasses, a crystal one for the major, and for himself a tumbler I knew well as a family heirloom. It had a heavy bottom, and when you tried to tip it over, it inevitably stood up again. Made of pinkish-purplish glass, it had a single, small ornament on its side — a Polish white eagle. They drank, and, noticing the eagle on my father's tumbler, Major Hühne said, "Herr Professor, I understand the symbolism of the white eagle on your untippable tumbler. It's certain your Poland will come back. I wish you all the best — but never show that glass to any other German." Such an expression of tolerance was rare in those days.

The sheer barbarity of German rule in wartime Poland is difficult to describe, and from September 1 on, there seemed to be no end to it. It encompassed every facet of the Polish nation's life and was aimed at the complete elimination of the Polish language, customs and traditions, the suppression of cultural life in all its manifestations, the eradication of national wealth by open robbery, and the destruction of human life. In the *Ostdeutscher Beobachter* (*East German Observer*), a newly established, hate-spitting Nazi daily, one could read the countless new *Verbote* (bans) that now defined our lives. All Polish associations, unions, and federations were outlawed. Church services in Polish were forbidden and Polish religious holidays abolished. All Polish schools and universities were closed, as were Polish theatres and cinemas, restaurants, and cafés. It was now prohibited to publish periodicals, newspapers, or books in the Polish language, and Poles were not allowed to own radios, gramophones, cameras, or bicycles. The city's theatres, concert halls, cinemas, streetcars, parks, and many public places such as squares and designated sidewalks were *nur für Deutsche* (for Germans only). Those considered enemies of the Third Reich — a broad category which included intellectuals, artists, clergy, and leaders of every stripe, even Boy Scouts — were either jailed, or tortured and murdered in the notorious Fort VII, one of a series of forts surrounding Poznań. Officially a Gestapo prison and temporary camp for civilians, it was in reality an extermination camp in which it is estimated the Nazis murdered between 10,000 and 15,000 Poles by execution (including by guillotine) and in primitive gas chambers. Few returned from this place of horror. It is said that one of my father's colleagues, Professor Kalandyk, then in his seventies, met his end here after being ordered to strip and run about in the snow as target practice for the SS. The Collegium Maius, which had housed the Institute of Musicology, was slated to become Hitler's headquarters for the *Ostgebiete* (eastern territories).

The closing of Poznań University meant that my father was out of work. In October 1939, he was arrested by the Gestapo, and my mother's efforts to find those authorities responsible for apprehending and holding Polish intellectuals, artists, and scientists were futile, as were her inquiries at the gates of Fort VII. She would cry and call my father's name in her sleep, and sometimes talk incoherently to him. I tried to convince her that he'd soon be back with us, but the more I talked, the more desperate she became. My father was detained for several days and released on October 30. His release papers were signed by SS *Obersturmbannführer* (Major) Wagner, leader of *Einsatzkommando* 15/VI. On his return, my father appeared exhausted, shaky, and dispirited. He was unwilling to look my mother and me in the eye, locked inside himself. Mute and distant, he seemed to be a different person. Sensing his mood, neither my mother nor I asked any questions, which was just as well, because next morning he seemed to become almost himself again. In a strangely impersonal tone of voice, he told us that he had been manhandled and endlessly interrogated, until at one point he lost his voice. Of course, we were overcome with happiness to have him with us again, but with this joy came something I encountered many years later while reading Orwell's *1984*: a darkness of fear. I was also to encounter a lot of it in Nazi Germany.

In those days, one's fate was often determined by sheer luck — or the lack of it — and on this occasion, a case of mistaken identity worked in my father's favour and facilitated his release. Among the identification papers he presented to his interrogator was a now obsolete card dating back to the early 1900s and attesting to his former membership in the *Reichsmusikkammer* (Reich Association of Composers). This association had been established in the 1870s when Bismarck's brutal Germanization policies suppressed Polish cultural institutions in Prussian-occupied Poland and young Polish composers could protect their copyright only by joining a German professional association. The major, reading my father's name only cursorily and giving the card no more than a fleeting glance, asked him, "So, you are the composer Heinrich Kaminski?" My father was familiar with the work of this German composer, whom he considered a "tireless graphomaniac [who had] counterpointed himself to fame and fortune [with his] industrious pseudo-Bach" compositions. He was about to correct the major's error when the latter, evidently in some way pre-disposed by hearing himself say the Kaminski name, brightened a little and said, "Well, that changes things; otherwise you would have been sent straight to a KZ [concentration camp]." Writing about the incident a few years later in a letter to me, my father concluded: "Goddamn it! By a hair! Suddenly I felt hot and cold. I asked, 'A KZ? Why?' to which he replied, 'You'll know more when we talk next time. But not today.' As you can see, my competitor unknowingly saved my life."

Only weeks after my father's release, on November 23, an event occurred that was to change my parents' lives, and mine as well. My mother was ordered to appear at the offices of the *Volksliste* (Register of German Nationals), where she was told to sign a declaration of her German origin and was given a bright red ID card. There were four types of ID cards, easily recognizable by their distinct colours, and issued according to the bearer's degree of "German-ness," based on criteria established by Nazi decree. Groups One and Two included persons whose German ethnicity was beyond question, while Groups Three and Four encompassed those of uncertain or doubtful "German-ness." In many such cases, these were Poles with German names who were forced to sign the declaration under threat of being sent to a concentration camp, or persons in mixed marriages. But there were also those who wanted to save their possessions and felt indifferent with regard to nationality. My mother was regarded as German because she was born in Königsberg (today Kaliningrad) and attended German schools. But her red Group Four ID card identified her as being of doubtful German nationality, and I must say that this designation was amazingly accurate. She spoke perfect Polish and moved exclusively in Polish society circles. Her voice students were all Poles. Lastly, she had married a Pole and raised me as one. We received Polish food coupons, which represented only about one third of the nutritional value of those given out to the German occupiers.

A great many Polish families who had to survive on the Germans' leftovers became victims of starvation, and their death rate, especially among the youngest children, rose to levels never seen before. By contrast, families of German origin brought by the Nazis from abroad to settle in confiscated Polish properties showed rapidly rising birth rates. Asked by his henchmen what to do with those starving, crippled, and incurably ill Poles still alive, *Gauleiter* Greiser suggested in all seriousness, "Machine-gun them." Our own food situation was helped by Zosia's skill in dealing with black market sources, so that we were even able to share some of those modest purchases with our building's caretakers, an elderly couple. But Christmas dinner that year was a meagre affair, consisting of only a thin soup and a few other scraps saved up for the occasion. It was the one time that I saw tears in my father's eyes.

From friends, those who had so far managed to avoid arrest as Polish intellectuals, we learned of the horrifying events that had taken place during our absence. The rumours about gunfire in the city, which we had heard just before boarding the train out of Poznań in September, had reflected the truth. German residents of Poznań had launched a concerted assault on the Polish population, especially those wearing Polish uniforms, military or not. Soldiers and officers, railway personnel, mail carriers, even streetcar conductors and Boy Scouts were all targeted. These German civilians — all of them Polish citizens, with the rights and privileges accorded minorities by the Polish state — had their own organizations, German-language schools, libraries, and assembly halls. With the rise of Hitler in Germany, they absorbed the Nazis' racist ideology that viewed Jews and Slavs alike as subhumans. Well before the beginning of the war, they had become organized as a clandestine Fifth Column called *Selbstschutz* (self-defence), ready to spring into action armed with weapons smuggled in from the German Reich, and helped by German agents and saboteurs who infiltrated Poland. Once the invasion of Poland had begun, members of the *Selbstschutz* engaged in sniping at and machine-gunning Polish civilians from rooftops and church towers or rounding them up for execution. Typically thorough, German photographers documented such executions, choosing the moment when the bullets hit and the victims' bodies collapsed. The pictures were then released worldwide to expose ostensible "Polish atrocities" and camouflage the truth.

In February 1940, more horrors were revealed. A Copenhagen daily newspaper, *Politiken,* published the eyewitness account of an Englishwoman, Miss Baker-Beall, who had been living in the town of Bydgoszcz at the beginning of the war. On the morning of September 3, armed German civilians had attacked Polish troops, who had returned fire. A street battle ensued in which 238 Polish soldiers and 223 Germans were killed. Shortly thereafter, the Wehrmacht entered the city, followed by German police, SS, and Gestapo. These last three units began a mass murder of Poles in the city market square, killing 10,500. A further 13,000 were deported to concentration camps, where they perished. Over 2,000 Jews were executed. Those murdered included a group of Polish Boy Scouts between the ages of twelve and sixteen, who were executed against the wall of a church along with a priest who joined them in death. The town's many merchants and civic leaders, including the mayor, were also murdered. After the war, this report was confirmed by other surviving witnesses.

Without a doubt, Poles not only defended themselves to the best of their ability, but also tried to avenge the mass murder of innocent Polish civilians. Not as well armed as the German executioners, they could hardly pay them back in kind or carry out the same sort of genocide as the Germans had perpetrated. The German propaganda machine published the figure of 58,000 German civilians presumed to have been victims of Polish violence. Hitler himself later raised the number to a staggering 60,000. Polish authorities objected to this number, taking it down to about 2,000. Historians on both sides of this conflict are still trying to separate documented truth from unproven assertions.

Nazi Propaganda Minister Joseph Goebbels excelled when it came to twisting the facts of real events to make the Polish people appear as blithering idiots. Two such events in particular stand out, as both were perpetuated assiduously and, even today, are widely accepted as the truth. The first myth stemmed from a Polish cavalry attack, during which a German infantry formation was wiped out. German armoured vehicles arriving on the scene then opened fire on the cavalry, killing twenty troopers and the unit's colonel. The next day, Italian war correspondents, there to cover the incident, were told that the Poles had been killed while charging German tanks on horseback. This confabulated version of the event was then spread around the world and even became the basis for a German feature film. A second lie, which gained credence through repetition, was that the entire Polish Air Force had been annihilated on the ground, owing to the fact that the aircraft had supposedly been parked in plain view on an airstrip. An incident in which some small private and sports aircraft had been destroyed formed the basis for this fabrication, the truth being that the Poles had, in fact, carefully camouflaged their fleet of outmoded but agile P-11 fighter aircraft in forested areas. They had certainly held their own in dogfights, downing 165 of Germany's vastly superior Messerschmitts and Dornier bombers in the seventeen days preceding Poland's defeat.

In those cold, dark days, we were glad when friends came to visit us. One of them was my father's old friend, Juliusz Kręglewski, former owner of a school supplies business and now dispossessed by the Germans. Another was Stanisław Kubicki, a close colleague of my father's from before the First World War. Both of them had been born in the 1880s into well-to-do Polish upper-middle-class families. They were raised in an atmosphere of national patriotism at a time when Bismark's forced Germanization of Prussian-occupied Western Poland suppressed the Polish language and disallowed it on all levels of education, from primary schools to universities. In order to obtain a high-level education, both my father and Stanisław Kubicki were compelled to attend Berlin's Kaiser Friedrich University; my father to study musicology with Max Bruch, Kubicki to study Slavistics with Alexander Brückner. They were not the only Polish students at that university, and, quite naturally, their common nationality brought all of them together socially to form an ad hoc group to discuss matters of common interest, as well as problems besetting their Polish homeland. In time, the group was joined by the future world-famous pianist Artur Rubinstein.

Following the First World War (1914–18), my father left Germany and settled in Poland, now liberated from German oppression, to eventually assume the professorship of musicology at the newly established Poznań University. His friend, Kubicki, however, stayed in Berlin and retained his German citizenship for purely political reasons. Possessed of a strong social conscience and witnessing the plight of postwar Germany's proletariat, he drifted toward Socialism and farther, joining the German Communist Party. He rose in the ranks to become an assistant to the party's leader, Ernst Thälmann, but in March 1933 left Berlin to escape the Nazis' mass arrests of all Communist functionaries and return to his native Poland — still carrying his German passport. Probably helped by Party comrades, he stayed in Poland and visited us a few times around 1935, and also in 1940. Then he disappeared from sight. Later, a mutual friend told my father that Kubicki had joined the Polish Resistance, using his valid German passport to facilitate his underground activites, until his Communist past caught up with him. Seized by the ever-vigilant Gestapo, he was probably tortured before his ultimate execution in Moabit, a prison in Berlin. It was only in 1957, when my father came from Poland to visit me in Canada, that I learned of Kubicki's fate.

Another visitor was a former student of my father's, Lieutenant Adam Wieczorek, who during the September 1939 German invasion had commanded a battalion of Polish tanks. Wounded and taken prisoner, he escaped from captivity and found a temporary refuge in our home. He wore rather ill-fitting and clearly secondhand workman's clothes, and stayed with us for only three or four days before leaving in the dead of night. After the war, Wieczorek told my father that he had joined the *Armia Krajowa* (Home Army — Poland's large and fully organized underground army) and fought in the 1944 Warsaw Uprising.

Life was harsh, and I'd grown despondent. In whispered conversations with my parents, I occasionally voiced doubts about Poland's future, but even amid the despair and misery around us, they never gave up hope

Lieutenant Adam Wieczorek, Second Tank Brigade, Polish Army, a family friend who stayed with us briefly after escaping from German captivity. He was an inspiration to me, lifting me out of my despondency at Poland's defeat.

of a better tomorrow. I recall an occasion when, reacting to my dark thoughts, my father merely whistled the first few notes of the Polish national anthem, which begins with the words, *"Jeszcze Polska nie zginęła, póki my żyjemy."* ("Poland is not yet lost while we live.") It helped.

Three rather important events coincided in February 1940. My father was approached by Dr. Kurt Lück, a German writer and historian, who, before the war, had been active in Poznań's German minority organizations. Despite his Nazi convictions, Dr. Lück was unfailingly decent in his dealings with us. Eyeing the life-size self-portrait of our friend, Kazimierz Jasnoch, that hung in my father's study and showed the artist in full Polish uniform, he gave my father some good advice. "Herr Professor," he said, "may I suggest you take that portrait down and put it somewhere where it cannot be seen. It would be wise if you did that." More importantly, he asked my father to do research for a book he planned, on the subject of "The Mythos of the German in Polish Folklore and Literature." And since, despite help from friends and our trusty Zosia's black-market skill, our financial resources were virtually exhausted, Dr. Lück's offer came just in time to save us from ruin. The money was sufficient to keep us alive for quite a while.

The second event followed from the first. My father approached a Polish physician, Dr. Rakowski, who lived across the street from us and, fortunately, had not been evicted by the Germans, to ask if the doctor could operate on me and remove the piece of shrapnel that was still embedded in my left thigh. At first Dr. Rakowski was skeptical, mainly because as a Pole he no longer had hospital privileges. The operation would have to be performed illegally, at his home, where he had a small surgery. However, he finally agreed, and the operation was performed under local anesthetic, with his wife assisting. After a week spent convalescing in the guest room of their apartment, I was able to cautiously hobble across the street back to our home and was helped up the stairs to our apartment, where I recovered fully in a little more than a month.

It was then that the third important event occurred. It was an unexpected visit by Zenek, who, having fought as an infantry sub-lieutenant in the previous year's battles, had managed to escape from a POW transport and return to Poznań. In the course of his

In the spring of 1940 I was convalescing from the removal of shrapnel in my leg. My casual pose belies the brutal Nazi occupation we were living under. Poles weren't allowed to own cameras, but my friend, Kazio Wendland, who took the picture, worked in a photo lab that had been put under German ownership and managed to "borrow" one.

subsequent visits, he and I became close friends, and eventually our conversations turned to an important matter — the emergence of a Polish underground resistance movement. Still in its organizational stages and being formed primarily in the General Gouvernement, it was guardedly extending its activities into other parts of German-occupied Poland. Zenek also told me that the Polish government-in-exile was encouraging the formation of armed groups of partisans and that this would most likely occur in the near future. This is exactly what happened. Eventually these groups formed the *Armia Krajowa,* which fought the Germans every step of the way, up to and including the tragic end of the 1944 Warsaw Uprising.

Zenek had developed some connections with the still modest but slowly growing black market, and this helped the situation in our home. He was also a pragmatist who, very much like my father, saw the necessity of understanding the enemy in order to fight him for the freedom of our country. This, he told me during one of our conversations, included the knowledge of the enemy's language, history, customs, and traditions. Of course, he knew that my father had studied in Berlin before the First World War and had written his PhD thesis in the German language. Zenek also knew that my mother had been born in Germany and attended German schools, and that she spoke fluent German. But he was fully aware that she not only spoke perfect Polish but had also raised me as a Pole and heartily detested the German invaders. Such linguistic and cultural heterogeneity was not uncommon in Poland. During the over 126 years of German occupation in Western Poland, many generations of Poles had been forced to learn and use the German language — and applied that skill toward resisting the occupier.

I'd heard my mother say on a number of occasions that being born and growing up in a particular place had little to do with one's real roots. In the case of her own family, most of these roots were decidedly non-German. Her father, Armand Harder, was a direct descendant of mid-nineteenth century Swedish immigrants to Germany, and her mother's family, whose name was Retti, had come from Italy even earlier. In her own opinion, she was half-Swedish and half-Italian, born in Germany and now a citizen of Poland. This may have sounded like a strange mixture, but it wasn't. In Europe, racial interfusion was, and still is, as frequent as, for instance, in Canada. A perfect example of this was the case of the so-called Bambry, a people whose ancestors had been brought to Poland in the early seventeenth century and received crown land to settle on in counties around the city of Poznań. They were hard-working, industrious farmers from the area of Bamberg in Germany, who brought with them their language, customs and traditions, and greatly contributed to their host country's prosperity. Over the centuries, they had blended in with the Polish population and adopted the Polish language, but retained their family names and traditional costumes. In time, the women's colourful dresses, with all their ribbons and lace and many petticoats, gave way to the fashions of the day, but they reappeared on special occasions, such as religious celebrations. The family names, however, remained proudly unchanged throughout the centuries, even though their bearers had become completely Polonized. A classic example of the Bambergers' Polonization was Poznań's well-known Leitgeber family, Polish nationalist to the core and Catholic by tradition. In fact, our Zosia's family name was Bamberowicz, clearly indicating its origins. However, because of the German names inherited from their Bamberg ancestors, thousands of young, male Bambry over the age of eighteen were forcibly drafted into Hitler's Wehrmacht in the 1940s, despite their deep-rooted Polish patriotism and the fact that they neither understood nor spoke a word of German.

Whatever scant knowledge of German I possessed came from the curriculum of the Collegium Marianum, the school I had attended until the war broke out. Even though still unable to use the language with any degree of ease, I possessed a good ear for its sound and needed only some practice to speak it more effortlessly. My father's library included several books in German, some of them works dating back to the turn of the century and therefore printed in German Gothic letters. It took me a day to get used to deciphering the curlicued characters, but after that, I could read them as quickly as the Roman ones. I spent a few weeks reading aloud, and this method of practice helped me acquire a much better feel for the pronunciation and — even more importantly — the difficult grammar of the German language. In all this, I was encouraged by Zenek, as well as by my father.

5 MESSENGER WORK
AND SMALL SABOTAGE

I understood that learning a foreign language was not just a way to kill time or keep myself amused. I was recovering my health, and although the bomb explosion in September of the previous year had permanently weakened my eyesight and damaged nerves in my left leg, I was quite capable of functioning as normally as before. But at home the financial situation had become critical once again — the money from Dr. Lück was running out, and I saw the need for me to pitch in. I felt that my knowledge of German had improved to the point that I could apply for work practically anywhere in any kind of business. Instead, I was directed by the official German *Arbeitsamt* (Employment Bureau) to go to work as a messenger boy in the office of the *Deutsche Arbeiterfront* (German Labour Front), an organization established in 1933 to replace all the old, established German labour unions, which had been outlawed by Hitler. The office I worked in was a branch of that large organization and charged with planning German settlements in the newly conquered Polish territories from which their rightful owners had been evicted. The office staff consisted of two directors, three urban planners/architects, a secretary, and now me. Since no German could possibly be asked to do the lowly work of a messenger, the office had to make do with a Pole who just happened to speak German almost acceptably. I was given a bicycle on which I traversed the city between various Nazi Party and government offices (even though the two were essentially synonymous), and, sometimes, private businesses, which were now run by Germans who had replaced the dispossessed Polish proprietors. Mostly I carried parcels, large sealed envelopes, and occasionally big rolled-up maps and plans of future settlements. The work wasn't difficult, and the pay was miserable, to say the least.

One day, I had just delivered a package and was walking back to the office. En route, I stopped at Matejko Street and stood with some other pedestrians at the curbside, looking on as a Luftwaffe company marched by, preceded by some kind of a flag, possibly the unit's pennant. Watching the march pass, I forgot a regulation which stipulated that all Poles must take off their hats or caps as a sign of respect for any military formations of the Master Race that might be passing by. I hadn't noticed whether or not others had bared their heads, but now, suddenly, I was hit on the head, and my cap was snatched off by a *Feldwebel* (sergeant) who stormed from the ranks, threw me into the gutter, and then stomped and danced on me, shrieking the usual "Polack" curses and giving me a kick on the head that broke two of my teeth.

In civilian life, he may have been a mild-mannered, decent person, loving toward his family, but now he turned into the embodiment of a *Furor Germanicus!* Was a part of him German, and the other a Nazi, with either part available for duty depending on demand? And then I think of the vicious *Furor Hispanicus* in ancient Mexico, and of the *Furor Britannicus*, and the *Gallicus* one, the *Furor Americanus* and *Mongolicus*, all the great *Furoris* — and then a little voice inside me asks: "Wasn't there ever a *Furor Polonicus*?"

Was German brutality as we knew it during the occupation of Poland an inborn, yet unweaned national characteristic? Was the intentional cruelty applied in Gestapo torture chambers an inborn trait? Hitler's regime created an educational system in which absolute ruthlessness in dealing with opponents became a credo. Small wonder then that this kind of education would later have a bearing on any German boy heading into battle and singing, "We will march on till all crashes down, for today we have Germany and tomorrow the whole world."

A telling incident was witnessed by our housekeeper, Zosia, in the summer of 1941. Crossing the street, she saw a girl playing hopscotch on a sidewalk and a man, clearly deep in thought, walking toward the girl. Inadvertently he shuffled over the hopscotch lines and destroyed their pattern. The girl faced him and shouted, "Stupid Polack! See what you did!" Stunnned and angry, the man slapped her. She moved back and in a whiny voice said, "I'm sorry. I didn't know you were a German."

Our magnificent radio, an Elektrit Majestic that used to give us wonderful reception on all wavelengths, had been confiscated by German police back in November 1939, and whatever news we got from the rest of the world came from friends who had providentially hidden their radios and listened in secret to what the BBC provided in its Polish-language programs. Not much was happening in the West, and we waited impatiently, hoping in vain for the long-promised French-British offensive against Germany. But the "*Sitzkrieg*" continued. Much of France's military force spent the winter of 1939–40 behind the safety of the Maginot Line, while England sang a new hit, "We're gonna hang out the washing on the Siegfried Line, if the Siegfried Line's still there." There was a war between Finland and the Soviets, and in our hearts, we were certainly with the Finns, whom we saw as victims of the same kind of aggression as we had become subjected to.

The expulsion of the Polish population from Poland's western territories and the outright annexation of all of Western Poland into the *Grossdeutsches Reich* (Greater German Empire) brought with it unexpected consequences for those Poles kept there as subservient forced labour. Considered subjects (though not citizens) of the Reich, they fell under the governance of the Reich's April 30, 1940 law pertaining to *Wehrpflicht* (compulsory military service). This meant that if they were able to carry arms, they were forcibly drafted into the Wehrmacht. For the benefit of those compelled to fight on the German side, the Polish government-in-exile declared that they were not bound by any oath imposed under duress, and that there was only one duty they must observe, that of allegiance to their own country, Poland. Obviously, very many, if not most, of those Poles already drafted used every opportunity to cross the front lines and join the Allied Forces.

Sometime in June 1940, there was a great celebration in the office of the chief planner, Herr Mahnke, on the occasion of the German victory over France. It started in the evening, with all kinds of uniformed Nazi Party bigwigs in attendance. The secretary, Fraülein Meyer, and I were sent home, but told to come to the office the next day to clean up the premises after the festivities. We did, and found an incredible mess — smashed glasses, spilled drinks, half-empty bottles amidst leftover food (the likes of which I hadn't seen for a long time), and vomit on the floor, in short, evidence of a pretty revolting Nazi victory festivity. Fortunately, it was a Sunday and we could take our time to do a good job of cleaning the place.

As I was collecting toppled-over glasses from Herr Mahnke's drafting board, I noticed that some food and red wine had been spilled over a stack of maps and plans of Zamość, an area surrounding the old Polish city of the same name, and renamed Himmlerstadt by the Nazis. While Fraülein Meyer was busy cleaning all sorts of debris off the floor in another part of the office, I took a good look at the map. It showed the positioning of proposed German settlements adjoining the city, with numbers giving their future residential capacity as well over 100,000 persons. A note in the margin stated it was a given that the Polish population would be expelled from the city and that all Jews would be locked in a ghetto *"zur weiteren Bestimmung"* (decision pending). I don't know what made me memorize that interesting document, but the next time I saw Zenek I showed him a sketch of what I had seen and remembered. He looked it over carefully, sat back, and after a while said: "I think it's time you got to know a few things." He then proceeded to ask me whether I was willing to join a "certain organization," the exact nature of which he was not going to divulge just then; but he was sure, he said, that I was smart enough to figure out what it all meant.

To make a long story short, that was the day I joined the Polish Resistance. I was seventeen, filled with passionate hatred of the enemy on one hand and overwhelming enthusiasm for the cause on the other, hardly aware of the dangers into which I might be walking, possibly taking my parents with me. I was sworn in a few days later.

It goes without saying that I told my parents nothing of my decision to join the Resistance. This was something that concerned only two people:

Zenek and me. If someone higher up in the organization knew of me, I was not aware of it. In keeping with the degree of secrecy and caution needed to carry out our activities without endangering each other, Resistance members adopted false names, preferably short ones that would be difficult for outsiders to understand if spoken quickly and quietly. As well, one's contacts were limited to one or two other members only, to keep to a minimum the amount of information that could be extracted from any member under torture. As a result, in all the time that I knew Zenek, I never did learn his real name. Some time in mid-September 1940, we met in an abandoned shack near a bridge over the Warta River. To my surprise he brought with him my friend Kazio Mettler, whom I hadn't seen since the beginning of the war. Kazio also turned out to be a member of our organization, and the two of us were to be instructed in what was called "small sabotage." In contrast to major sabotage, the aim of which was to destroy military objects and installations serving the German wartime economy, the idea of small sabotage was to remind the German occupiers of the enduring Polish presence, ensure that they felt a constant sense of unease and generally undermine their self-confidence. But this had to be done with caution. Although well over half of Poznań's Polish population had been evicted and shipped east to the General Gouvernement, there were still about 150,000 Poles in the city. Aware of this, occupation authorities kept their vigilance at a very high niveau.

This in turn meant that the Resistance in the Poznań region, although active, had to restrict itself to low-level activities such as printing and distributing primitive two-page bulletins with German translations of news clandestinely obtained from the BBC's Polish-language broadcasts. In addition to military situation reports, which at that time dealt with the Battle of Britain and the outstanding role that Polish fighter pilots were playing in it, such bulletins included details of the most recent German atrocities in Poland, such as the ongoing murders of scientists, writers, artists, landowners, political leaders, and clergy as well as the country's Jewish citizens. These bulletins would be discreetly slipped into the mail slots of formerly Polish and now German-inhabited apartments, in hopes of contributing to the new occupants' level of discomfort.

I volunteered to distribute these bulletins, but Zenek vetoed it, saying I was too tall and therefore too conspicuous to carry and distribute such dangerous material. Besides, he said, there were other things he had in mind for me, though he didn't specify what they were. What I was allowed to do wasn't much to my liking, but I reminded myself that it at least helped to do undermine the enemy. After the 9:00 p.m. curfew (which applied only to Poles), I'd quietly walk the streets and, in the heavy darkness of a strictly enforced blackout, engage in minor vandalism to German-owned parked cars. It was wartime, and there weren't too many of them around, since non-Germans were not allowed to own them. But there were enough to do damage to by, say, sticking a knife into a tire or two, leaving a nasty scratch on a car door, or ripping off a windshield wiper: in a word, making the occupier's life as unpleasant as possible. Only once did I encounter a police patrol, but the two uniformed cops were too busy talking and laughing at some evidently funny story to pay any attention to me lurking in the dark.

Another small-sabotage tactic was to secretly apply virtually indelible white paint to the eagle that was part of Poznań's city crest, displayed in bas-relief on every black, cast-iron lamppost in the city, yet another reminder to the occupiers that Polish patriotism was still very much alive. Yet another way to shake the German "order" was to disrupt its communications. This was a particularly dangerous job, since it involved some exposure to public view, but it proved to be very effective in creating chaos within the German military telephone system. A few of the overhead cables, of which up to ten or more ran parallel, would be cut and randomly spliced among themselves. Thus, a coding room might become connected with the kitchens, an armoury with a field hospital, and so on. To my recollection, a Resistance member, dressed in a German uniform and courageous enough to perform the task, did this twice in the area of the Poznań citadel.

This low-level resistance activity (although we did not know it at the time) also included deadly work carried out by a daring group of scientists and lab assistants from the Faculty of Medicine of the (formerly Polish) University of Poznań. Although the laboratories and research facilities of their departments of bacteriology, pharmacology, and chemistry had been either taken over or savagely destroyed by the Germans, they used their professional knowledge and whatever resources were still available to them to secretly generate bacteria and slow-working poisons. These were discreetly added to restaurant food served to German Party and police officials, as well as higher-ranking Wehrmacht personnel, especially well known for their barbarities in persecuting the population. Waiters, obviously members of the Resistance, spiked the food before serving it. This group was active from 1940 until 1942, when the Gestapo tracked it down. Its members were executed, as were their families — parents, wives, brothers, and sisters. The Nazi Party took their children to the Third Reich to be "Germanized."

The abduction and Germanization of an estimated 200,000 Polish children was yet another facet of the Nazis' attempts to increase the dominance of the Master Race. Children whose blue eyes, blond hair, and pleasing build caught the attention of SS-trained experts in racial purity would be kidnapped by SS units, German police or the Wehrmacht and given to a denationalizing institution. Beaten for speaking Polish and forced to undergo a process of Germanization, they were eventually adopted by German families, preferably ones committed to the Germanic-Nordic racial doctrine. Very few of these children found their way back to Poland after the war, and most remained completely unaware of their origins. Other Polish children between six and fourteen years of age were treated with another kind of cruelty, abducted to be used as slave labour in factories, construction, the armaments industry, and in agriculture, replacing some of the German workforce drafted into the Wehrmacht. Forced to work under inhuman conditions, they were routinely mistreated and starved, often forced to work outdoors, even in extreme cold, wearing only rags. Many died of hunger or froze to death. Jewish children, if not murdered by SS *Einsatzkommandos* in mass executions, died of hunger in the streets of the ghettos or perished in gas chambers.

I saw Zenek less often in those days. Asking where he'd been and what he'd been doing was out of the question. But I suspected that he travelled to Warsaw and Kraków on the organization's business, because whenever I did see him he had news about what was happening in the General Gouvernement, be it the Germans arresting and killing our people, or our success in sabotaging some major German military installation.

Meanwhile, the *"Sitzkrieg"* had ended. On May 10, 1940, the Wehrmacht began its blitzkrieg against France, Holland, and Belgium. By the end of June, all three had surrendered, and the British Expeditionary Force had been mauled on the beaches of Dunkirk. Poland stood alone. Having lost a brief war against Germany's overwhelming might, her armed forces now began to fight again, this time at Britain's side. In a classic example of treachery, the Romanians joined the ranks of Hitler's axis coalition in November 1940. Little did we know then that in time Britain, too, would leave us to Stalin's tender mercies.

In the late autumn of 1940, I was ordered by my employers to deliver a small parcel to the former Holy Transfiguration hospital, located at the very large St. Bernard's Square, in one of Poznań's older districts. The hospital had formerly belonged to a Dr. Meissner who, despite his German name, was a leading figure in the Polish National Democratic Party. His hospital had now been taken over by the Wehrmacht. As I approached the square, I had to get off the bicycle and push it, since the old and narrow streets leading to the square were blocked by long lines of military vehicles, mostly big trucks with tarpaulin covers. Soldiers and police stood around chatting among themselves, and no one paid attention to me as I made my way toward the square. But once I reached that huge, open space, I saw that it was packed with a mass of people, some standing, others sitting on suitcases and various bundles, most of them talking in low voices, their faces showing bewilderment and concern. It was an enormous crowd that filled the square, guarded on the periphery by police armed with bayonet-mounted rifles. I didn't have to guess who these people were: the *Ostdeutscher Beobachter* (*East German Observer*) had often displayed pictures of Jews forced to wear the Star of David on the sleeves of their jackets or overcoats. Since I was outside the police cordon, I could move freely, although I was stopped at one point and ordered to identify myself. I did so by showing the parcel I had to deliver to the hospital nearby, and I was let go. Walking along the perimeter of this mass of humanity, I thought that these Jews, like all those Poles before them, had been evicted from their homes to make room for Germans and would be sent off to the General Gouvernement, maybe to Warsaw or Lublin, or some other such place. Of course, as I later found out, I was terribly wrong in this assumption. The sight of a hand waving made me stop suddenly: Hania Hirschberg, the girlfriend of my classmate and buddy Adam Majkowski, was trying to get my attention. I cried out, "Hania ..." and moved to get closer to her, but a policeman hit me with his rifle butt between my shoulder blades, screaming, "*Hau ab, du Dreckpolack!*" ("Beat it, you dirty Polack!") He pushed me away, and I fell over my bicycle. When I got up, I tried to find Hania again, but she had disappeared in the multitude. Deeply shaken, I delivered the parcel. The memory of Hania waving at me, and of the despair I saw in her face is with me to this day. Poznań's Jewish community was very small, consisting of some 3,000 persons in a city with a pre-war population of about 270,000. I don't know if anyone from that community survived. I can't help hoping and thinking of Hania as being still among the living. The Gestapo arrested Adam Majkowski; his fate remains unknown.

6 THE ASSIGNMENT

I was still seventeen, a minor, and therefore out of the authoritarian grasp of the Nazi bureaucracy. However, since my mother had been compelled to sign the *Volksliste*, there was the real danger that once I reached the age of eighteen in 1941, I could be drafted into the Wehrmacht and forced to serve the enemy we so passionately detested. My parents and I discussed vague, often hopeless, plans of my escaping to some safe country — Hungary, perhaps Romania — and from there to God knows where else. But by then the Germans were everywhere, and the difficulties in crossing borders had become monumental.

Meantime my father had found work in the cataloguing department of Poznań's great and rich Raczyński Library, so that between his income and mine, our financial situation became almost bearable. It was only several years after the war ended that I learned from him, and later from a contemporary witness, that throughout his tenure at the Raczyński Library he had repeatedly prevented the Germans from plundering the library's priceless collection of rare, ancient volumes by hiding them in his briefcase or simply under his coat and later depositing them with old friends he trusted. These volumes included some examples of late fifteenth- and early sixteenth-century printing, then newly invented, and a number of priceless manuscripts, often with religious content. My father also saved a few mid-sixteenth-century maps of the world from being stolen by the German pilferers. After the war, these rarities were returned to the reinstituted Raczyński Library, or so I've been told.

In early March 1941, German eastbound rail traffic suddenly began to increase, and it soon became quite apparent that much of what these transports carried was not at all of a peaceful nature. The main railway line leading from west to east and passing through Poznań's central station ran partly through the suburbs, and the traffic it carried could be observed with fair accuracy. At a certain point, the line ran between high, sloping embankments covered with grass and dense bushes, perfectly suited to shielding from sight anyone who wanted to reconnoitre unseen. Of course, the nine o'clock curfew and the blackout interfered with our vigilance, but Kazio Mettler and I (and later Tadek Staś, who joined us at the end of March) each managed to spend a few hours counting the freight cars. One couldn't see what was inside the boxcars, but objects stacked up on flatcars and covered by camouflage-patterned tarpaulin started to evoke our interest. From ostensibly innocent boxes and box-like objects, they gradually began to acquire more ominous shapes: those of armed personnel carriers, military vehicles of every kind, and finally, tanks. Our observations were handed to Zenek, who took them without

My companions in the Resistance, from left to right: Kazio Mettler, Henryk (Henio) Komorowski, and Tadek Staś.

a comment and presumably forwarded them to someone higher up and more important. In spite of all that, I still went about my messenger work, just as before.

The two Polish daily newspapers published in Poznań had, of course, been liquidated by the Germans and replaced by a single one, the German-language *Ostdeutscher Beobachter* (*East German Observer*). It pumped out news about the warm friendship between the Third Reich and the Soviet Union, crowing songs of pride about having conquered France, Belgium, Holland, and, later, most of the Balkan peninsula, including Greece. There was, of course, ample space on that daily's pages to vent hostility against Poles and Jews, but by and large the newspaper constantly appeared to serenade Germany's communist bosom friends. Thus it wasn't surprising that, in addition to German eastbound rail traffic, we occasionally saw trains moving westward, presumably loaded with grain and other foodstuffs, and obviously also transporting oil in huge containers piggybacked on flatcars. Watching that to-and-fro rail traffic, we became aware of the letters *CCCP* on some of the westbound boxcars. Assuming these letters denoted "something Russian," I asked a former classmate of mine, a boy of Russian descent named Oleg Jefimov, about the meaning of those letters. He said they were the initials of Soviet Russia's name: Union of Soviet Socialist Republics. We speculated as to whether Nazi Germany and Soviet Russia, were exchanging arms for food or food for arms, but Zenek just laughed and said, "We'll soon find out."

Hitler attacked the Soviet Union on June 22, 1941, and Zenek gave us the word from above that we were not favouring either side in that conflict. After all, in 1939 Germany and the Soviet Union had collaborated in partitioning our country and were both, obviously, our enemies.

At Zenek's request, he and I met regarding a matter that he called exceptionally important. He began by asking about my fluency in the German language, and I said that having worked for more than a year in a German office I was able to speak the language fairly well. He wanted to know if I thought I could pass in an exclusively German social environment, and I said yes, I thought I could. Then he asked if I'd be prepared to undertake some work that would require me to blend into that environment and at the same time work for the Resistance. I replied that this was already the case, even though I didn't actually "blend" in with the personnel of the office I worked in. He waved this aside and said that what he meant was a lot more serious and infinitely more important. I pressed him for details, but he wanted my answer first. Youthfully impetuous, I said yes.

It was only now that he began explaining to me what that work involved. I was to live in enemy territory, meaning in Germany itself. There, I was to find a suitable occupation to provide a cover and establish myself in the community. I would need to find inconspicuous lodgings with a discreet landlord or landlady, preferably outside the city's limits and if possible in a building some distance away from others. (In today's parlance, such an accommodation would be called a "safe house.") Once in a while, I might receive a postcard or a brief note in an envelope, telling me in a pre-arranged way and in German of a person who would come to visit me (an "uncle," "cousin," or some other "family member") and stay overnight, leaving the next day. I was to help that person in any way required, with food, directions, and any necessities (if obtainable), et cetera. I remember asking Zenek if the visitors I was to house and take care of were messengers of some sort, but he only shrugged and said "maybe."

Another task I was given was to find a radio — not the popular *Volksempfänger* (People's Receiver) that was tuned to only one Nazi government-approved wavelength and usually poured out light music and war propaganda, but a proper sort of radio with a choice of bands, most importantly a shortwave one on which the BBC Polish-language broadcasts were transmitted. I was to transcribe these broadcasts, and then, extracting from them the most important facts (dealing mainly with Allied and now also some initial Soviet successes), copy these transcriptions by any means possible and distribute the copies to the nearest Polish forced-labour camps.

Having been forcibly taken by the German occupiers from Poland to Germany to work as slaves of the Third Reich, these camps' wretched inmates were both in despair about their future and filled with deep hatred toward their oppressors. Factual information about the course of the war, especially concerning the Polish forces' participation in it, was to be a means of keeping up their spirits, boosting their hope for a better future and an eventual return home. The masses of those slave labourers, spread throughout Germany in countless camps and forced to work for the enemy, de facto constituted a Fifth Column which was capable of not only slowing down all manner of war production but also sabotaging it outright, to the detriment of the German war effort. That such acts of sabotage took place in a great many factories and even in agriculture became a proven fact, although by now it's obviously impossible to establish to what degree these actions were motivated by the reading of illicit information smuggled into the labour camps.

Another one of my functions, Zenek explained, would be to monitor and record the regimental numbers worn by the German Army's enlisted men and noncoms on the upper sleeve of their uniform, just below the epaulette. These numbers identified the wearer as a member of a particular regiment. For example, the number 172 meant he belonged to the 172nd regiment, and white edging on his sleeve cuff designated it as an infantry regiment. I forget the colour of the cuff edgings worn by tank unit personnel, but I recall that red ones identified artillerymen. I was to keep my eyes open for these numbers whenever and wherever I could — walking along the city's streets, waiting for a streetcar or travelling in it, but especially in the vicinity of any complex of barracks. Zenek, who had instructed me in all my other tasks, did not tell me what counting regimental numbers had to do with any Resistance activities, and it was only some time later that I understood its significance. A sudden, unexpected agglomeration of similar regimental numbers could indicate the presence of a regiment or a battalion on leave in the city from frontline duty, perhaps en route from, say, Norway to the Russian front or to Italy. Also, since any such troop movement would be of interest to the Allies, it was important to inform them of it. This information would be imparted to a courier passing through, so there was a chance it would reach the proper authority in time for action to be taken. In the context of a great armed conflict, a tiny, almost infinitesimal bit of knowledge may not have been of much importance to those who made weighty strategic decisions;

but when confirmed by several other sources (which, of course, existed), it could contribute to advance, change, or halt an already-planned operation. Within my recollection, I was able to convey this type of information only a few times to couriers passing en route to the West.

Yet another task, more general in its nature, involved keeping an eye on and making a note of events and particularities that affected the population's daily life. This included monitoring the general mood of the German people, their overall attitude toward the Nazi Party, and thus, toward the Führer himself. Their opinions about the conduct of the war were also very important, as were those concerning their day-to-day existence, especially in view of increasingly severe economic restrictions of wartime. In this context, I was to note the quantities of food available to individuals and to families with children. Since all food was controlled by a coupon system, it would be easy for me to follow the fluctuations of its availability. All this information was to be passed on orally to the travellers I was to shelter.

Was I able to do all this, Zenek asked, and confidently I said yes. But with most of the what and why of the mission explained, the where and when still remained to be settled. This, as I recall, happened a few days later. This time, however, Zenek surprised me by approaching the subject from a different angle. He asked me if I remembered a classmate of mine named Tadek Beutlich. Yes, I said, of course I remembered him — a skinny fellow, a bit older than me, kind of quiet, who had once told me that he wanted to study painting. Then the war came, and I lost track of most of my school buddies. Well, said Zenek, Tadek Beutlich was now in Dresden, studying painting at the *Staatliche Kunsthochschule* (State Academy of Art). With that German-sounding surname, his family had probably been forced to sign the *Volksliste* and had been given the red Group Four ID card (the one that branded them as "doubtful Germans"). Now officially called "Thaddeus," Tadek had become an art student in hopes of eluding the long arm of the Wehrmacht. And, since he was now in Dresden, and Zenek even had his address, I might he able to stay with him until I found my own accommodation. Did I think that was possible? he asked. I said, yes, it was, especially since Tadek and I had been the best students in our school's art class, and often discussed art that we'd seen in galleries. It was something we definitely had in common, I said, but — somewhat bewildered — asked how and where he had gotten all this information about Tadek. In answer, he only smiled wordlessly and shook his head.

How would my parents react, Zenek wondered, and I told him that they'd probably be relieved. Now that I was already eighteen, the necessity of finding a way to escape the tentacles of the local German draft board had become more pressing than ever, and diving into the grey mass of civilian life in Germany itself seemed an excellent ploy. The question of when I was to leave could only be answered when my papers were ready. Zenek assured me that real specialists would prepare them: people from the now-defunct *Polska Państwowa Wytwórnia Papierów Wartościowych* (PWPW, or the State Printing Concern), where postage stamps, stock certificates, et cetera, had formerly been printed. I recall being amazed that our resistance movement, which had begun so small, had grown so large and efficient that it was now able to produce absolutely genuine-looking documents!

I was also assured that money was no problem; I would be given 500 Reichsmarks to get me settled in and started in Dresden, and further funds would come my way more or less regularly until I found reasonably well-paying employment. My papers arrived in late September 1941, carried no doubt by one of those courageous, daredevil Resistance couriers, who constantly risked their lives facing German railway police patrols, Wehrmacht gendarmerie, and the Gestapo. What I received was a "Stateless Passport," issued (like the Nansen passports) to those who did not have a formal nationality. It was made out in the name of Hansjakob Schreiter and was a masterpiece of forgery that even featured my photo. Apart from that, I had only a copy of my own genuine 1923 birth certificate, duly translated from Polish into German and stamped by the German authorities in already-occupied Poznań.

I met Zenek for the last time on the day before my departure for Dresden. He had wanted that meeting to give me some last-minute instructions concerning my first days in Dresden. What he had to tell me was short and to the point, and, as I had done with all information coming from him, I was to commit it to memory. He gave me the name and

With its turrets, frescoes, and three-storey loggia, Poznań's exquisite Renaissance City Hall exemplified the soul of the city known as the "Cradle of Poland." Virtually demolished in 1945, it was restored in the 1950s.

address of a contact in Dresden, a man whose name was something like Krajewski (although after all these years I'm not sure of it anymore) and who lived in Kanalgasse. I should try to find him soon after my arrival in the city. Zenek also said that I might be required to undertake other, still unspecified tasks, of which I would be informed in due course. Naturally, he refused to say what they might be.

I left on an evening train to Berlin. My parents saw me off at the train station, my father suppressing his tears, but my mother letting hers flow freely. In a low voice she said, *"Bóg z tobą, moje dziecko."* ("God be with you, my child.") It was the last time I saw her alive.

Part 2

IN THE THIRD REICH

7 GETTING STARTED IN DRESDEN

I arrived in Berlin at Schlesischer *Bahnhof* (train station) and made my way to Anhalter *Bahnhof*, from where I took a train that arrived in Dresden early the next morning. The apartment building on König Albert Strasse where Tadek Beutlich rented a room was not hard to find. But for some reason of his own, Zenek hadn't wanted me to notify Tadek of my arrival ahead of time, so I wasn't sure how my old buddy would receive me. However, I need not have worried. His landlady opened the door, I introduced myself and asked her to announce me to Herr Beutlich, which she did — and suddenly there was Tadek, still in his pajamas, with a big grin on his face, welcoming me with open arms and with the obvious question of what had brought me to Dresden. Just as obviously, I couldn't tell him the real reason for my being there, but I had a good answer ready anyway. I told him I was avoiding the German draft board in Poznań and hoping to sit out the war in Dresden. He chuckled and said that studying at the Academy gave him, too, the opportunity to steer clear of the Wehrmacht. He was quite agreeable to sharing his room with me until I found some work and proper lodgings of my own.

It was probably a day or two after I moved in with Tadek that I went to the address Zenek had given me at our last meeting. Kanalgasse, not far from Postplatz in the centre of the city, was a short, narrow street with small buildings, most of them quite neglected and old, some clearly cheap tenements, others given over to a few rather grubby bars. It all truly embodied poverty in the midst of a beautiful city that was rich in history, culture, and tradition. Yet, when I got to my contact's address, I found the old and creaky stairs leading to the upper floor scrubbed clean and the man's two tiny mansard rooms positively immaculate, with gauze curtains and a nasturtium in the window.

I introduced myself in German, but when I produced my papers — only the legal ones — the man replied in Polish, which we then spoke for the rest of the visit. He was fluent in the language, though with the almost imperceptible trace of a German inflection. I told him I had come from Poznań to settle and work in Dresden but, as sternly advised by Zenek, I mentioned neither names nor anything about the true purpose of my being in this city, nor did I ask any questions of my host. Even today, I smile inwardly, recalling the conversational minuet we performed while this man was probing my credibility. Gradually our chat became personal. I told him an (obviously) brief story of my background and he told me about himself, but at no point did either of us touch on the subject of the Resistance movement.

He was an employee of the *Reichsbahn* (German State Railway) and had been born in Westphalia of Polish parents. His father had left the German-occupied part of Poland toward the end of the 1800s to find work as a coal miner in Germany and had even served in the German army during the First World War. Nevertheless, he had taught his two children to speak and read Polish, so that the family had kept the connection to its origins alive, even while immersed in German language and culture.

I already knew that the German railways had to employ hundreds of formerly Polish railroaders, mainly locomotive engineers and firemen, to temporarily replace German railway personnel who had been drafted into the Wehrmacht. My host had earlier worked in some obscure Reichsbahn office, but was now employed as a translator between the German railway administration and the Polish engine drivers and mechanics who had been drafted to work for the railway system.

I must have been found trustworthy because, after an hour's polite chit-chat, the man told me that I should be prepared to receive "distant relatives" who would stay with me overnight before travelling farther

Here I am with Tadek Beutlich (right) in October 1941 on the Brühlsche Terrasse in front of the Dresden Art Academy.

west. He gave me some food coupons to buy bread and whatever else was available, so that I could have a modest evening repast and a breakfast the following morning. After that, I saw him only a few times, for reasons I no longer recall.

My search for work occupied me totally in my initial days in Dresden, but it was an exercise in futility. Everything in industry was now geared to the war effort, and anyway, I would have proven totally useless working in a restaurant or selling merchandise in a store. Naturally, I had to obey the law, which stipulated that a newcomer to an area had to register with the local police department. I did this, presenting my birth certificate as ID, but I had to think fast when it came to filling out the form's section dealing with "profession." After a few seconds, and purely on impulse, I wrote down "freelance artist," which, to my great relief, was accepted on the spot and without any questions. Only when I left the police station did I realize how tense I'd been throughout that very first encounter with the authorities. But my German had not been questioned, my birth certificate had been given only a quick glance, and I was now legally a resident of Dresden, eligible to receive a full allotment of food coupons.

I found the city to be absolutely enchanting. Even the somewhat heavy nineteenth-century buildings looked comfortable amid all the delicate baroque charm of the various palais and other structures dating back to the reign of August the Strong who, as I well knew, had not only ruled Saxony (of which Dresden was the capital), but had also been an elected king of Poland. August had won the Polish throne by switching from Protestantism to Catholicism, Poland's predominant faith. He also had brought the hitherto healthy Polish economy to ruin by ransacking its resources to fight wars, vastly enrich Saxony, and create the thing of beauty that became Dresden.

Eventually, I got to know Tadek's colleagues and also Professor Dietze, who was in charge of the second-semester painting class that Tadek attended. Dietze, a competent painter of the old school, was an elderly, friendly man who saw my interest in art and asked if I, too, painted. I admitted to drawing a fair bit, and he said that he'd like to see some of my work. I hadn't drawn anything since before the war, when Tadek and I had made a couple of forays out of town to sketch landscapes. I felt a little uncertain and made vague excuses, but Tadek told Dietze that I was actually quite good. Then he turned to me, saying I should show the professor what I could do. I gave in, bought a sketch pad and spent some time drawing architecture in the *Zwinger*, a beautiful, early eighteenth-century baroque complex, and in the *Grosser Garten*, a huge and beautiful municipal park. I took altogether maybe a dozen drawings to Dietze's studio in the Academy. He found them good enough and invited me to take part in some classes he conducted in the evenings. These classes were attended by a small group of students who wanted to further their skills in this extracurricular way, under the supervision of a good teacher. Tadek was a member of that group, as were four young women whose names — amazingly! — I still remember. Among them was a vivacious and bright woman by the name of Franziska Ulich with whom, in time, I found much in common.

Aside from pursuing the purely academic studies in Dietze's classes, I began to draw on my own, mostly images of the war horrors from 1939 that were still vivid in my mind, and personal depictions of the misery of the Polish population under German rule. Franziska saw those drawings and told me that my pen-and-ink technique was reminiscent of Alfred Kubin's style and that the social content of my drawings reminded her of Käthe Kollwitz's graphic work. Naturally, I was flattered, although I had never heard the names of these artists before. I confessed to not knowing anything about them, and, since we were nearing Christmastime, Franziska presented me with a collection of Käthe Kollwitz reproductions. I still have and cherish that portfolio with Franziska's inscribed dedication.

At the end of November I left Tadek's cozy room and moved into a rather dismal but inexpensive room on Dürerstrasse. I had also landed a deadly boring, though reasonably well paid, job at Goehlewerk, a factory belonging to the world-famous Zeiss-Ikon Company. This company manufactured a great range of optical instruments and — as I was to find out — highly interesting objects made of metal, whose purpose I was eventually to learn.

A self-portrait of Franziska Ulich.

79

Clearly realizing that I'd be spending Christmas cooped up in my gloomy room, Franziska invited me to a Christmas Eve supper at her family's home in Hellerau, an attractive park-like suburb of Dresden. All I could take along as a present was a drawing of mine, but even so, it was accepted with genuine grace and pleasure. That evening marked the beginning of my deep and abiding friendship with that family, which consisted of Dr. Franz Ulich, his wife, Ruth, their young son, Herrle, and, of course, Franziska. (An older son, Ernst, was serving in the Wehrmacht in France.) They were to play an extremely important role in my life throughout the remaining war years and for some time after.

It was a pleasant meal, modest in its substance, but followed by what Franziska called an "unexpected dessert." Dr. Ulich turned the radio on to a Swiss station, which, after playing a Christmas carol, announced that as of a week before, the Third Reich was at war with the United States of America. This was followed by the replay of Hitler's speech, in which he let the world know of his joy about the successful Japanese combined navy and air force operation against the American naval base on the Pacific island of Hawaii, and that in keeping with the Third Reich's mutual assistance treaty with Japan, Germany was now at war with the United States. Stunned, we sat in silence until Dr. Ulich stood up to turn the radio off, saying "The man has lost his mind!"

Working at Goehlewerk meant getting up at six in the morning, and, after a frugal breakfast (often even without it), travelling by streetcar all the way across town to report at the factory at eight o'clock. I could only guess at the number of workers of whom I was one, but I estimated it to be more than three thousand. They were overwhelmingly young people, of both sexes and various origins, many of them being of eastern European or Balkan, but also some French, ancestry. Just like the Jews, who were forced to wear the Star of David on their clothing, the Poles had to wear an equally humiliating purple-coloured "P" on a yellow background, while the Ukrainians wore a white "OST" against a light blue background — this, to distinguish them from the German higher-positioned workers and supervising personnel. For some reason, the Yugoslavs were not required to display any sign of ethnic origin. Of course, my masterfully faked papers shielded me from having to wear this kind of ethnic stigma.

Along with a few dozen *Ausländer* (foreigners), I was employed in one of the quality control departments. Using sensitive testing instruments, we checked various small, finely machined and quite mysterious metal parts, and separated them, based on the degree of their accuracy. The perfect ones were deposited in a "good" box, while the faulty ones were dropped into a "bad" container. One of these parts was a nickel-plated, three-millimetre-thick pointed object, about an inch long and with a kind of collar in its middle. Only somewhat later did we learn what lethal purpose it served. German overseers supervised the production, walking up and down the length of the tables and stopping now and then to see how well we were doing our work. The work was deadly dull, the boredom of it all-pervasive and wholly reminiscent of the assembly line in Charlie Chaplin's movie, *Modern Times*, which I had seen just before the war.

On my left sat a young Serb by the name of Mirko, and on my right, an equally young Polish woman (actually more of a girl), named Halina. But while Mirko was usually in good spirits, Halina was mostly depressed and filled with hatred for the Germans, who had not only shot her small brother for possessing a hunting knife, but had also caught her in a street roundup and forced her to work for them in this godawful factory. She was housed together with some fifty other young Polish women in a special camp, from which — always under German supervision — they had to travel by streetcar to work and back. Interestingly, we both came from the same area in Poland. I came from Poznań and she was from Żnin, a town near which my godfather had his estate. Needless to say, being such close compatriots created an even closer bond at work. For me, her situation was of more than passing interest, considering that my Resistance activities (which I still hadn't begun to pursue) required me to learn more about exactly the kind of camps as the one in which Halina was forced to live. It was for this very reason that I began to cultivate our acquaintance even more cordially. Halina, in turn, was only too happy to have someone to talk to while we both did that mindless work, even though our conversations were conducted in whispers and often interrupted by the overseers.

Of course, we couldn't be seen to be too elated by the news of the Wehrmacht's defeat in early December 1941, virtually at the gates of Moscow. German reports of that debacle were, of course, thoroughly sanitized, but Dresden's hospitals were suddenly filled with soldiers with frozen limbs that required amputation and with frozen faces which, while healing, looked like grotesque earless and noseless masks from some infernal carnival. Despite his generals' warnings, Hitler had envisaged only a blitzkrieg campaign lasting three to four months and ending with a victory parade in Red Square. As a result of the Führer's confident expectation of an early end to the war, his Wehrmacht marched into battle wearing summer uniforms, only to later see its soldiers perish in Russia's deadly frost. Following this catastrophe, a desperate action was begun in Germany and — under duress — in all German-occupied countries, to collect civilian winter clothes and keep the Wehrmacht warm in Russia. In the course of that massive operation, my father was stopped in one of the Germans' street roundups in Poznań. A soldier pulled the beaver fur coat off him and, to complete this act of robbery, forcibly wrenched my father's signet ring from his finger. A family possession dating back many generations was never to be seen again.

Early in 1942, Halina and I had a little chat about the occasional visits paid to Goehlewerk by small groups of German naval officers. Neither she nor I knew what this signified, so I turned to Mirko, asking if he knew what the *Kriegsmarine* (navy) was doing in our factory. He gave me a knowing grin, and whispered back that a friend of his who understood German had overheard a supervisor talking with an overseer about the navy formally making a last check before taking possession of the latest shipment of navy-ordered *matériel*. I conveyed this to Halina, who spread the information among those of her Polish women co-workers whom she knew well enough to trust implicitly.

I do not know how she found out that the pointy little objects we were testing were actually parts of torpedo firing systems, but the news shocked us both, since (as I knew and told Halina) Polish navy ships were fighting alongside the British fleet — while here we were forced to contribute to their possible destruction! In feverish whispers, we discussed ways of doing something about it. We had almost given up when I suddenly remembered the idea of "small sabotage" and explained it to Halina. Within seconds, we had a solution: if firing pins came up as faulty, we'd put them in with the perfect ones, and conversely, we'd smuggle perfect ones in with the faulty. We did not know how many of those missiles would fail to explode on impact, but even if it were only one, it would be a small victory for the young woman from the Polish countryside, and for me. We crossed our fingers.

It was from Halina that I learned about conditions inside the camp in which she and all the other women lived. The winter was exceptionally cold, and one small stove could not compete with the frosty wind whistling in through the wooden structure's uninsulated walls. The women tried to fill the cracks with whatever was available, but it wasn't enough. Paradoxically, rather than suffering the conditions of what passed as a shelter, they preferred to be at work, even in modestly heated factories. They received food twice a day: in the morning, a few grams of bread made from indeterminate ingredients and ersatz coffee made from roasted and ground turnips. The evening meal consisted of a watery soup of unknown origin, handed out in small, beat-up tin containers. To keep each other warm at night, the women doubled up in two-tier raw wood beds with straw mattresses. Halina would not speak of the camp's hygienic conditions and of her fellow camp inmates' state of health.

She later told me that she'd persuaded some of the other women testers to follow our "small sabotage" method and that two of them had agreed to co-operate with us. But, realizing the great danger in involving others, I asked her to stop them right away. I had no way of knowing if Mirko suspected anything. After all, he was not part of our quiet conspiracy, but almost close enough to notice what we were doing. Nonetheless, I thought at the time that he would not have forgotten the April 1941 bombing of Belgrade and the murderous German invasion of Yugoslavia. He certainly didn't display any friendly feelings toward that jackbooted lot.

I was in regular correspondence with my parents. The German officers quartered in our home usually stayed for only a few months or weeks, to then be transferred somewhere else and make room for another group.

The war dragged on, with England holding out and the Soviets making life very difficult for the Germans all the way from besieged Leningrad to the Black Sea. Dresden was quiet and serene in its beauty. Franziska, Tadek, and I went to a couple of symphony concerts, and we attended Dietze's classes more or less regularly. From my parents' letters I learned that Zenek was visiting them now and then. He had my address, but I never received any mail from him. In late February 1942, I got sick with a bad case of the flu. A day or two later, a nurse appeared on behalf of my Goehlewerk employers, to check up on me and make sure that I was really ill. She found this to be true, and I thought that this might be a way to leave Goehlewerk behind me. I told her that I was afraid of tuberculosis, which, I said, seemed to run in my family. The nurse became quite agitated and said that, if this was the case, I should be under medical care and certainly stay away from work, where I could possibly infect other people. She packed up her stethoscope, blood pressure meter, and whatever else she'd brought along, and left quickly. I chuckled to myself, knowing that there were not too many doctors left in Dresden (since many of them had been drafted and sent to the front), so that in effect I was free to do with myself as I pleased. My ruse worked. Goehlewerk released me from employment, my flu eventually abated and then disappeared, and it was time for me to find something else to do.

Franziska, as always enterprising and helpful, found me a place to live in Hellerau — two tiny rooms, each not quite three and a half metres square, on the second floor of a small, pretty house owned by a Frau Heinich, an old, sweet-tempered widow whom I instantly liked. Most conveniently, the house, Auf dem Sand 31, was a mere two houses away from the Ulich residence. Franziska also arranged for me to have my dinners with her family; I surrendered most of my food coupons to Frau Ulich, keeping only those that could be used to buy wartime bread (the dreadful quality of which I'd rather not describe here), which I toasted on my wood stove.

Almost simultaneously, I found a job that more or less suited me, working as a film animation artist at the Boehner Film Studios. The films produced there were not the usual animated movies, such as the ones I

Frau Heinich, my landlady in Hellerau.

knew from the pre-war days of Mickey Mouse and Snow White. These were stereo, three-dimensional, and highly specialized films, and watching them required the wearing of Polaroid spectacles. It was a patented process, owned by Boehner Film and (as in the case of all German industry of that time) used for military purposes. When I responded to the newspaper ad looking for people with art schooling and found out the nature of Boehner's productions, I knew that this workplace would be not only interesting, but also relatively safe. The job was not at all dull, mainly because I was surrounded by some fascinating people — artists, technicians, cameramen, film editors, film directors, and stage designers. The studios were in the suburb of Gorbitz, far away from Hellerau, but with the excellent, and still-functioning, Dresden transit system, I could reach my destination in forty-five minutes, including a transfer.

The first film I worked on dealt with the stellar coordinates and was produced primarily as an educational tool for navy personnel, to enable

Helping a colleague in 1943 at Boehner Film cope with stereo animation.

them to navigate even in the event that their navigational instruments should fail. The stars were drawn as white dots, about four millimetres in diameter, on great cellophane sheets. Their celestial travels were shown in three dimensions so persuasively that, when filmed, edited, and projected onto a screen, the illusion of depth was enough to make an audience gasp in amazement. To me, the work — which required great, almost mathematical accuracy — was not overly interesting, except, of course, for the result on the screen. Even so, it was a far cry from the deadly boredom of my former job at Goehlewerk. Soon, Franziska followed my example and got a job at Boehner Film, in the same department in which I worked, also drawing little white dots.

Meanwhile, Tadek, Franziska, and I became close friends. We not only attended the Dietze class together, but also went for walks around old Dresden, and frequently went for a watery, wartime beer or two at the Pschorr Bräu restaurant in the oldest part of the city's downtown. Needless to say, we also visited the fabulous *Staatliche Gemäldegalerie* (State Gallery of Art), then still open, with almost religious regularity.

It had now been six months since Zenek had asked me if I would be willing to go to Germany and work for the Resistance. In that time, I'd done what I was expected to do: I had established a legal domicile in Dresden, made friends, and gotten myself an interesting and fairly well paid job, working at something which was officially considered *kriegswichtig* (essential to the war effort). Was I perhaps ready to begin the work I had been sent by the Resistance to carry out?

8 MY RESISTANCE WORK BEGINS

A postcard arrived from some obscure town in occupied Western Poland, announcing in perfect German and in cordial terms that "Onkel Ernst" or some cousin would like to stop in Dresden on such-and-such a day to see his nephew. Could he come by in the evening, when I'd be home from work? Not even the most observant postal censor could have found anything suspicious in this plain, innocent text, which also included my "uncle's" date of arrival.

Having made sure Franziska wouldn't pop by my place, I waited for my visitor until after dusk. When the bell rang, I ran downstairs to open the door before Frau Heinich got there. I'd been wondering all along what my "uncle" would look like, but I wasn't prepared for the complete and utter ordinariness of the person standing in the doorway. Everything about him, including his face, was absolutely average — an incalculable advantage for a person whose life depended on not being noticed. He looked to be in his thirties or forties, wore slightly threadbare clothes, shoes that had seen better days, and a grey, semi-military cap of the kind that was becoming very popular among the wartime German working class. He greeted me with a somewhat accented *"guten Abend"* ("good evening") and, as I let him in, I saw that his cap bore the winged-wheel emblem of the Reichsbahn. No names were exchanged.

We shook hands, and I led him upstairs to the spare room I had prepared for him. Regrettably, there was no bedstead, and I apologized for being able to offer him only an old spring mattress to sleep on. He shrugged, smiled, and said he'd seen worse — sleeping on the bare ground or on straw was most often the only choice. We were now speaking Polish, and I invited him to come to my room across the tiny hall, where I had some bread that I'd saved up and some cooked vegetables ready for him, as well as a small pot of herbal tea, which I quickly heated up on my wood-stove. After he had wolfed down this modest meal, I asked him how things were back home, but he wasn't overly talkative. He said only that the situation was not good, that the German oppression could be felt in every aspect of life, but that the Poles were more hopeful of the war's positive outcome, now that even America was on the Allied side. His knowledge of conditions in Poland was unfortunately restricted to the enclave of the General Gouvernement, so I didn't ask about the situation in Poznań. In any case, I could read about it between the lines of my parents' letters.

Of course, I already knew how to exercise self-restraint in conversations with people like Zenek and other friends in the Resistance. You had to be careful in your questions and answers, because any information acquired or imparted could later become highly dangerous under possibly intense interrogation. Even knowledge about details of this man's mission belonged to the category of "unmentionables." What we could talk about, however, was the mood and attitudes of Dresden's population regarding the course of the war. As far as this was concerned, I was able to tell him that there was no perceptible shift of opinion, at least not from what I overheard of conversations in public places and at work. But some people in the film studio in which I worked had expressed circumspectly whispered pessimism about the Wehrmacht venturing much too far into southern Russia — and then promptly corrected themselves by saying that, of course, the Führer knew what he was doing in heading for the oil fields of the Caspian Sea. It goes without saying that I avoided taking part in those speculative conversations.

My visitor left next morning after a skimpy breakfast and just in time to get to the railway station and catch his train. Where he went from there, I had no way of knowing. Only toward the end of the war did I learn that the Polish Underground's communication system had its bases and outposts in such cities as Stockholm, Budapest, Bucharest, Constantinople, Cairo, Bern, Marseille, Paris, and Lisbon.

Couriers en route between Poland and England travelled along three principal routes. The northern one led from Baltic ports, such as Danzig (now Gdańsk), Gdynia, or even Stettin (now Szczecin) and, in one case, even Kiel, to Sweden. From there the route led to Norway and across the North Sea to Britain. The Polish Resistance had people posted along land routes, and sea crossings were accomplished on fishing boats, coal freighters, or other kinds of vessels under non-German flags, whose captains had been suitably paid for looking the other way.

The southern route, the longest and most cumbersome of all, went either through Prague into Austria or through Bratislava into Hungary. In the first case, it led from Austria into northern Italy. The second variant, which took couriers across the north of Yugoslavia into Zagreb, also led into northern Italy. From there, couriers would work their way along the Mediterranean coast to Perpignan, on the French side of the Pyrenees. Here, they would either bribe a willing skipper to take them along the Spanish coast to Gibraltar or risk the long walk across the treacherous Pyrenees and the Guardia Civil–infested Spanish mainland. From Gibraltar, couriers would be taken by Allied vessels or aircraft on the next available passage or flight to Great Britain.

A third route, the shortest, but also most dangerous, led directly across Germany into Belgium and from there to the French coast. Here, couriers were either picked up by small aircraft or taken by fishing boat across the English Channel. Toward the mid-point of the war, some couriers, sabotage experts, special operations (SOE) agents, and even important political contacts between the Polish government-in-exile located in London and its underground representation in Warsaw, began to be parachuted into German-occupied Poland or night-landed in remote parts of the countryside. This form of transport was certainly faster, but in its own way was probably just as dangerous as the couriers' slow land-and-sea journeys.

I was, of course, acutely aware of the danger in providing stopovers for individuals travelling from Poland to the West. There was no way to ascertain their credibility, not even by the use of passwords. The latter were often changed in the mail I received to announce the arrival of "Cousin Hans" or "Mother's half-brother, Willy." These names later served as the visitors' passwords, to which I would reply by casually stating the family relationship (cousin, half-brother, or whatever) given on the postcard or in the letter. But even passwords could have become known to the German *Abwehr* (counter-intelligence) or the Gestapo, which had its own effective ways of extracting information from arrested members of the Resistance. My "guests" spoke only of events taking place in the General Gouvernement, of mass arrests and executions, of the persecution of Jews and their annihilation in death camps, whose many names and locations had by then become known. Much was also known about the Gehenna of Poles persecuted by the Soviets and Ukrainians and forcibly transported to Siberian labour camps. Understandably, my overnight guests never spoke about the exact purpose of their travel or mission. Of course, they memorized whatever I could tell them about the rapidly worsening living conditions in Saxony and, presumably, in most of Germany. Clearly, they also absorbed information I was able to impart about a growing number of foreign troops now replacing the Wehrmacht's steadily growing casualties: Kalmucks, Tatars, Ossetians, Chechens, Mongolians, Uzbeks, Nenets, and others who during the twelve years of Hitler's Thousand Year Reich were all seen as *Untermenschen* (subhumans).

Contrary to the impression one may get from the above, only a few Polish couriers stopped by in Hellerau. I remember them only vaguely as appearing in the evening and vanishing in the morning. To be on the safe side, I'll say that between 1942 and November 1944 no more than three to six couriers from Poland stayed with me in Hellerau (though I'm not fully certain about these numbers). The end of the Warsaw Uprising in October 1944 curtailed Resistance activity and ended most of the courier travel.

Even though these stopovers represented a rather infrequent sort of traffic, I incessantly worried about the presence of two relatively close neighbours. One of them was an elderly but active minor Nazi Party leader who had a fairly good view of Frau Heinich's house entrance. The other

Looking out my window over peaceful Hellerau, it was hard to believe there was a war going on.

was also a Nazi, a retired bureaucrat named Geyer, who used to hoist the swastika flag every time the radio announced a German victory, no matter how insignificant. His house was only a few metres away from Frau Heinich's home, and from a second floor window he had a view into my room. Whenever I had a visitor, closing my window and drawing a curtain became mandatory. Just one word from Herr Geyer to the Gestapo about suspicious individuals calling at Frau Heinich's address would have had consequences I hesitate to name even now, so many years later.

The published accounts of some of these couriers shed light on the many perils they faced as well as the scope of their assignments. In Jan Karski's *Story of a Secret State*, published before the end of the war, the author describes his adventures in travelling from Warsaw to Britain to inform the Allies about the mass murder of Jews that the Germans were perpetrating in occupied Poland and to request more weapons for the Polish Home Army's fight against Hitler's Reich. Jan Nowak's memoir, *Courier from Warsaw*, a work somewhat different in scope, deals in part with the author's exploits as a courier dispatched by the Polish Underground authority to plead Poland's cause with the likes of Churchill and Roosevelt, only to find that those two worthies had already handed Poland to Stalin during the 1943 Tehran Conference, in return for the Soviet Union's staying in the war.

For me, *Courier from Warsaw* contained a surprising personal note. Having overcome considerable difficulties in slipping across the border from Germany into Switzerland, courier Nowak arrived at a Polish outpost in Vezenas, near Geneva, to find himself in the company of a Major Młodzianowski and, to my surprise, also of Captain Kazimierz Jasnoch, an artist connected with the Resistance's Polish liaison in Switzerland. There was no doubt in my mind that it was the same Kazimierz Jasnoch I had known throughout my childhood and teen years in pre-war Poznań, whose life-size self-portrait in his Polish officer's uniform had once hung in my father's study and whom I'd last seen at his estate in Borsk just before the outbreak of the war. By then he must have been in his sixties, so he would have been well advanced in age when he and Nowak met in Switzerland in the early spring of 1945. In late 1946, he surfaced briefly in Poznań in search of any information that might help him locate his wife, who had been one of my mother's students. Although my father was able to help, he learned nothing of Jasnoch's story, which — given the Polish Communist regime's brutal behaviour toward former Resistance members — would certainly have included facing considerable risks in order to return from Switzerland to Poland. My postwar inquiries about his subsequent fate, directed to the General Sikorski Institute in London, remained unanswered.

By now, everyone in the Ulich family was aware that I was a Pole, but it simply didn't seem to matter to them. Although outwardly discreet, they were open in expressing their staunchly anti-Nazi opinions in my presence. They understood my attitude toward the German occupation of Poland and were horrified by the persecutions of Poles and Jews which were taking place there. Shortly after that first visitor-courier had spent the night at my place, I had a conversation with Franziska's mother, Frau Ruth Ulich, about conditions in Poland. In the course of our talk, I found that she possessed knowledge far more extensive and detailed than mine. Amazed by the amount of information she had, I asked where in the world she had gotten it, and she replied — quite casually — "Oh, from the BBC, of course." Momentarily stunned, I realized that here was a solution to my problem of obtaining information from the West. I didn't even have to ask permission to listen to the BBC broadcasts. Frau Ulich herself suggested it.

The Ulich's magnificent Grundig radio was capable of receiving foreign stations from many parts of the world, but we were primarily interested in news coming from London. Of course, there was massive German jamming of the airwaves, but even so, a good half or more of what we wanted to hear came through that hellish whistling and squawking noise. Mostly, the speakers' voices sounded as if they were coming from under water — and even then covered by the whooshing of waves — but they would sporadically emerge with some clarity for brief spans of time, ranging from mere seconds to as long as half a minute. We listened to BBC's Polish- and German-language broadcasts, although the former were incomprehensible to my hosts, and I had to translate for them the most interesting parts, including those pertaining to the activities of Polish armed forces on the Allied side.

There was an additional benefit to those translations. I was able to make brief notes, which I could then transcribe and, if necessary, widen in scope for discreet distribution among the Polish labour camps around

Dresden. Halina, my friend from Goehlewerk, had given me their locations; there were three in the Dresden suburbs of Freital, Radebeul, and Klotzsche, and one in a small resort town called Bad Schandau, situated on the Elbe river some sixty kilometres southeast of Dresden, in a beautiful mountainous area popularly known as "Saxon Switzerland."

It was now that the other part of my mission was to begin. According to the instructions I had received before leaving Poznań, I was to take my time and never appear to be in a hurry. Clearly, with a height of 192 cm, I could not look quite as average as I would have wished. To compensate, I had to rely on my behaviour, always making sure that I acted as if whatever I was doing was right and suitable to the time, place, and occasion. This was obviously crucial when approaching and exploring the best ways around the labour camps, looking for discreet places to plant my — as yet primitively produced — BBC transcriptions.

The clandestine listening sessions at the Ulich family's home were irregular and always arranged spontaneously, but they took place at least two or three times a week. Usually the audience consisted of Dr. and Frau Ulich, Franziska, and me. Occasionally, twelve-year-old Herrle was allowed to join this small group. The big Grundig radio stood in the somewhat crowded little family room, with a large picture window overlooking the garden behind the house. Just as in Britain, there was a total blackout throughout Germany, and in the evenings this picture window was covered from the inside by a large, thick blanket, which did more than simply prevent light from escaping to the outside. It also protected us from the eyes of busybodies and effectively kept the squeaks and howls caused by the jamming from escaping to the outside. A primitive aerial, a long copper-wire coil stretched inside the attic, most likely improved the quality of those transmissions. Of course, we all knew that listening to "enemy" broadcasts was punishable by an indefinite stay in a concentration camp — or even by death.

The subject of concentration camps first came up in a conversation I had with the Ulich family, when Franziska happened to mention that a man named Chrambach, a writer living a few houses away, had been released from such a camp and was now secluded in his home, evidently quite incommunicado. I had already heard it whispered at work that prisoners with relatively minor sentences were sometimes let go, but only after signing an oath not to divulge anything they had witnessed or experienced during their stay in the camp. This in itself spoke volumes about the barbaric treatment of inmates populating those horrible places. Over time, I found that most Germans carefully avoided speaking of concentration camps. Just the same, it had become known that when a prisoner died or was killed during incarceration, the form letter sent to the family invariably gave "pneumonia" or "stroke" as the cause of death. Sometimes this was attached to a cardboard box supposedly containing the deceased's ashes, so the existence of crematoria in the camps became public knowledge. But in 1941 and 1942, no one knew yet that a different kind of camp was being established on occupied Polish territory and that this signaled the beginning of a mass murder on a scale never even heard of before. Toward the end of the Second World War, the German public appeared inured to the existence of concentration camps and their reputed "unpleasantness." Even when the real horrors of Nazi-conceived genocide came to light, the news was met with disbelief and denial on the part of most Germans. Some of that denial is still around, not only in Germany itself, but in many other parts of the world. Needless to say, those friends and colleagues whom I could trust seethed with hate against the Nazi regime, but were helpless to take any action. The Gestapo seemed to have its people almost everywhere, and fear of it was all-pervasive.

Alas, poor Tadek, the Wehrmacht caught up with him and he was drafted. He spent some time in the military depot of Königsbrück, near Dresden, being trained to march, shoot, and salute. Franziska and I visited him there before he was shipped to the Russian front, from where I received a few terse letters. The next communication from him, quite some time later, was an enthusiastic postcard from Florence. His unit had been sent to Italy, but in the course of events, he was captured by the Allied troops and put into a POW camp. He was rescued from there and, as a pre-war Polish citizen, incorporated into the Second Polish Corps, part of the British Army. I was luckier than Tadek. The long, hairy arm of the Wehrmacht never did catch up with me, although the possibility that it might was a constant source of worry.

It was probably the beginning of April 1942 when I decided that the time had come to try to produce a bulletin compiled from BBC newscasts. Writing the text was not difficult, merely a matter of translating London's German-language broadcasts into Polish and condensing the Polish text into some brief paragraphs. The news dealt mostly with heavy battles fought by the Soviets to slow the German invasion of Russia and Ukraine, the German siege of Tobruk, and various actions in the Battle of the Atlantic. As I recall, around that time there were also Polish broadcasts dealing not only with Polish fighter pilots in combat over Britain and elsewhere, but also with purely political events taking place within the Polish government-in-exile in London.

The bulletin had to be short and touch only on the most noteworthy points. But, since I didn't have a typewriter or a copying machine, I had to write the text out by hand and use carbon paper to produce three, and sometimes four, copies of this single-sheet bulletin. Naturally, I handprinted the entire text in Roman characters, since handwriting could be too easily traced. The problem of sporadically distributing those bulletins without in any way changing my daily routine — which included my work at the Boehner studio and, of course, my frequent appearances at the Ulich family's home — could be solved only by careful planning. Needless to say, all my clandestine activities had to be kept hidden from them and especially from Franziska, with whom I spent the weekdays at work and weekends at the Ulichs' home. Most of the time that I spent by myself was in the evenings, after dinner at the Ulichs. My landlady, kindly old Frau Heinich, used to retire around nine o'clock. In any case, she was quite disinterested in what I did, when and where I went, or whom I entertained. The occasional courier visitors (who, by the way, all spoke fairly good, though accented, German) were accepted by her as my friends or family members. We also made a deal by which these visitors would be admitted by her only if they appeared before she retired, and afterwards by me. She was the soul of discretion and never came upstairs to my rooms. And she certainly never read any mail that arrived for me from eastern Germany or occupied Western Poland, with greetings from "cousins," "nephews," or (in one case) from my "sister" — and, of course, from my parents, who were trying to survive in the misery of occupied Poznań.

I decided to make my first foray into the unknown to drop off a single copy of my arduously produced news sheet at a Polish labour camp in Radebeul, a northwestern suburb of Dresden. Since the streetcars ran as late as 2:00 a.m., I could leave Hellerau just past 9:00 p.m., reach my destination in approximately one hour, quickly perform my task, and be back home around midnight. I was not alone in that streetcar. There were, I think, a few soldiers on leave and a dozen or more women, probably on their way to work the late shift in some factory or other. Male workers had become a rarity, since most of them had been drafted into the Wehrmacht and were now enjoying the doubtful pleasures of the war in Russia. At Postplatz, a square in the very centre of the Dresden, I changed to a different line. When I got off the streetcar in Radebeul, I found myself in the darkness of a total blackout. Fortunately, Halina had given me the precise location of the camp, so despite not being able to see any street signs, I could still find the three low-slung huts, which were separated by a wire fence from the residential and commercial buildings surrounding them — unmistakably the camp I was looking for. I walked slowly around the enclosed area, slipped my twice-folded bulletin under the fence and sauntered away slowly, in the casual manner of someone just out for an evening walk and some fresh air. On my way back to Hellerau, I wondered who, if anyone, would pick up that folded piece of paper and read it later on. Halina had told me that most, if not all, forced-labour camps had German gatekeepers — old men way past military age who spent all of their time inside their little gatehouses, listening to the radio, reading their magazines, and snoozing a lot. They rarely ventured out for an inspection of the camp's grounds and certainly wouldn't stoop to pick up any litter. Keeping the grounds clean and free of such rubbish as stray pieces of paper was the responsibility of camp inmates. Knowing this, I was confident that my very first clandestine bulletin would reach the right recipients.

The Freital camp was quite far away, at the other side of Dresden proper, and I could travel there only by the train that left the Dresden-Neustadt station at six in the morning and arrived at Freital twenty minutes later. This left me sufficient time to carefully check out the camp's surroundings and plant my bulletin in an appropriately discreet place before boarding a train back to Dresden at around seven-thirty. I would be back in Hellerau a little over an hour later, around a quarter to nine. From what I remember, I made those trips to the Freital camp only on Sundays, when Boehner Film Studios gave their employees a day off. But, these trips to Freital were possible only under cover of darkness. When summer came, I decided to abandon them.

The Polish labour camp in Klotzsche was the easiest for me to reach. Located on the edge of a small municipality adjoining Hellerau, the camp was surrounded by the usual barbed wire and quite a few trees and bushes, so smuggling my subversive literature under the wire fence was relatively easy. Moreover, it never took me more than thirty minutes to walk from my place to the camp.

9 A CLOSE CALL AND A NEW PASSPORT

Bad Schandau, about forty-five minutes by train from Dresden, was a Saturday afternoon destination for me, since Boehner Studios did not require us to work past one o'clock. But access to the Polish labour camp there presented problems of its own. It was fairly exposed on two sides, and on the other two faced a nondescript piece of ground, with just a few scrubby bushes. These provided no cover at all for anyone wishing to approach the facility as unofficially as I did. The only way I could do it was to brazen it out, pretending to be looking for something among those miserable bushes and only gradually approaching the fence to plant my bulletin.

For my second foray to this camp, I employed a perfectly innocent piece of camouflage: my sketchpad, in which I drew the various weeds and thistles growing by the camp's fence. Of course, there was nothing more harmless than an artist studying and sketching the wonders of nature. To study them more closely, I had to bend down nearer to where the wire fence touched the ground. Slipping my "literature" into the camp took no more than a split second. To this day, I'm amazed at the disarming naïveté of those people who walked past, smiling, and even giving me a friendly wave. This incident pretty well summed up my existence in those days. Being a stranger in this foreign land, I instinctively assumed a chameleon-like persona, blending in with the environment and becoming part of the landscape.

On one particular Saturday in April 1942, having managed to smuggle my newsletter into the Schandau camp, I walked back to the railway station to wait for the regional train that would take me back to Dresden. I think I was quite satisfied that my second (or perhaps even third?) trip to Schandau had been successful, and I'd been glad to see that, just as before, the previous bulletin was no longer where I'd placed it — proof to me that it had been picked up and done its work as a source of information for the camp's inmates.

Along with a small crowd of women and their children, some teen-aged Hitler Youth boys and girls, a few older men in work clothes, and a couple of soldiers evidently on leave, I stood on the platform, expecting the train to pull into the station in a matter of minutes. Suddenly, the roar of car and motorcycle engines was heard approaching from what seemed like all directions. It came in fact from the area behind the little station building at the other side of the tracks. The noise suddenly died down, and a number of police and black-uniformed SS men rushed through the station door and from behind the building, raced across the tracks, and jumped onto the platform. In a matter of seconds, they had formed a half-circle facing the group of people waiting there. It all happened so quickly that there was hardly time for anyone, myself included, to grasp what was taking place. An old man stepped forward, faced the SS man who appeared to be the leader of the action, and asked in an irritated tone of voice what was going on. But the SS man shoved him aside brusquely, ordering the women and children to stand to one side and all males to form a line on the other side. This done, he and an SS subaltern began examining the papers of every man and teenaged boy and of the two sol-diers as well. The workmen's tool bags were minutely examined, as were the soldiers' knapsacks, carry bags, and even gas mask containers. Those who wore headgear had their hats or caps searched with exemplary thor-oughness. Some were asked to turn their pockets inside out and display the contents. Shoes and boots had to be taken off and examined. Women and children were exempted from the search.

Then and there, on that railway platform in Schandau, I changed. In less than a millisecond, my youthful arrogance gave way to a fear so all-encompassing I could almost taste it. Never before had I been so terrified, not even when I was wounded and blinded by the bomb explosion in the marketplace in Kutno. The closer that the SS man came toward me, the more that fear grew. Strangely, though, I recall that I wasn't shaking. But as I stood there motionless, waiting with my false passport at the ready, I was overcome by the sudden realization that in one of my pockets I was carrying a document testifying to my true identity: my birth certificate issued to Jan Jakub Daćbóg Kamieński. If I were to be searched, and the two documents compared, my prospects of survival would be nil. The SS man took my passport, looked at the photo, looked at me, and asked, "*Sprichst du Deutsch?*" ("Do you speak German?") "*Ja,*" I said, with a deliberate accent, "*aber nicht sehr gut.*" ("Yes, but not very well.") He grunted something, returned my passport, and moved on to the next man in the row.

No one was arrested in that incident. The SS and police roared away, and the train arrived to take us back to Dresden. There were mumbles and whispers about the possible purpose of the unexpected action, and a few low-voiced remarks about the impertinent behaviour of those in authority, but all that abated once the train reached Dresden *Hauptbahnhof* (central train station). It was only the next day that the reason for that police and SS action became known.

Bad Schandau is situated south of Dresden, in a beautiful area of sandstone hills, rocky riverbanks, and mesas popular with tourists and other lovers of the outdoors. But during the Third Reich, this area also served more sinister Nazi purposes. In a mental hospital, housed in Schloss Sonnenstein, high on a mesa above the town of Pirna, over 13,000 mentally ill or disabled "patients" were killed by injections of Phenol or in gas chambers. On the mesa overlooking the town of Königstein, the gloomy thirteenth-century fortress (which had served as a prison since the late sixteenth century) had been turned into a POW camp for high-ranking officers, mainly French, captured during the German invasion of France in May and June 1940. Among those prisoners was General Henri Giraud who, obviously with outside help, had managed to escape the Königstein camp on the night preceding my visit to Bad Schandau. The episode on the train platform was part of a frantic search for his collaborators.

Of course, I never mentioned the incident to my friends in Hellerau; they hadn't even known that I was away in Bad Schandau. But the news of

General Giraud's escape — and of the embarrassment this had caused the Germans — quite naturally became an interesting few paragraphs in my next bulletin. Giraud eventually managed to reach North Africa following the Anglo-American landings in November 1942. He then commanded French forces in Italy, but quarreled with de Gaulle and retired in 1944. After the war, he remained a member of the War Council and received a medal for his escape.

The general's sensational escape was not the only bright light on the war's otherwise gloomy horizon. Hitler had already declared war on the United States in 1941, and thus one more nation had become part of the Alliance to which we Poles also belonged. The Royal Air Force was now bombing German industry and German cities. Still, the Wehrmacht continued to march victoriously ever deeper into Russia and Ukraine, and I had to blunt this news by stressing in my bulletins all the positive developments on the Allied side. The BBC never stinted in emphasizing these achievements either and sometimes blew them out of proportion — it was the kind of psychological warfare practiced by all belligerents.

No one in Dresden believed that the city would ever be bombed. After all, it was thought, the British were a civilized people who respected the beauty and artistic value of that lovely city on the Elbe. Hamburg, Cologne, and Berlin were being bombed most thoroughly, as were many other industrial German centres, but Dresden remained virtually untouched. As I remember, very few travellers from Poland stopped by my place in Hellerau during that time — perhaps only two individuals, weeks or months apart, mostly undemonstrative, and quite inconspicuous. Whatever scarce news they brought with them from occupied Poland was always grim and depressing. They spoke of mass arrests and executions, and of shootings carried out indiscriminately and publicly and often involving up to a hundred or more victims at a time. These bloodbaths were invariably confirmed from London in Polish-language broadcasts. Among other things, we heard about "special SS units" on the rampage, burning entire villages to the ground, often with the villagers crowded into churches and incinerated alive. The persecution of Jews was also gaining in intensity and cold-blooded bestiality.

As I recall, it was a lovely spring in the Elbe valley. There were flowers everywhere; parks and playgrounds were full of women with their children; the zoo was crowded; even the paddlewheelers were still busy carrying holidayers between Dresden and Meissen, and as far as Rathen, not far from the Czechoslovakian border. To a visitor who came through Dresden and stayed with me overnight, I reported my observations of the population's mood and the fact that the numbers of younger men had visibly diminished. On the streets of Dresden, one now saw mostly elderly men, those past military age. Regarding the mood of the population, I could only say that it underwent swings motivated, no doubt, by news given out by Wehrmacht Headquarters. German successes in the battle for Kharkov brought with them hopes for an early conclusion of the war in the East. Conversely, the RAF's 1,000-bomber raid on Cologne at the end of May raised despair and hate against the British. But I did hear some discreet murmurs about it having been revenge for the massive 1940 German raid on Coventry and the destruction of much of that historic city. Clearly, it was also meant to avenge the Luftwaffe's Blitz on London.

In movie houses, the war was shown in newsreels that always preceded feature presentations. Victorious German troops, dust-covered but smiling, pressed forward, while thousands of Russian soldiers, defeated and now in rags, dragged themselves in the opposite direction, toward POW camps from which most of them would not come out alive. Crushing everything in their way, German tanks rolled eastward to the musical accompaniment of Liszt's *Les Préludes*, a piece of "heroic" music that could easily have been written for just such occasions.

Sometime in June 1942, an air raid alarm rang out in Dresden and its suburbs, the second or third such occurrence since the beginning of the war. The all-clear sounded a few minutes later, but the incident left the population in a state of temporary panic and, later, astonishment that the enemy had flown that far into the Reich's territory. Even so, my civilized colleagues at the Boehner Film Studios were confident that "they" — meaning the RAF and the Americans — would never deliberately attack the pearl of baroque beauty that was Dresden.

Around this time, I began to worry about the duality of my names — the real one on my birth certificate and the false one in the stateless passport the Resistance had issued me back in 1941. So far I had used the passport rarely, only on occasions when it had helped me get out of potentially sticky situations. Everywhere else I was known by my real name. The fact that it ended with the letters *ski* never seemed to raise any eyebrows; it was not a problem. What I did find very difficult, however, was having to constantly watch myself and use the correct name in accordance with any given situation. The more I thought about it, the clearer the idea of combining my real name with a stateless passport became in my mind.

It turned out to be easier than I thought. In the Dresden phone book I discovered that the County Office was also in charge of issuing passports. When I went there to make inquiries, I found it occupied not by the arrogant officials I'd been expecting, but — to my great relief — mild-mannered, elderly men at work behind their desks. Most had no doubt been brought back from retirement to replace younger civil servants now serving in the Wehrmacht.

I was directed to the official in charge of issuing passports, a kindly sort of gent, to whom I explained my business. Presenting my birth certificate, I told him I had been born in Poland, but that since the Polish state no longer existed and since I was not a German citizen either, I needed proper identification in the form of a stateless passport. My well-reasoned (I hoped), yet simple, request was evidently convincing, because the man nodded agreement and told me to wait while he took down all the necessary particulars. That done, he said I could pick up the passport the next day. I don't recall whether I already had my photo handy or if I brought it the next day to have it affixed to and stamped into the brand-new passport. But I do remember the feeling of immense relief at having succeeded in carrying out this potentially risky coup. It became clear to me that this elderly civil servant's mind was still functioning in the old-fashioned way, with dealings between officialdom and the public based on mutual trust. Had I encountered a much younger official, perhaps even one with a Party button in his lapel, a very thorough examination of my case would certainly have landed me in a concentration camp, or worse. Nonetheless, I was still nervous and filled with apprehension when I went to pick up the new passport on the following day. Might something have happened to stop its issuance and validation? Had that nice old man's superior reversed the decision? Had anything changed since the previous day? But nothing like that happened. I got the passport, paid the fee, thanked the old gentleman, and left. Then I sat on the front steps of the building and waited for my pulse to return to normal.

In my bulletins, I did my best to explain that German successes in the East and in Africa could be only temporary and that, since America was now in the Alliance, the war's final outcome was certain. Victory would be ours. However, I had learned something I hadn't known while still in Poznań, but later heard commented on in the BBC's Polish broadcast. About a half-million Poles had been dragged by the Soviets from their homes in eastern Poland to Siberia, where they now toiled as forced labourers. Obviously, this was material I should have used in my news bulletin, but I hesitated. Supposing that, among the Polish forced labourers whom I was supplying with bulletins, there were some from eastern Poland's Soviet-occupied areas? This news would make them despair about the fate of their families. In the end, I decided not to publicize this information. The way I saw it, my function was to bolster the spirits of my compatriots. It would have been wrong to deepen their misery.

In the summer of 1942, following the disastrous Canadian-British raid at Dieppe, two or three wooden barrack sheds were erected on the terrain next to the Boehner Films studio buildings. A chain-link fence was put up around the area, and a large group of POWs, mostly British, New Zealanders, and a few Canadians moved into the camp. The Brits and Canadians had been taken prisoner during the Dieppe debacle, while the New Zealanders had been captured in North Africa. Any contact between studio personnel and POWs was verboten, but the camp's proximity to the studio made some interchange unavoidable. Eventually, apart from such items as chocolate or cigarettes (of the POWs' Red Cross parcel provenance), information was also exchanged — not just the official pap, but real news coming via the BBC. Those who risked communication with the POWs included Herr Best, an elderly gentleman who spoke English rather well, Franziska, who knew some English words and phrases, and

The desk where I wrote Underground literature.

a few other studio employees. These exchanges, verbal or involving tangible goods, were always quick and occurred while the two parties just "happened" to be walking on either side of the chain-link fence. I didn't speak any English, but I did recall a few words from the many American movies I'd seen before the war. Using these words, gesturing, and adding some German, I was able to communicate well enough to be understood. I guess it was some time in November 1942 that I was able to tell a loitering British POW, "America land in Africa" and quickly walk away, carrying with me the picture of that young man's expression of open-mouthed and wide-eyed delight. While I never admitted to such a sin, I was amazed to find among my colleagues three or four who confided to me that they sometimes listened to foreign broadcasts.

The number of German casualties had been rising steadily throughout 1942, and by 1943 the sight of wounded and even crippled soldiers became quite common. Newspapers filled a lot of space on their numerically ever-shrinking pages with fallen soldiers' death notices: "For Führer and Fatherland, our dearest son died in battle ..." et cetera. It was commonly known that even gravely ill civilians could not be easily admitted to hospitals. Wounded soldiers had precedence.

Sometime, maybe in September 1942, Franziska and I were returning from work when our bus had to stop at a railway crossing to let a snail-paced and long military hospital train pass on its way through Dresden. Some of the windows were painted over, but most were quite clear, so we could see the passengers' faces staring out at us. They were pale and drawn, some quite expressionless, others almost completely covered with bandages, except for the eyes and mouth. Some soldiers, with arms and even torsos bandaged, appeared ghostly white against the dark interior of the railway cars. As the train moved from right to left across our field of vision, macabre and surreal, not a word or whisper was heard inside our bus. The driver had turned off the engine, so all that could be heard was the clickety-clack of the train's wheels. There were maybe twenty or so passengers in that bus, and only when the train had passed did someone give out a loud whisper: *"Scheisse!"* ("Shit!")

To me, this episode was an eerie reminder of what I'd already seen in the spring of 1941— slow-moving trains carrying weapons, heavy war equipment, and troops eastward through Poznań, while I (probably together with a friend) sat on the embankment and counted the railway cars. I couldn't help wondering if among those crippled wretches I'd just seen, there weren't some whom I had witnessed travelling eastward toward glory in battle, now returning defeated, broken in body and spirit.

Franziska watched that train in complete, stony silence. But when we reached Hellerau, she sat on the steps of her house and wept.

10 THE TURNING TIDE

In November of that year, Soviet forces encircled the entire German Sixth Army at Stalingrad. I knew there would be jubilation in the forced-labour camps, and the details of the Stalingrad trap which I described, originating as they did from the BBC, were more precise and accurate than those disseminated by the German propagandists in the Wehrmacht's daily reports. Someone who came through Dresden at that time talked about long trains going east across the German-run General Gouvernement, carrying troops and war *matériel* to reinforce the hopelessly bogged-down front and perhaps relieve the Russian pressure on Stalingrad. The mood in occupied Poland was, according to this informant, not much better than in the previous three years of the occupation. The positive news about American landings in North Africa and of the Germans' hopeless situation in Stalingrad was overshadowed by the fury of atrocities continuing in the General Gouvernement — mass executions of Poles and the unremitting emptying of Jewish ghettos, whose inhabitants were herded by the thousands into long trains of cattle cars and transported to camps from which no one ever came back. The Polish railway personnel reported that the trains were full on their way to those camps, but empty on return. The conclusions to be drawn from this were only too obvious.

We were nearing Christmas 1942, and I wanted to take a little gift to Halina, my acquaintance from Goehlewerk. I decided to intercept her at the end of her shift. Halina was housed in a women's hut in the Radebeul camp, but I decided that it would be best to hand her the present as she left Goehlewerk together with the other young women in her group. I forget what time it was when the gates opened, but it was already dark, and it was hard to find her in that crowd; obviously, the blackout didn't help. But finally I recognized the light-coloured kerchief she always wore when outside the plant. I sidled up to her and pressed the cigarette package into her hand, at the same time asking, in a whisper, how she was doing. Before she could reply, I was suddenly gripped by the arm and restrained, while the group of women kept moving, faces averted. I was being held by a man in uniform, and one glance out of the corner of my eye told me who and what he was — on his left sleeve he wore a small, diamond-shaped insignia with the letters *SD*, which stood for *Sicherheitsdienst* (Security Service), the intelligence branch of the SS. As the workers walked by, the man demanded to see my papers, and I handed him my stateless passport. But since it was almost impossible to see anything in the dark, he pulled me over to the guard's booth at the gate and told an armed policeman to shine his flashlight onto my passport and face. He compared me with my photograph, checked the stamps and validations of my having registered with the local police, then turned to me and asked if I spoke German. "Yes," I said, "but not very well as yet." He asked where I worked, and I told him I was employed by a film studio which, I stressed, was in the *kriegswichtig* (essential to the war effort) category. To prove it, I showed him my studio ID card. This appeared to impress him somewhat, but then he asked what I was doing talking to that "Polack" woman. I didn't think he had seen me slip Halina the cigarettes, but I had to find an answer to the question about my speaking with her. The brilliant idea came to me in about two seconds. I said something about chatting her up, thinking that perhaps she and I … "you know how it is," to which he grunted something I don't remember and said, *"Hau ab!"* ("Beat it!") I made myself scarce, walking into the darkness and sending up thanks for letting me get away with it once again.

It was only when I was back in my room in Hellerau that my nerves snapped. I shook uncontrollably for quite a while before I could calm down, realizing that things could have gone very badly for me. Compared to what had just happened, the small episode at the railway station in Bad Schandau had been child's play. There, I had been but one in a whole crowd. Here, I had been facing danger alone, with the Gestapo man's attention totally concentrated on me. I was nineteen years old, but although I had already gone through some truly scary experiences, I still retained a few characteristic teenage traits, among them a vague denial of my own mortality and a childish idea of heroism — derived from fairy tales, history books, and pre-war movies about St. George slaying the dragon or Napoleon's Polish cavalry charging Spain's Somosierra Pass. They were all fearless, so I had to be like them. But in Bad Schandau I had found out that I wasn't a hero — and now I knew that the thing called "fear" would be with me constantly until the war was finally over.

With this realization, I discovered a lot about myself. Running away was unthinkable, and desertion carried the stench of treason. But living with fear was in itself a frightening prospect. In Bad Schandau, I'd been careless to carry two different identification documents in one pocket. And there had been other occasions on which I hadn't been careful enough, hadn't taken the time to make sure the coast was clear, when dropping off those ever-so-risky news bulletins at the labour camps. Was Halina trustworthy? Had Mirko kept his mouth shut? The trouble was, of course, that I had no way of checking up on these people. I could go only on instinct or mere supposition. My mentor, Zenek, would have recoiled in horror at my lack of caution.

The working hours at Boehner Film were regular and allowed me to devote some time to artistic activities. I painted very little, but my newly discovered interest in woodcut inevitably led me to explore this medium. Its expressive power suited me well, especially in those turbulent times. I found that, for the grim depiction of wartime tragedies, woodcut allowed me to vent my innermost feelings about what had befallen my own country and, by implication, all other countries under the German heel.

Terse news about the calamitous German defeat and capitulation at Stalingrad was transmitted through public loudspeakers that until then had served to trumpet news of Germany's great victories on land, sea, and in the air. On the cold, rainy morning of February 3, 1943, as I stood on

Dresden's Postplatz waiting to change streetcars, the loudspeakers broadcast the sombre announcement that the Sixth Army had been forced to give up its heroic struggle, fighting courageously "to the last man." No mention was made of either the losses — though by now everyone knew they were horrendous — or the numbers of those who might have survived the Stalingrad hell. This time, the Wehrmacht report was followed not by the usual triumphant sounds of military "oompah" marches, but by the darkly tragic funeral march from Beethoven's *Eroica* symphony. By playing this solemn music, the Nazi Propaganda Ministry was de facto proclaiming that it regarded the still-surviving soldiers of the Sixth Army as already dead, along with their fallen comrades! Many average Germans held the view that this was beyond comprehension and demonstrated unbelievable coarseness on the part of the broadcasters writing such scenarios. Moreover, as I was told, the faith of a lot of loyal Party members was badly shaken. It was with cold satisfaction that, after hearing the news on the BBC, I wrote in my bulletin about the Stalingrad debacle. The BBC broadcast the number of Germans killed, wounded, and taken prisoner as 260,000, and it was this figure that I wrote down and delivered as information to the Polish forced-labour camps.

Tucked away in my library, a somewhat tattered and oft-repaired copy of Theodore Plievier's *Stalingrad* reminds me not only of the deadly trap into which Hitler sent his entire Sixth Army, almost all of whose soldiers died in combat or perished in Gulag camps, but of the man who gave me the book in May 1946. Dr. John Ulrich Schroeder was a lawyer, a friend and neighbour of the Ulich family, and like Dr. Ulich, an old-time socialist. Shortly after the collapse of Hitler's Reich and the Communist creation of Soviet-occupied East Germany, he was appointed judge-prosecutor in the case of several Nazi party functionaries as well as SS bullies and policemen, accused of killing some three hundred Russian prisoners of war a mere two days before the arrival of the Red Army at the town of Bautzen, about eighty kilometres east of Dresden. This act of mass murder, carried out publicly, was evidently so gruesome that even Schroeder, a mild-mannered, kind man, was moved to impose the death sentence on all the killers. They were hanged within the confines of the Bautzen labour camp. Schroeder, deeply shaken by this experience, left the legal profession and became a hermit in his own home. The last time I saw him was when he presented me with the *Stalingrad* book. He died shortly afterwards, in 1947.

By 1943, the mood among the German population had changed from joyous pride and unswerving faith in the Führer to confusion and even mystification. It was no longer "The Führer knows best" but "What now?" One could overhear this in whispered remarks and see it in people's faces. The propaganda machine beat the drums of confidence in the future, but the damage had been done. The firm belief in an ultimate victory was showing some cracks — slight, but rapidly widening. Also around that time, news leaked out about two Munich students who, following the Stalingrad catastrophe, had printed and distributed leaflets calling for the Nazi regime to be unmasked and overthrown. For this, and for having organized a resistance group called the *Weisse Rose* (White Rose), Hans Scholl and his sister Sophie were sentenced to death and beheaded with an axe. Among my colleagues at the film studio, the small group of intellectuals became noticeably thoughtful. As for myself, I had no idea that any kind of even mildly active anti-Nazi resistance existed within Germany itself. Yes, there were people like my friends the Ulichs, who were decidedly hostile toward the Nazi regime, but did not overtly risk their lives. It was only in July of the following year (1944), when an attempt to kill Hitler unfortunately failed, that the whole world learned of the existence of a major conspiracy against him and his gang. Possibly motivated by the heroic example of the two Munich students, the coup was staged by a group of high-ranking officers of the Wehrmacht's General Staff, who until then had faithfully served Hitler and his regime. They had followed the Führer's orders to march into Austria and Czechoslovakia, and on September 1, 1939, had obediently clicked their heels when he commanded them to invade Poland and thus unleash the enormity of the Second World War.

In my own little bailiwick, I managed to achieve modest success by finding a means to actually print my bulletins. Through the good graces of Herr Eckhardt, the friendly old printer who ran the Academy's graphic printing shop, I was able to obtain an ancient but still-functional hand press. In this way, I could produce up to six or eight copies without having to write the text by hand, through carbon paper, over and over again, as I'd been doing until then. Herr Eckhardt thought this hand press probably dated to the early nineteenth century and was most likely used by amateur artists, or even by children, as an educational toy. He also made me a present of a tinful of printer's ink, a squeegee that just about fitted the frame, and an old tamper for inking the template. I wanted to pay him, but he refused any sort of payment, saying that he was glad to be rid of the piece of old junk. After the war I found out he, too, had been an old socialist and an acquaintance of Dr. Ulich's.

Obviously, the printing of my journalistic efforts had to be done very late in the evenings and at irregular intervals. It was also important to make absolutely sure that, apart from the now rare, but always pre-announced travellers from Poland, no one turned up at my door unexpectedly while I was engaged in my clandestine activities. Franziska regarded my need for evening solitude as a strange quirk, but respected it just the same.

As mentioned before, my tiny second-floor apartment in Frau Heinich's house consisted of two rooms. The one in which I lived had two windows and contained a small table and chair, a stove, and my bed. But since it was directly under the roof, the upper part of two of its walls sloped at an angle of about forty-five degrees. There was additional space behind those walls, and it was there that I kept a two-foot-high stack of paper and all the other supplies needed in the printing process. The other room, across a little hall with a cold-water tap and a wash basin, I had designated as the guest room. It was empty, except for a mattress and a couple of well-used pillows. Eventually, I scrounged some sheets and pillowcases from Frau Heinich, to make my Polish guests feel more comfortable. Late that spring, I bought an old, somewhat rickety Adler typewriter from Günther Nitzsche, a friend and colleague at the Boehner Film Studios. Now I no longer had to laboriously write out the texts of my bulletins by hand.

In April 1943, the BBC and the German Rundfunk (radio) broadcast news of an armed uprising in the Jewish ghetto in Warsaw. The Ulich family and I listened to both sources and found that, although the Polish broadcasts from London gave this heroic event considerable attention, the BBC's German-language service barely allowed it any airtime. The reason for that may have been other occurrences that overshadowed that tragedy — the surrender of all German forces in North Africa, and the destruction by the RAF of Germany's Eder and Möhne dams, a spectacular raid that caused catastrophic flooding of the German countryside and a considerable loss of human life.

As well, much attention was devoted to news of the German discovery in Katyń Forest, on Soviet territory, of mass graves containing the bodies of some 4,000 Polish officers. On the Allied side, the immediate assumption, eagerly supported by the Soviet military authorities, was that the Germans themselves had committed this crime. After all, they were already well known as specialists in mass murder. The Polish government-in-exile requested that its Soviet counterpart ask the International Red Cross to investigate the matter, but the Soviets responded by breaking off diplomatic relations with the Polish government. The BBC's coverage of Polish affairs and of the Poles' participation in the war against Germany was severely curtailed and became downright hostile. The British government sided with the Russians, who were clearly a far more powerful ally than the many thousands of Poles fighting in the Allied ranks. Someone coming from Poland on his way west at around this time told me that most Poles were sure the Soviets were the perpetrators of that atrocity. They were certainly capable of it, as they had shown throughout their history.

Several more thousands of Poles — officers and non-commissioned officers, as well as a great number of civilian officials of all ranks — had also been imprisoned during the 1939–41 Soviet occupation of eastern Poland. Their places of incarceration were known, and initially there had even been some correspondence between them and their families in German-occupied Poland. Now, all this kind of contact ceased, and the fate of these prisoners became — and remained — unknown. High-level inquiries by the Polish government-in-exile in London elicited only stony silence from the Soviet side. It was with a heavy heart that I delivered my BBC radio news transcript to the Radebeul forced-labour camp: I knew that the father of my friend Halina had been among the prisoners in the Ostashkov POW camp, from where she had received a card from him. A warrant officer in reserve, he had been mobilized in 1939 and captured by the Soviets after the war was over, in October of that year. It was almost certain that he was among those missing.

In the summer of 1943 another national disaster left Poles around the world in deep mourning and despair — the death of Polish prime minister and chief of Poland's Armed Forces, General Sikorski. Moments after taking off from the Gibraltar landing strip, his plane had inexplicably plunged into the water, killing all aboard, except for the Czech pilot who, amazingly, escaped unscathed. Sabotage was commonly assumed in the German printed and radio news. They gleefully blamed the British secret services for getting rid of a now-inconvenient Polish ally who dared to ask embarrassing questions of Britain's powerful Soviet friends (whose forces, admittedly, bore the heaviest burden of the war). When quoting British radio commentators in my bulletins, I moderated the harsh, often insulting, tone in which they belittled and discredited the Polish side in that conflict, trumpeting that the blood of those killed in Katyń was on German, not Soviet, hands. I did not want to distress the already despondent, wretched Polish forced labourers any further. For my part, a great deal of the admiration I had felt for Britain right from the start of the war was now rapidly fading. Did our pilots, who had valiantly and successfully fought off the Germans in the Battle of Britain, deserve to be humiliated in this way? Our sailors on the Atlantic and the North Sea and the thousands of Polish ground troops under British command were still loyally doing their duty. Surely, these men and women must also have felt the sting of derision coming at them through the BBC and officially from Whitehall alike. It was the first — though, I thought, maybe not the last — time that I diluted the language of my bulletin.

Some postwar historians describe the July 1943 Battle of Kursk as one of the greatest armed conflicts in all history. This opinion is confirmed by statistics that came to light after the war. Over two million men, German and Russian, with several thousand tanks and tens of thousands of artillery pieces, fought this epic battle, resulting in stupendous losses on both sides. As expected, the initial German reports were triumphant, but it soon became clear that the days of those easy 1941 victories were now over.

Along with my friends, Franziska, the Ulich family, and some colleagues at the Boehner Film Studios, I had learned to "read" between the lines delivered by the sombre-voiced German radio announcers and commentators. The BBC declared that the German offensive was failing at every step and would probably lead to a disaster equal to that of Stalingrad. I still recall quoting that assumption in my news sheet. When Kursk vanished from newscasts and newspapers, the German public was left in a state of some confusion. The news of heavy fighting and "frontline straightening" (i.e., retreats) at the Eastern Front wasn't exactly encouraging. On the other hand, the endlessly repeated mantra *"Der Führer weiss am besten"* ("The Führer knows best") appeared to mitigate a deep feeling of unease. Many restaurants, as well as public institutions such as galleries, libraries, and museums, had closed their doors since Goebbels's declaration of a "Total War" in February of that year. Most of the students at the Academy had been ordered by the authorities to work full-time in similarly designated *kriegswichtig* jobs in factories, public transit, postal services, and so on. They were not alone in this. Students at the Polytechnic, the Music Conservatory, and the Theatre Drama School had also been forced to break off their studies and devote themselves to the *Kampf um den Sieg* (struggle for victory). Movie theatres, of course, remained open, in order to present a flood of war propaganda films and the *Wochenschau* (*Weekly News*), which dealt mainly with German military triumphs against the evil forces of the decadent West and the Bolshevist dangers from the East. To this day I cringe when I hear Liszt's symphonic poem, *Les Préludes*, remembering how its romantic, though sometimes heroically strident, tones used to accompany the silver screen's pictures of German soldiers storming enemy trenches, blowing up Soviet tanks, or burning villages, or of iron-crossed aircraft shooting down Allied planes and returning victorious to their bases. Allied losses in the air were always announced in double digits, German losses invariably as no more than twos or threes. Walls of public buildings now carried the slogan *"Führer, befiel! Wir folgen Dir!"* ("Führer, command! We follow you!")

If memory serves me correctly, it was in the late autumn of 1943 that a small, mundane event interfered with the Ulichs' and my habit of listening almost daily to the BBC broadcasts. One late evening, when Dr. Ulich turned on that excellent and always reliable Grundig short-wave radio to the BBC frequency, not even the sound of jamming could be heard. The reason for this failure was a burnt-out tube, one of several that in those days used to be a vital part of a radio receiver. This calamity meant that listening to the BBC was out of the question, at least until a replacement for the defunct part had been found. The likelihood of finding a new tube, however, appeared doubtful, since all production of communication technology was geared to serve the German war effort and was not available to the civilian population.

For me, this situation meant that I could not avail myself of my prime source of information and now had to stop printing and distributing the primitive little news sheet which, I hoped, had helped to keep up the spirits of those downtrodden workers. I had been told that they sometimes were allowed to receive postcards from their families and write cards in return. But, being subject to strict censorship, these postcards were invariably no more than a sign of life ("I'm well, and hope you're well too") and devoid of any other information. However, even without the benefit of BBC newscasts, I was able to learn about some events taking place in German-occupied Poland. Just before Christmas 1943 or at the beginning of 1944, I heard about a marked increase in partisan activity in the General Gouvernement and in the formerly Polish eastern territories. Many German munitions and troop trains were being blown up or derailed, and urban guerilla warfare had increased in intensity, not only in Warsaw itself, but also in cities such as Radom and Kielce, and in scores of smaller centres. Unfortunately, German reprisals resulted in mass executions of Poles, often with as many as one hundred Polish hostages being shot in revenge for the killing of one German official. The liquidation of what remained of the Jewish population was also increasing in intensity. I was told of Poles condemned to death and executed by the *Armia Krajowa* (Home Army), the Polish Resistance's military arm, for denouncing Jews to the Germans. Information I received from an overnight visitor told me far more about conditions in occupied Poland than the BBC would have been able — or was now willing — to impart.

At that time, the BBC's radio signal consisted of four Morse code taps signifying the letter *V*: three short, one long, or ... – . Tapped out on two drums, they sounded exactly like the first four notes of Beethoven's Fifth Symphony, interpreted in German lore as *"Schicksal schlägt an die Tür"* ("Fate is knocking at the door"). Goebbels read this correctly as British propaganda announcing the end of the Hitler regime and ordered countermeasures. In a widespread campaign, the letter *V* was featured on posters and other displays as "V for Victory" — a German victory, of course. On one of Warsaw's squares, a huge *V* was erected, made of plywood and heavy canvas and painted the colour of steel. Within hours, and to the joy of Warsaw's population, it was a pile of smoking ashes, courtesy of the Polish Resistance.

With the radio out of commission, Dr. Ulich now began bringing home the *Dresden Neueste Nachrichten* (Dresden Latest News) when he returned from work. The daily paper featured regular Wehrmacht reports and it was from this source that we learned about the American landings at Anzio at the beginning of 1944. And since Italy had already declared war on Germany, this landing appeared to be one more portent of a coming German defeat. I think it was then that I began to fully understand the personal dichotomy in my friends', the Ulichs', attitude toward the war. From the moment I had met Franziska and her parents, I was aware of their firm anti-Nazi point of view. Even the initial exchange of thoughts between us, careful as it was, had given me the impression of a deepseated compassion and tolerance toward all humanity, regardless of race, religion or nationality. On a personal level, the Allies' landings in Italy — Sicily, Salerno, and now Anzio — increased not only the virtual certainty of an Allied invasion in the north of France, but also of possible danger to the life of the Ulich's older son, Ernst, who was serving there in a signals unit. In spite of that fear, however, they were anxious to see such an invasion succeed.

Some time in March 1944, through a friend of a friend, Dr. Ulich managed to obtain a replacement for the burnt-out radio tube. Our listening sessions recommenced, but German jamming of the BBC broadcasts had intensified to such a degree that it became almost impossible to make any sense of the bits of words that floated through the earsplitting noise of interference. There was no way I could continue informing those practically incarcerated Polish workers about events taking place in our country and of the war that our soldiers were currently fighting in Italy and, as partisans, in Poland. Moreover, some forced-labour camps were now guarded day and night by armed police patrols, and, even with all my feelings of patriotic duty, I became careful not to risk my life for a cause that already appeared more than half won. Of course, my conscience bothered me, but then I'd recall Zenek's admonition from years before: not to take unnecessary risks and play the hero when heroism was not called for. Interestingly, he did not mention a longing for death while under torture, but he didn't have to. It was obvious anyway.

11 THE CHOKING MOLOCH

As I recall the course of events in the fateful year of 1944, it still looks to me like the slow, but gradually accelerating, agony of an ugly Third Reich Moloch choking to death on what it was attempting to swallow. It seemed as if hardly a day passed without a Soviet offensive, an Allied landing, an American triumph over the Germans' Japanese ally, or savage USAAF and RAF bombing raids on German cities. The Germans retreated from Leningrad and were pushed by the Red Army all the way back into Poland. The end was even more clearly in sight by June 6, when the long-awaited Allied invasion began in Normandy. It went without saying that this raised the level of Frau Ulich's worry about her son, and for quite a few days she remained inconsolable, despite everyone's efforts to comfort her.

For me, the date of July 20, 1944, is doubly significant. On that day, a handful of the Wehrmacht's General Staff and a few highly placed civilians finally bestirred themselves to save what was left of Germany by attempting to assassinate Hitler. Moreover, at that very time, my father was visiting me in Dresden, after a separation of almost three years. He arrived a few days, perhaps even a week, before July 20, and throughout his stay we took the time to tour the city. By then I knew it well, and he remembered it from over forty years before, when he had spent several months there researching material for his doctoral thesis. Franziska accompanied us in all our sightseeing, and her parents received my father in a true spirit of friendship and respect. The presence of a grand piano in the Ulichs' home led to ad hoc intimate evening concerts, which did much to develop a warm, personal relationship between him and the Ulich family.

Clearly, after years of being apart and exchanging only carefully worded letters, we had much to talk about. My mother's health was failing, she was losing weight, the doctors who hadn't been drafted by the Wehrmacht were helpless, and hospitals were filled with casualties from the front. Despite the help of friends and Zosia, black-market food had become increasingly difficult to obtain, and what was available on food coupons was proverbially just enough to starve on. The number of arrests among the Polish intelligentsia had increased dramatically, as had the number of executions, including public ones. My father had managed to keep his job at the Raczyński Library, but Wehrmacht officers were now only rarely being quartered in our apartment.

The Hallelujah news of an assassination of Hitler almost immediately turned into deepest disappointment when the German radio broadcast a speech by Joseph Goebbels, triumphantly crowing that Hitler had survived the attempt on his life, suffering only a few scratches. At this, Frau Ulich, who had been worrying about her son stationed in France during the Allied invasion, recovered her usual temperamental nature. She stood up from her chair, slammed a fist on the table, and let out a wail of despair: *"Das Schwein lebt noch!"* ("The swine is still alive!"). I remember thinking afterwards how this outcry, quite uncharacteristic for such a highly sophisticated lady, truly came from the heart. She was certainly not alone in her feelings. Some of my colleagues at Boehner Film had expressed similar emotions, though only in whispers and looking over their shoulders. Franziska, being Franziska, voiced her thoughts in far more blunt ways, speculating on methods she would use to slowly kill Hitler, personally of course.

My father left Dresden on August 1, the day on which the tragic, more than two-month-long Warsaw Uprising began. We recommenced our correspondence, but by the beginning of the next year, even this would no longer be possible.

The mass executions and murders of conspirators in the coup against Hitler began immediately and were exultantly announced on the radio and in newspapers. Among those apprehended and killed for taking part in the conspiracy was General Fritz Lindemann, whose brother was a close friend and law firm colleague of Dr. Ulich. And since Hitler had ordered that, in some selected cases, even entire families of the conspirators were to be liquidated, the danger that Dr. Ulich's friend might also be executed was obviously very real. Clearly, this could have led to an investigation and possibly brought Dr. Ulich under suspicion of collaboration with the conspirators. A few tense weeks went by. As it turned out, Herr Lindemann was only perfunctorily interrogated by the Gestapo and then let go. It's hard to say why he was given his freedom — maybe because the Gestapo already had their hands full with ever more arrests and interrogations and the various forms of torture that always accompanied such procedures.

One late summer evening in 1944, as I was walking in Hellerau, probably returning from the Ulichs' to my rooms, I heard unusual sounds in the distance. Curious, I followed them and discovered that they were coming from the vicinity of the Klotzsche camp. I was able to make out the dark shapes and slitted headlights of a large truck and what looked like a *Kübelwagen*, a command vehicle used by the Wehrmacht, parked at the camp's main entrance, its engine running. German commands filled the air — coarse, snarling, and not to be disobeyed. I virtually melted into some nearby bushes, still able to hear and watch what was going on in the camp, which consisted of three large huts, one for the men and two for the women. Each hut had a small, separate room, with some basic amenities to accommodate an *Aufseher* (guard), responsible for keeping order and a semblance of cleanliness in and around the huts that housed his charges. Back in 1941, when I had already started working at Goehlewerk, my coworkers Mirko and Halina had described to me their living conditions, mentioning, among other things, the guards, whose average age seemed to range between sixty and seventy. Now, as I crouched in the bushes, a frightening thought rose in my mind: what if an *Aufseher*, in making his tour of a hut, had found something incriminating — a prohibited object, an illegal radio, maybe letters that had slipped through censorship, perhaps even printed Underground material? The latter possibility had, of course, occurred to me before, at the time when I began to distribute that risky literature. I recall adding a line to every bulletin's text, something like "Burn immediately after reading," but I had no way of knowing if that advice was followed.

The commotion, with its yelling and screaming, lasted for almost two hours, during which I didn't dare to leave my hiding place. When it finally abated, I was sure I'd see people being led away and driven off in the truck, but nothing of the sort happened. Talking among themselves, the Germans, presumably an SS contingent, got into their vehicles and left. Not until after the end of the war did I learn that this raid had been only one in a general *Aktion* (operation) that the SS and police had carried out in most labour and POW camps.

Ever since my arrival in Dresden, and especially after meeting Franziska and her family, I had become aware of Germans who were very, and sometimes even startlingly, different from those who had jackbooted into my country in that tragic September 1939. I had grown up with the history of German-Prussian repression, throughout the nineteenth century and even later, of everything that was Polish. It was this past history of forced Germanization under Bismarck and now its far more brutal 1939 Nazi follow-up that had shaped my attitude toward the entire German nation. In this I was clearly not alone. The occupiers had introduced a system of virtual slavery far exceeding in cruelty that of the Stalinist Gulag network. At its mildest, the Nazi system in occupied Western Poland resembled a kind of layer cake of intolerance levels, similar to what once could be found in the American Deep South with its "Whites Only" signs and its drugstore counters at which Blacks were still forbidden to sit. We encountered an equivalent in the many signs proclaiming *"Nur für Deutsche"* (Germans Only).

Needless to say, I brought my suspicions and resentments with me when I arrived in Dresden. Some of what I felt proved to be justified. Ochre-coloured and gold-adorned Nazi Party officials' uniforms could frequently be seen amidst the graceful baroque architecture, and one constantly encountered the Third Reich's swastika flag flying from public, and even clearly residential, buildings. And yet, interestingly, rather than flapping their right arms and saying *"Heil Hitler"* by way of greeting, as Germans in occupied Poznań did, most citizens of Dresden still used the old-fashioned *"Guten Tag."*

In time, after Tadek Beutlich had introduced me to his artist friends, I began to understand that there was also a different kind of German. Quietly intellectual, many of these young artists saw the world in colours other than Nazi brown. They spoke of their views only carefully and indirectly, but I knew that they were seething inwardly when they touched on the subject of the Nazi repressions of works of contemporary, progressive artists such as Ernst-Ludwig Kirchner, Otto Dix, Karl Schmidt-Rottluff, and hundreds of others who didn't cater to the petty bourgeois tastes of

Before he was shipped to the Russian front, Franziska and I visited Tadek Beutlich, here in his hated Wehrmacht uniform, at the military depot in Königsbrück.

the Nazi hierarchy. Later I was to discover a few Germans who, when listening to official announcements or Wehrmacht reports on the radio, said nothing, but merely shrugged as if to say, "So what?" I realized that there were also Other Germans.

But it was my friendship with the Ulich family that ultimately convinced me of the existence of Germans quite different from the hoi polloi, the masses who blindly followed their Führer and just looked on while his orders to kill millions were obediently carried out. The decent Germans who befriended me, even though they knew I was a Pole, reminded me of the years after the defeat of the 1830 Polish Uprising against Russian rule, when many of the insurgents had found refuge among the then-friendly citizens of Germany. In fact, when I visited Dresden's Friedrichstädter Cemetery I found many Polish graves, including that of my father's Uncle Telesfor, who had become a successful merchant of high-quality household metalwares. His son, Tadek, born in Dresden, had a distinguished military career, fighting in the Polish Legion (under Austrian command), then in the Polish Army, and after 1939 in the *Armia Krajowa*.

Throughout the turmoil of these years, correspondence with my parents continued with reasonable regularity. Because the mail was subject to censorship, we wrote to each other in terms as general as possible, and on safe subjects, such as the weather, fine arts, and music. Sometimes I was able to read between the lines and detect their feelings of helplessness and frustration, especially because most of their Polish friends had been robbed of all their possessions and deported to the General Gouvernement. In one letter, my mother wrote (in German, of course), "We are now completely surrounded by German newcomers from Latvia and Estonia, who have taken over the properties of those who have lived here since time immemorial." In another letter, my father wrote, "I've been told that the lovely place where you have spent so many happy holidays has now been given to the Hitler Youth organization, 'to educate young boys in the proper spirit.'" Here my father was referring to Turew, Aunt Uja's estate, where I had last been in the summer of 1939. Much later, long after the war, I found out that Aunt Uja, an old woman suffering from severe arthritis, had later that year been brutally kicked out of her home into the frost and snow of the worst winter in decades and eventually transported by cattle car, together with many thousands of other forced deportees, to the General Gouvernement. The manor was ransacked and virtually all the furniture, most of it exquisite antiques, stolen and replaced by furnishings in abysmal Nazi taste. The approximately 2,000 books which comprised the library, among them priceless volumes with records of parliamentary debates of the Polish *Sejm* (Parliament) dating back to the mid- to late-seventeenth century, were taken from their shelves by the Hitler Youth boys, thrown from the windows down onto the wide space in front of the building, then doused with gasoline and burned.

As far as Germany's future was concerned, the writing was clearly on the wall, and most Germans seemed to know it or, at least, sense that the pompous slogans and "oompah" martial music had a false ring. Little Frau Heinich, my landlady, who listened all day to her *Volksempfänger* and usually believed every word, now anxiously asked me if I thought Germany might lose the war. Not to upset the old dear, I told her that she had nothing to fear and that the Reich would soon reconquer all the lands it had temporarily vacated in the East. She smiled happily and waddled off again to listen to her radio.

I had always considered her to be sweetly naive in matters other than her small garden with its vegetable patch. But now she appeared to be having doubts about the world around her. And if my landlady's thinking was going in that direction, what about everyone else, maybe even Party members who ran around consoling themselves by endlessly repeating catchwords from Hitler's speeches?

In the war being fought on the airwaves, German announcers maintained a studiously earnest tone, making an exception only for the highly popular *Wunschkonzert* (Request Concert). Based on requests from either soldiers at the front or their families, the show was full of blatantly cranked-up good humour and light music ranging from popular folk tunes to film-music favourites. But as the war dragged on and claimed ever more lives, the program's forced jollity became a dismal farce, a "dance of the dead with the near-dead," as my friend Günther Nitzsche so aptly called it. Years later, incidentally, the son of this program's musical director, a reporter by the name of Manfred Jäger, was a colleague of mine at the *Winnipeg Tribune*.

Meanwhile, the Red Army pressed on westward and by the end of July stood only a few kilometres east of Warsaw. On August 1, 1944, Polish insurgents began an uprising in that city, hoping for the solemnly promised Soviet help in defeating the German occupation, liberating the Polish capital, and creating a national government in a free, sovereign Poland. To this day, I find it difficult to think of, let alone write about, the treachery of the Soviets, who stopped the Red Army at the gates of Warsaw, to simply stand and watch as the Poles fought not only the German Wehrmacht and Waffen SS but also thousands of East European criminals in German uniforms. Despite some help in the form of weapons and munitions airdropped by a group of American and British bombing aircraft (some flown by Polish pilots all the way from Italy), the Warsaw Uprising ended in defeat after sixty-four days of uninterrupted, murderous fighting. On the Polish side, military and civilian losses came to approximately 200,000. In Germany, Minister of Propaganda Joseph Goebbels himself wrote a sanctimonious front-page article in the official government weekly organ, *Das Reich*, hypocritically expressing some understanding for the valour of the insurgent Poles and then pointing at the true face of the double-crossing "Bolshevist Red Menace" against which the German Reich was struggling. The article ended with an impassioned plea to defend Germany to the last man, in order to prevent it from suffering the same fate as Poland had received at the hands of the Soviets in 1939.

Obviously in panic at the prospect of the Red Army unstoppably rolling over the now-enfeebled German defences, the Wehrmacht's High Command preposterously, or just naively, attempted to get the Poles to collaborate by force of arms in fending off — or even only slowing down — the Russian advance sufficiently to allow Germany to replenish her forces' ranks, such as still remained in action. All the Germans got in reply from the Poles was mockery and laughter.

By now, it was common knowledge that, to fill the Wehrmacht's dwindling ranks, the Reich's military recruited volunteers from nations friendly to Germany and to Nazism in general. At Hitler's urgent plea for European unity, volunteers — even from nations previously invaded by Germany — rushed to join the Nazi SS or their own national formations to fight side by side with the Wehrmacht against Soviet Russia. With Hungary and Romania already in Hitler's ranks, the Belgian fascist, Leon Degrelle, organized Flemish and Walloon brigades to fight on Germany's side. Vichy France supported Nazi Germany with volunteers in the ranks of the Waffen SS, while Franco's officially neutral Spain put a superbly equipped "Blue Division" at Hitler's disposal. Other collaborators came from eastern European countries, such as Lithuania, Latvia, Estonia, Slovakia, and Ukraine, to serve as concentration camp guards and, occasionally, to help with the torture or outright killing of inmates. In Russia itself, the so-called *Hiwis* (short for *Hilfswillige*, meaning "willing to help"), who were often deserters from the Red Army, were used by the Germans to perform mundane, easily supervised tasks: digging trenches, burying the dead, driving trucks, delivering field-post mail, and, surprisingly, even fighting on the German side. Quisling's Norwegian SS division also played its supporting role.

Boehner Film Studios' production line now also included work on a feature film based on the timely subject of espionage. Those of us who toiled over stereo animated instruction films for the navy went on drawing little white circles and stars on sheets of cellophane, sometimes watching projections of proof strips of film to check the accuracy of our eye-straining work. Every now and then, someone would take a break, maybe go for a walk outside and wave to the Allied POWs on the other side of the chain-link fence, or saunter over to the sound stage where a feature film was being shot. Its title was *GEKADOS*, an acronym formed from a designation used on military documents: *Geheime Kommandosache* (Secret Command Matter).

The film's action was supposed to take place in Paris, the simulation of which wasn't actually difficult, since there were many sites in Dresden that, with careful editing, could double for views of Paris, both for interior and outdoor scenes. It also helped that a lovingly constructed facsimile of a Parisian bar/nightclub was added for authenticity, including a small band and a singer warbling the then-popular French hit, *"Parlez-moi d'amour"*

("Speak to Me of Love"). The plot was simple. A beautiful German secretary in some important Wehrmacht headquarters is seduced by a sneaky Frenchman and made to hand over to him some highly sensitive documents. The love affair thrives until the lady's ex-lover, a suspicious and patriotically motivated *Abwehr* (counter-intelligence) officer, catches the pair in flagrante delicto in a hotel room. He shoots the Frenchman, the lady dives out the window, and the officer tearfully reports the incident to his superior. I saw only snippets of that shoot, and the rest of the plot was told to me by one of the film editors, Miss Ponto. *GEKADOS*, however, was not the only motion picture that, apart from the animation I worked on, was in the shooting and editing stage. It seemed downright idiotic that at a time when the Allies were already well into Germany, the Red Army leaned against the border of East Prussia, and France had been liberated, a Boehner Film producer named Engel was putting the finishing touches on his film about tobacco production in Ukraine, while another producer named Dinkel was just beginning the final edit on a film dealing with German submarines attacking Allied convoys. It was all a mass delusion, an all-encompassing game of pretend, such as children play when they close their eyes and assume that what they don't see does not exist. Yet everyone knew that the Soviets already had a bridgehead across the Vistula, and that their next offensive was imminent.

By late September 1944, the German High Command, and maybe even Hitler himself, finally recognized the Third Reich's almost hopeless military situation. The staggering losses incurred by the Wehrmacht over the years had depleted its ranks, and there were practically no more reserves available. A decision was made to create the *Volkssturm* (People's Storm), a kind of last-gasp militia consisting of civilian men up to sixty years old, and boys aged fourteen years and up. Also included in this miserable conglomeration were the lame and crippled and those unable to serve in any real armed forces. Pitifully equipped with obsolete weapons and the odd *Panzerfaust* (an anti-tank weapon), they wore civilian clothes and were identified as "military personnel" only by armbands marked "Deutsche Wehrmacht." But the armband did not give them true military status, and as civilians bearing arms they were, in the event of capture by

In July 1944 with my father at the grave of his Uncle Telesfor in Dresden's Friedrichstädter Cemetery.

the enemy, subject not to imprisonment as POWs, but to immediate exe-cution. In any case, the *Volkssturm* hardly mattered in the defence of Nazi Germany and in most cases melted away like snow in midsummer.

Neither Christmas 1944 nor New Year's 1945 seemed in any way remarkable. In October 1944 there were a few minor Allied bombing raids on Dresden's rail yards and some factories, but that was far away from the city centre and the bucolic world of Hellerau. To be sure, Leipzig and especially Berlin had been severely affected and there were thousands of victims. But even at this late stage of the war, Dresden appeared to be a sanctuary, supposedly sheltered by the Allies who were, after all, civi-lized people (weren't they?) and who knew this city as "Florence on the Elbe" — a place of beauty, culture, and all things admirable. Bombs on Dresden? It was unthinkable.

The Eastern Front was now in central Poland, and for a time there seemed to be little action. BBC commentators speculated that the Soviets had reached the planned objective of their offensive and were now using the greatly overextended supply lines to replenish manpower and war *matériel*. But this lull in fighting didn't last long. On January 12, the Red Army under Marshal Konev broke out of the Baranov bridgehead on the Vistula and crashed through the German defences. It was now on its way west, toward Germany proper.

I don't remember what day of the week this was, but it was clearly an event that belonged in the category of "where were you when such and such happened?" I can still see myself walking along the street early in the day and encountering Franziska, who was running toward me to breath-lessly give me the news: "The Russians have broken through!" Of course, this was a development that we had expected, so I was not surprised, nor was I impressed at the enthusiasm with which she told me of it. She'd always quite openly displayed her pro-Slavic sentiments, which I used to view as her fierce reaction to the all-encompassing Nazi Teutonism that pervaded every aspect of life in the Third Reich. Although certainly not a communist, she was sometimes more radical in her political views than her pragmatically socialist father. Now, on this memorable day, she again told me that she could hardly wait for the Red Army to march in and do away with the Nazi beast. For my part, I replied that a Russian occupation could not be expected to become a celebration of brotherly love, but might, as it had after Poland's defeat in October 1939, turn into an orgy of rape, plunder, arrests, executions, and mass deportations.

Naturally, I was worried about my parents. It was impossible to tell when the Red Army would reach Poznań and how what was left of the Polish population there would be treated. Right at the beginning of the New Year, I had received a Christmas parcel and a letter from home. It was the last I was to hear from my parents for quite some time. I wrote back, but I doubt that my letter ever reached its destination.

Part 3

"IMPROVING FORTIFICATIONS"

12 FORCED LABOUR

On January 13, the day after the Soviet breakthrough at Baranov, the head of Boehner Film Studios called me to his office and told me to pack some personal belongings and report for duty at Dresden's central railway station on the following day. I was to join a contingent of civilians who were being sent east to Silesia to help reinforce what could become a defence line "just in case the Russians get that far." Stunned, for a moment I didn't know what to say. Then I asked why it had to be me rather than someone else from the studio's personnel. "Well," said the man, "you seem to be the only one here who looks to be in fair health. The rest of the crew is either *unabkömmlich* (indispensable [to the war effort]), crippled, or simply too old." There was no way out, I thought, unless I went into hiding. But the war could still go on for a long time, and where would I hide? And how could I survive? There was nothing for it: I had to go and would have to use my wits to get through whatever situations I might face. I hated myself for buckling under that pressure — especially because I was now supposed to actively help those Nazi barbarians who had devastated my country and butchered as yet untold numbers of my compatriots. Later on, it occurred to me that if I were to just go into hiding and by some miracle even survive until the end of the war, my disappearance would, of course, become known, and my friends and even studio colleagues might find themselves in very deep trouble indeed. As it was, my association with the Ulich family had already been putting them at risk ever since we had first met more than three years previously. Unwittingly, they had become my co-conspirators, and I carried the responsibility for their fate. I found myself in a dilemma that forced me to constantly weigh my genuine friendship with that family — and especially with Franziska — against the duty to which I was sworn and had taken on a few years before. Needless to say, it was an almost permanent, soul-wrenching balancing act, and the memory of it troubles me even now, well over half a century later.

On January 14, together with thirty-nine other male civilians, I boarded an eastbound train consisting of freight cars as well as several flatcars loaded with tanks and armoured personnel carriers. All but two of the freight cars were already occupied by troops, and we civilian conscripts were herded into the two remaining ones. No one knew anything about our final destination, and our minders, two low-ranking Nazis wearing Party uniforms and carrying side arms, kept their mouths tightly shut. With twenty passengers plus luggage per boxcar, space was tight, and an ad hoc system was established, under which some of us stood while others sat on their bundles or suitcases, changing places at hourly intervals. There being only one bucket to serve the needs of so many passengers led to speculation that this might be a reasonably short trip, and oddly, this black-humoured joke turned out to be an accurate prediction. Our journey lasted no more than five hours. The train stopped at a tiny station almost in the middle of nowhere and unloaded us, before moving on in an easterly direction.

When we had left Dresden, the city had received only a small amount of snow, and the temperature was above freezing. Now, only a few hours later, we stood in deep snow under a sky the colour of lead, trying in vain to protect ourselves against the freezing wind coming from seemingly all directions. Even the two Nazi officials appeared stunned by it all. But then the one who had more gold on his hat and was evidently more important and better informed told the group to follow him along what appeared to be a road. It was only two kilometres to our ultimate destination, but trudging through snow halfway up to our knees and carrying our belongings made the distance feel twice that far.

While we laboriously made our way ahead, I asked one of the men in the group why we were being escorted by uniformed and armed Nazi Party functionaries rather than by, say, military personnel. He told me that, since all the military were now needed at the front and most male civilians had been drafted into the *Volkssturm,* the Party was now looking after many aspects of general administration, additional policing, guard duties, and civil defence coordination. This, he added with a note of cynicism in his voice, kept individuals like our two guardians warm and cozy and away from the front. The Party, he said, certainly protected its own.

It was getting dark by the time we reached our destination. Located on low ground between gentle rises in the land, the building in which half of us conscripts were to be housed was a former barn, now equipped with a small iron stove and a supply of firewood. Straw was spread out generously on the bare ground for us to sleep on. The rest of the group was accommodated in an evidently abandoned school building nearby, in a couple of classrooms from which benches had been removed. The two Nazis occupied the teachers' quarters, which were also deserted, but contained a still-functioning kitchen, in which a couple of sullen-looking women cooked our meals on a massive wood stove.

Like everyone else, I had brought some food for the journey, but not knowing how long the train ride would take, I had eaten very little of it. Small wonder then, that at the end of that trip, I was not just dead tired, but hungry enough to eat my supply and more than one portion of a soup prepared by the two women. From them I also learned a few facts about the eerie, deserted place in which we found ourselves. The village, located some twenty-five to thirty kilometres north of Breslau, capital of Lower Silesia, was called Katzberg and consisted of the above-mentioned school, a Protestant church, a small store, and a post office, all of which served a considerable number of outlying farms. The ghostly stillness of this abandoned place was the result of an order issued on the evening of January 12 by the Nazi *Kreisleiter* (district Party leader) to immediately evacuate the whole area, taking along everything needed for survival — household goods, bedding, clothes, food, some farm animals — and flee westward, away from the approaching front and the Red Army. The order must have been followed to the letter, since there wasn't even one farm in the area whose owner had remained. The teacher, the pastor, and the storekeeper had also left in a hurry, and only these two women — a mother and her daughter — had stayed on, ordered by the Party to cook for a contingent of men who were to work on "fortifications," whatever that meant. I asked the daughter, a big, handsome woman well into middle age, if they were "from here," meaning from Katzberg. She said no, they were from Blüchertal, a village only a few kilometres to the northeast. At this point, her mother, probably into her seventies or older, murmured something I couldn't hear well enough. I asked her to repeat what she'd said, and she uttered a single word, something like "Zhavoine." Her daughter shrugged and said that her mother meant the village's old name, one that had been changed to "Blüchertal" many years ago. It was only much later that I thought about it and remembered what I'd learned from the history books that I used to read with such interest. This part of Silesia had been Slav territory since time immemorial and belonged to the Kingdom of Poland until the first half of the fourteenth century, when conflicts between Silesian princes made them incapable of defending themselves against external pressures from abroad. With Silesia now outside the Polish state, German influences grew in that region and reached a peak of intensity in the second half of the nineteenth century, when the ruthless Germanization policies of Prussia's chancellor Bismarck resulted in the liquidation of the last traces of a Slavic past in Silesia and in all other Polish territories seized by Germany over the centuries. Thus the ancient name "Opole" (by the field) was changed to "Oppeln," "Oleśnica" to "Oels," and "Zhavoine" (which had actually been "Zawoine") to "Blüchertal" (*Tal* = valley), named after the Prussian General Blücher, who helped to defeat Napoleon at Waterloo.

Sleeping on straw was no novelty to me. After all, the Luftwaffe had accorded me that doubtful pleasure back in September 1939, when they had bombed the town of Kutno and sent me to an overcrowded hospital, blinded and with a shrapnel wound. But here, the circumstances were different, and so was the company. In Kutno, I had been lying on the floor, between beds occupied by heavily wounded and dying Polish soldiers, some only moaning softly, others crying out to God and their mothers.

Now, in this Katzberg barn, the ground was just as hard as the floor in the Kutno hospital, and the straw had a familiar feel to it. But the people in whose midst I now found myself were almost all Germans, native Saxons — quicker, wittier, and more industrious than their compatriots in, say, Prussia or Bavaria. They were not a bad lot. Most of them were factory workers and low-ranking office employees, men who were found physically unfit to serve Führer and Fatherland at the front and now had to exert themselves in other ways. I still remember a few of them, not by their names but by the infirmities that saved them from active military service. One of them was a relatively young welder who had lost an eye. Another, a farmer, had gotten a foot crushed in the gears of his tractor. Yet another man was the victim of a childhood illness. A youngish fellow who, for some reason, attached himself to me, told me about his lower middle-class background and about his physical condition, some sort of "itis," ostensibly serious enough to keep him out of uniform. He seemed quite curious about me, but the few years I had spent in the Resistance had taught me extreme discretion in dealing with strangers. Sometimes I viewed even couriers passing through with suspicion, if only because of a strange gesture or the particular inflection of a word. In talking with this individual, I restricted myself to what could be called "basic truths" — my real name, place of birth, age, and profession. All these things were interesting in and of themselves and could be discussed ad infinitum without having to debate politics or the war, which Germany was clearly losing on all fronts. Not that he didn't try to make me talk about it, but I always waved him off by mentioning *kismet*, the Turkish word for "destiny," and adding that we'd have to accept what had been preordained for us.

It was quite late on the evening of January 14 that, after filling up with soup and country bread, this bedraggled, disorganized crowd of wheezing, coughing, foot-dragging semi-invalids and reluctant draftees was divided into two groups of twenty each and sent off to their quarters, one group to the schoolhouse, the other to the barn. I was in the latter group and fortunately found a place to sleep only a few metres away from the little stove that was supposed to keep the building warm. Clearly, we were going to have to sleep in our clothes and get used to it. The barn was not very large, but sufficient to accommodate this entire group. There was, of course, a big barn door, but it didn't shut very tightly, and we had to stuff straw into the cracks to keep out the howling wind and blowing snow. But no one really seemed to care about the elements. Totally exhausted, we barely managed to bundle ourselves into whatever additional clothing we'd brought with us — sweaters, three and even four pairs of woollen socks, scarves wound around necks, caps pulled down on foreheads. This we did by the dim light of a lantern which one of the two Nazi party officials held while the other directed traffic, so to speak, and handed out blankets. That done, they both left hurriedly, and it was only now that some of the men's true feelings came out into the open. It was a kind of deep rumble of voices, from which one could distinguish a word or a sentence here and there: "There they go, the *Goldfasane!*" (golden pheasants — the commonly used derogatory nickname given to Party functionaries on account of the gold and ochre colours of their jackets); "Those bastards ..."; *"Schweinehunde!"* ("Swine!"); "For them, always the best — warm beds for themselves, straw for us!" On the surface, this appeared to be pent-up animosity against the two Nazis, but I felt that it went much farther, and that it was directed against the Nazi Party itself, maybe even ... just maybe ... against the Führer, this hitherto untouchable deity. However, moments later this collective expression of discontent died down, exhaustion prevailed, and I heard only a few snores before I also fell asleep.

Early the next morning, we woke up to strange sounds coming from outside. Someone got up, opened a small gate in the big barn door, looked out, and said only one word: *"Flüchtlinge"* (refugees). The deep snow muted the sounds, but we could clearly make out the creaking of wagon wheels, some human voices, a dog's bark, and the odd mooing of a cow. As I looked outside, memories of exactly the same kind of scenes from September 1939 came back to me, recollections of terrified people with their hastily gathered possessions moving ever so slowly from danger into what they perceived as safety. In September 1939, it had been Polish refugees forced eastward by the threat of German armour. Now the refugees were Germans fleeing westward, away from the Red Army's T-34 tanks. In 1939, the Polish refugees had been victims of bloodbaths perpetrated by the German Luftwaffe. Now, in 1945, the fleeing German population faced snow, howling winds, and frost, none of which was about to abate. The endless column moved at a steady pace. Sombre-faced men walked bent into the blowing snow, leading the horses that pulled farm wagons loaded high with household goods of all descriptions, including bedding that protected the women and children from the cold. Now and then one could hear a baby whimper — the only human sound emanating from this dismal procession.

After breakfast, a skimpy affair, the snow eased off gradually, and the wind subsided. Faced with the never-ending trek of refugees, both of our Nazi "Führers" tried to put on airs of almost nonchalant unconcern as they handed us spades and shovels that appeared to be available in some quantity. We were then led about a kilometre down the road to a rise in the terrain where, we'd been told, "prepared positions" had previously been established. These so pompously named "positions" turned out to be shallow trenches, ranging in depth from about three to four feet and much too narrow to accommodate an average man with a rifle. In other words, this "prepared position" was a hurriedly and sloppily dug ditch — now completely filled with snow — which we drafted civilians were to open for the prospective defenders of what remained of the Third Reich. I was not the only one to see the absurdity of the situation. The old-timers among us who had seen trench warfare in the First World War were now openly, though grimly, laughing at their own efforts as they, like everyone else, shovelled the snow out of that ditch in purposely puny amounts, like children playing in a sandbox. Our two uniformed Nazi minders merely stood around, trying to look heroic, but clearly aware of the uselessness of the whole effort. They made no attempt to drive anyone on if he stopped digging for a couple of minutes or more and only rested, leaning on his shovel. One old man stopped working and addressed them, his voice raised: "Hey, you two, don't just watch! Help us save the Vaterland!" The rest of us stood still, grinning impertinently at the attempts of the two stone-faced Party minions to swallow the insult. The whole scene was a comedy par excellence!

From the modest hill on which we worked, or rather pretended to work, we could clearly see the endless column of refugees, some walking alongside their wagons, others perched on top of the possessions piled onto the vehicles. Had it not been for the sheer mass of humans, animals, and conveyances, some now pulled by tractors, this long line of misery would have moved much faster. As I gazed at that snail-paced spectacle, a man next to me said, in heavily accented German: "Now war goes other way, no?" I turned toward him and saw that he was probably in his late twenties. Tall, with a narrow face and blue eyes, he looked not exactly emaciated, but certainly undernourished. I nodded agreement and, with his accent in mind, replied in German that I thought he was quite right. We both smiled, and this was the beginning of my brief but unforgettable friendship with Yakiv Malik. I asked where he was from. From a small town called Razdol, in Ukraine, he said, adding that he was hoping to get back to his young wife and little son. Still wary of new acquaintances, especially those who approached me themselves, I was careful in what I said and, in talking with him, actually got more information from him than he got from me. But he seemed to be quite forthright with me, and I learned that he, like many thousands of Ukrainians, had believed the Germans who, during their 1941 invasion of Ukraine, then part of the Soviet Union, had promised its population a sovereign state, free from oppression and the forced Russification of Ukrainian culture and language. In this belief, he and a great many of his compatriots had volunteered to work in Germany. He had been assigned to a farm near Pillnitz, a suburb of Dresden.

We had been chatting for a while, not even pretending to work, but unmolested by the Nazis, when some snowflakes suddenly floated down from the grey sky. At first, no one paid much attention to them, but within minutes those few flakes grew into a veritable blizzard that would have turned opening those supposedly defensive trenches from silliness into sheer idiocy. The whole crowd was ordered to stop "working" and make its way back to our accommodations in Katzberg. Clearly, any further digging efforts would have been useless, and with all their pompous posturing the two Nazis became just as bewildered as everyone else. It was all too obvious that the snow would fill the primitive, shallow ditch in a matter of minutes.

The dismal column of refugees was still moving through the whiteout, slow and almost soundless. I guess it was some time between early- and mid-afternoon when we reached our accommodations in the village. In the barn, a big pot of water was heated up on the little stove, and we took turns having a much-needed wash. I have no recollection of a midday meal, but we were given a modest supper in the evening. Now that even the mere idea of "preparing positions" had become a thing of the past, we had time to kill, just lying around and talking about anything that came to mind. Interestingly, a general shift began to occur in the way opinions were voiced about the course the war had taken, and where responsibility lay for what had clearly become a catastrophe. Even when our Nazi minders made their appearances to check up on us from time to time, distrust of the Party and its regime was expressed almost openly and fearlessly. Hitler's name wasn't mentioned just yet, but the implication was clear. Old Goering jokes, once only whispered, were now gleefully revived, as were the viciously accurate names for Goebbels: *Schrumpfgermane* (shrunken Teuton) or the other epithet, *Klumpfusszwerg* (clubfooted dwarf).

I was still awake after the rest of the group had fallen asleep. I recall thinking of my parents and wondering how they might fare if the Soviets had reached Poznań. What about my friends? Kazio Mettler, Tadek Staś, Zenek, and all those former classmates of mine who had remained in Poznań when I left my hometown for Dresden? My departure to "improve fortifications" had been so sudden that I had barely been able to say goodbye to my friends in Dresden and Hellerau. If a courier had made an unexpected appearance at my door, I wouldn't have been there to receive him. The last such visitor on his way west had stayed with me overnight sometime in late November or early December 1944. Now, considering the rapidity of developing events, it was doubtful that any more emissaries would come from Poland, given the tragic failure of the Warsaw Uprising and the almost certain break in communications between the Polish government in London and the last vestiges of the Polish Resistance, whose existence I was no longer certain of. I also worried about the fate of those wretched young Polish forced labourers who, I fervently hoped, had gained some comfort, maybe even confidence, from the few sheets of information that I had clandestinely slipped under the barbed-wire fences in the dead of night. But all of a sudden, this whole activity with radio transcripts — the printing and the sneaking around in darkness to deliver them to this or that camp — faded in significance when seen against the enormity of events developing perhaps only two hundred kilometres to the east. In performing the task assigned to me by the Resistance, I hadn't really been doing anything of great importance. It was so puny, compared with the deeds of those who had risked or given their lives blowing up German troop trains, executing Nazi butchers in broad daylight, or fighting on the barricades of the Warsaw Uprising. So what if I had helped audacious couriers to get from point A to point B on their dangerous journeys between Poland and, ultimately, England? In reality, I had been just one of the thousands of minuscule cogs on the large wheel of the Resistance's fragile machinery.

13 ESCAPE AND CAPTURE

It was now January 16, and though the tragic flight of the refugees continued, their numbers had diminished. A more northerly route to the west was now bearing the brunt of panicked, fleeing humanity. Snow was coming down intermittently and, of course, there was no more talk about "preparing positions." But the Katzberg post office's telegraph and telephone lines were still functioning and could be used by our Nazi bosses to report to higher authorities and ask for further orders. We were advised of this by the senior one of the two, the one with the extra gold on his cap. Miraculously, he managed to reach Party headquarters in Breslau (now Wrocław). Having talked to someone in charge, he gathered the whole crowd of us civilian conscripts to give us our next assignment. We were to proceed in the direction of Breslau, on foot and using a country road reportedly still free of refugee traffic. If there were abandoned farms along that route, we were to feed ourselves with whatever we could find in the farmhouses. Also, if there was still any livestock left — horses and cattle — we were to take them with us and deliver them to a special collecting point in Breslau.

The reaction in this crowd of men who had been pressed into service was mixed. Some were glad to be getting out of the way of the approaching front and maybe even returning home to Dresden. Others were highly unhappy about having to cover the distance of up to thirty kilometres on foot. These were especially the older men, veterans of the previous Great

War of 1914–18, who knew a lot about long-distance marches in wintertime and were aware of their greatly reduced chances of survival, given the circumstances. Now the head Nazi drew himself up and declared that orders had to be obeyed no matter what and that malingerers would be dealt with according to wartime law. By this he meant, of course, that those who feigned sickness or inability to walk would face execution without trial. To me, at least, it looked as if having spoken with higher authorities and getting firm orders had stiffened the Nazi's spine and awakened in him the much-vaunted "Führer Principle," a key part of the Nazi Party's ideology. To emphasize the importance of his words, he patted the holster that held his Walther gun — enough of a gesture to shut everyone up and ensure his supremacy over us.

My own feelings were at that moment twofold. On one hand, I rejoiced in Germany's inevitable defeat. But then, knowing about the viciousness and brutality of the Soviet invasion of Poland in 1939 (carried out together with the Germans), I had no wish to fall victim to the Red Army steamroller. It was preferable, I thought, for me to await the end of the war in Dresden and then make my way back to Poland, specifically to Poznań, to once again be with my parents. I wasn't worried about marching the thirty kilometres to Breslau. Perhaps I remembered reading in some Boy Scout manual that, marching at an average pace, you could cover one kilometre in ten minutes. Of course, it didn't work out that way. We were to be taken down a country road that was almost completely free of refugee traffic and led in a southwesterly direction, but the road curved constantly, adding kilometres to our group's march. Like quite a few others, I worried about the condition of my boots, which were held together by glue and some strategically placed nails. The soles were already so thin that I was sure they'd get worn through in the not-too-distant future.

We left Katzberg around noon of the following day, January 17. Right away, it became clear that it would take us much longer than a whole day to reach Breslau. The snowdrifts, for one, were almost two feet deep in places, and this alone made walking extremely difficult. There was also the fact that a number of the older men couldn't, for various reasons, move as quickly and easily as the rest of us. The two women who had cooked our meals had provided us with some bread and a kind of marmalade for the trek, but it was hardly enough to see us through all the way to Breslau. They decided to return to their own village of Blüchertal. The old lady knew she couldn't possibly walk all the way to the city and made it quite clear that she wanted to go home.

The road we were marching on could be recognized as such only by the still undamaged power lines running alongside it; even the drainage ditches were completely filled with snow. After a couple of hours, we came to the first farm. Like all such properties in that region, it lay quite close to the road and consisted of a number of sturdy brick buildings — a barn, a shed for machinery, a horse stable, and a fine house that displayed a good level of material comfort. There wasn't much time to survey it all, but everything pointed to the owners' hurried departure. Willingly, we followed our instructions to go in and look for any food that might have been left by the absent owners, although I felt strange in the role of a marauder going through other people's property. On that day, we probably saw and searched close to ten farms, some large, some small, and all showing signs of panicky flight. There was food of all kinds — bread still in the ovens, smoked meat in iceboxes, and preserves in pantries — enough to feed us all for days. But there was a limit to how much we could take with us, burdened as we were by our own bundles and other luggage, so after we had eaten, we left what we could not carry.

From then on, we kept passing abandoned farms and looking for the livestock we were supposed to take to Breslau. It was just as well that none could be found. Only some hungry-looking and angry dogs seemed to be still guarding their absent owners' properties. Our Nazi minders kept urging us on, even though a few of the older men had begun to fall back more and more often. Occasionally, these urgings turned into outright threats, theatrically underscored by the wild waving of those Walther PPK guns. But even such threats had no effect on the ever-slower progress of the increasingly exhausted group.

Darkness came early and it became impossible to go on any farther. We had reached yet another one of those abandoned farms, and the Nazis decided we'd spend the night on the premises. But their bureaucratic instincts must have surfaced too, because they lined us up to conduct a head count. Having kept pretty well to myself, I hadn't paid much attention to what was happening within the rest of the group and only now found out that three men were missing. They were in their late sixties and early seventies, evidently unable to go on and desperate enough to risk what amounted to desertion. It was clear to anyone that they must have stayed behind in one of the farms we had passed. Our Nazis became simultaneously furious and confused. They screamed obscenities and threatened death to anyone who might have overheard the men plot their escape and hadn't reported it and to those who had actually seen them stay behind. Being faithful Nazi Party members, they had been entrusted with the job of putting forty civilians to work on "preparing positions" and, since that had fallen through, with leading them to Breslau, presumably to prepare some more "positions." But now — oh, horror! — they had only thirty-seven underlings and probably faced in their minds some kind of a brown-shirted Party abyss of guilt, perhaps even a demotion in rank, for letting such a terrible thing happen.

Eventually though, they realized that going back for those three oldsters could mean losing much of the time they had been given to get to Breslau. They decided to stay overnight after all and try to reach the city by evening of the following day. Some of us slept in a hayloft; others, myself included, were relegated to a cattle barn, which, unfortunately, had not been cleaned out. To me, the all-pervading foul smell didn't really matter. I was too tired to care.

It was now January 18, and we set out at first light. The snow began to fall again, and the country road, until now relatively free of traffic, suddenly became clogged by a long column of refugees moving in the same direction as our press gang. Like it or not, we had to adjust to the refugees' snail-like progress and did not reach a highway proper until around noon. Traffic was the heaviest I'd ever seen, with refugees moving westward, and the military trying to make its way to the East, toward the front — if, in fact, a real front still existed. What with the wagons, horses, and cattle of the refugees, and the Wehrmacht vehicles of varying descriptions — armed personnel carriers, the odd tank, even some 88-calibre guns — the confusion was beyond belief. My Ukrainian friend, Yakiv, speaking in his broken German, said that Napoleon's retreat from Moscow must have been just as chaotic. To this an elderly German added that compared with what we were witnessing, Napoleon's retreat had surely been no more than a picnic. Naturally, remarks of that nature were made only out of hearing range of our Nazi mini-Führers.

Watching this cavalcade of defeat, I was suddenly reminded of a picture in Poznań's newly established German daily from late October or early November 1939. It showed a column of Polish soldiers, now unarmed and looking grimly despondent, being escorted to a POW camp by grinning Germans carrying bayonet-tipped rifles. With all kinds of horrors and the war's gore shown in the background, the picture carried a triumphant caption: *"Mit Mann und Ross und Wagen hat sie der Herr geschlagen."* ("The Lord has destroyed them with man and horse and wagon.") Even today, I think back to that adage which so accurately depicted the chaos and depth of defeat. No one knows whether it was destiny or divine intervention that made the Germans suffer the same fate that their rulers had earlier inflicted on the Poles. But then, there is yet another saying that deals with such a course of events: "What goes around, comes around."

The traffic did move, even if only metre by metre. At a certain point, I saw a road sign with the information that we were nearing a large village called Hundsfeld. Never would I have imagined that fate would bring me to this place! While still in school, I had learned about the battle fought here in the twelfth century between an army of the German empire and forces of the king of Poland. This battle was so decisively won by the Poles that many scores of German knights were killed. Their bodies were left on the battlefield and devoured by starving dogs. The name "Hounds' Field" had survived centuries in both German and Polish languages. In the former it was called *"Hundsfeld,"* in the latter, *"Psie Pole."* Of course, there was now nothing remarkable about the place, and we moved through it at a steady, slow crawl.

We came ever closer to Breslau, a city that had played a very important role in the history of my family. The civil service career of my grandfather, Maximilian Antoni Dołęga-Kamieński, had taken him there, where he and his first wife, Angela (who died in 1886), and his second wife, Martha (née Węsierska), had raised a family of three sons and a daughter. My father and his siblings were obliged to attend German schools, but their domestic environment had provided them with the Polish language and a thorough appreciation of Polish history, culture and traditions. One of my father's brothers, Czesław, later became a businessman in Winnipeg. The other, Jędrzej (Andrew), became a Jesuit priest. His sister, Helena, entered an Ursuline convent at an early age. When my grandfather, Maximilian, died in 1910, followed shortly by his wife, Martha, their children attended both funerals and, according to family custom, had the two tombstones marked in the Polish language. In 1935, my parents travelled to Breslau to visit my grandparents' graves and found them practically destroyed and desecrated, the names on the tombstones chiselled off beyond recogniti-on, and the stones themselves scrawled with curses such as *"Sei verdammt, du Polack"* ("Be damned, you Polack") and with attempts to transform the emblems of Christian crosses into Swastikas. Breslau had for centuries had a high proportion of citizens of Polish background, bearing Polish names. Consequently a great many, and probably most, of their graves had been treated in the traditional Nazi way. My father's inquiries yielded the information that it was the Nazi Party that had organized the Hitler Youth and provided all the tools to carry out that act of barbarism. "What about restoring those tombstones?" I asked, but my father only shook his head and said he'd leave them as a grim memento for future generations.

And now, ten years later, I found myself nearing this city that held such deep significance for my family. Here, another surprise awaited me. It was already getting dark as our group neared a large complex of Gothic-style, red-brick buildings, with a great gate in front and a sign identifying this as the Ursuline Sisters' school of higher education for young ladies. I knew that my Aunt Helena, who as a nun had assumed the name of Maria Bronisława, had for years been living and teaching in an Ursuline school for girls, located in the Breslau suburb of Karlowitz (or Karłowice in Polish). I realized that the complex we were passing could only be the very convent in which she lived. I quickly detached myself from the slowly moving column and, careful not to be seen by our Nazis,

Martha Węsierska-Kamieńska and Maximilian Dołega-Kamieński with their three sons. From left to right: my father, Lucjan, Jędrzej, and Czesław.

ran through the gate, hoping to find out whatever I could about my aunt. I encountered a man, probably a gatekeeper, and breathlessly asked him about Mater Maria Bronisława. He informed me that the entire convent had been evacuated the previous day, but was unable to tell me its destination. I later found out that it was Lubomierz, a town in southwestern Poland. Hurriedly, I thanked him and ran back out onto the road to catch up with the group, which had meanwhile moved on.

Perhaps an hour or so later, we entered Breslau and came to a stop in some sort of a square already filled with people, all men. The sound of their voices, together with the now complete darkness of night and the blackout, created an atmosphere that was quite unreal and sinister. But what we learned as we stood there was even more frightening: Yakiv and I overheard a couple of men standing near us discussing the fact that Breslau had been declared a "fortified city" and would therefore be defended against the Red Army. The two men were clearly terrified, and, as the news spread through the crowd, so were many others. I remember turning to Yakiv and whispering: "I'm not staying here, how about you?" I will never forget his answer: "I'll go with you." After that, there wasn't much to be said. I felt him touch my arm and reach for my hand. For me, that handshake, too, remains unforgettable.

We knew that our group had entered the city from the northeast, and that we should be moving toward the west. In the all-pervading darkness, we could only hope and guess that we were going in the right direction. Slowly and cautiously, we picked up our possessions and began moving away from the crowd, at first sideways, crab-like, then with small strides, ready to stop instantly should the unexpected beam of a flashlight fall upon us, forcing us to return to our group. We could see such lights flickering here and there in the darkness and hear the guards' loud, commanding voices as they tried to keep the large crowd from scattering all over the place.

But luck was with us, albeit only temporarily. We managed to detach ourselves from the crowd and disappear into a narrow street leading off the square. Tall, evidently residential, buildings on either side could be seen silhouetted against what had now become a starry sky. They appeared deserted and no doubt the occupants had been evacuated. The snow that had fallen during the day had turned to slush, and every step we took could be heard loud and clear. It was a fairly long street, and we must have been cautiously walking for half an hour when, suddenly, a couple of flashlights were shined into our eyes, and we heard the command: *"Halt!"* We found ourselves facing four or five SS men in field uniforms, who held their burp guns pointed at us and demanded to see our papers. They examined them cursorily, told us we were coming with them, and pushed us into a group of maybe ten other civilians. We were led under that armed escort through a maze of more narrow streets, whispering with the other men. They too, we learned, had attempted to leave the city, but had been turned back by SS troops and police guarding an outer ring surrounding all of Breslau. Only women, children, and those clearly unable to bear arms and defend the city were allowed to leave. All more or less able-bodied males aged fourteen and up were to stay and fight the Red Army.

We were trapped. Yakiv became quite desperate, and I didn't feel overly happy with our situation, either. And yet, I seem to recall, even as we were being marched off by the SS, Yakiv and I exchanged a few whispered remarks about looking out for chances of escape. By no means had we resigned ourselves to our fate. Led along several streets and across intersections, we arrived at an old, quite decrepit two-storey building, which one of the men in our group identified as a Breslau *Nachtasyl*, a night shelter for homeless men, or (to put it bluntly) a flophouse. The SS men pushed us unceremoniously through the front door, and we could hear it being locked from the outside.

What I saw reminded me of the play by Maxim Gorki, *The Lower Depths*, which I had seen performed on stage before the war. Here, in this supposedly civilized, wealthy German city, I saw the dregs of humanity, squatting in the corners of a sizeable room, leaning against dirty walls, sitting on steps leading up to a second floor, some of them smoking, others eating what looked like dry bread. The old, worn-down linoleum floor was covered with slush and mud brought in from outside by the likes of us; the foul air stank of ersatz tobacco, sweat, and flatulence. Some of the men had probably, as we had, been caught by an SS patrol and brought here, to be kept under lock and key until needed to fire with outdated weapons at Soviet tanks. They all looked lost and very frightened.

Yakiv murmured that we had to find a place to sleep, even if it was on the floor. We pushed our way through to the staircase, climbed over some bodies, and then Yakiv found a tiny spot between two other men sitting on the steps. They protested loudly when he squeezed himself into that space, but then grudgingly gave in. I made my way up to the second-floor landing and found some space along the wall. The floor was muddy, so I looked around for something to cover it with. Luckily, I found a long plank about a foot wide. It was not much to sleep on, but it was better than nothing. Clutching my little suitcase with both arms, I lay down on the plank and fell asleep almost immediately.

14 ANOTHER ESCAPE

When I woke up, it was the dawn of January 19. Nearby, Yakiv was still sitting on the stairs, wide awake and no longer hemmed in by anyone. He told me in whispers that many of the men had been led away by SS escorts, presumably to be incorporated into fighting units. The SS men would be back soon, he said, to get the rest of those who were able to bear arms. This would include us, we realized; we had to try to get out of Breslau. To leave the place by the front entrance was out of the question; the armed guard posted there would stop us. Yakiv went down to the ground floor to see if there was a rear exit. There was a back door, but for some reason it was boarded up. I explored the second floor and found that the landing I'd slept on led into a narrow corridor with a dust-covered, long-unwashed window that gave out onto a small courtyard. Moreover, this window could be opened wide enough to allow access to the sloping roof of a shed just outside. Since that roof was covered with a thick blanket of snow, it was a perfect way out. A squeeze through the open window, then a snow-cushioned fall onto the sloping roof, and finally a drop of maybe two metres to the ground presented no difficulty to us. We waited until we were certain there was no one around to witness our escape and found ourselves outside in no more than a minute.

Once again, we had to guess which direction to take and — once again — luck was with us. Looking up at the morning sky, we could determine where east was by the much lighter colour of the cloud cover. That meant, of course, that we had to move in the opposite direction. We knew that, on the previous evening, we had crossed the Oder River before arriving at the square from which we had made our first escape attempt. But now we were caught in a veritable maze of streets running every which way, leaving us only able to navigate by pure guesswork. We made very slow progress, walking cautiously and staying close to the buildings. The skies had cleared and the sun was up. This worked in our favour, because we could be seen less clearly when moving on the shady sides of the streets. Three or four times we managed to avoid being caught by slipping into the entrances of tenement houses. Some of these were of the old-fashioned kind, designed for driving horse-drawn carriages through to courtyards in which, in former days, there had been carriage sheds and horse stables. These courtyards also connected with the backs of houses on the other side, so one could escape through these buildings and reach another street. The snow now dampened our footfalls, and we could clearly hear the voices of patrols approaching from around corners. This gave us time to dash into the nearest doorway. Other than that, the silence that now pervaded these once well-populated residential districts was total, and felt quite unreal.

We still had some bread, brought with us all the way from Katzberg, and ate a few bites, but with nothing to drink. We had become desperately thirsty, and it took us a while to find a still-functioning water faucet in the courtyard of one of the buildings. Having drunk my fill, and waiting for Yakiv to quench his thirst, I looked up at some of the windows. In one of them, I saw a man in uniform, though I couldn't tell whether it was Wehrmacht, police, or SS. It also could have been someone in hiding, but it didn't matter — we had to leave in a hurry. Only a short time before, we had heard the sounds of shouting followed by gunshots coming from an intersecting street, the clear sign of an SS or military police patrol dealing with someone trying to escape from the city. That was enough to make us doubly cautious.

By my watch, it had been over three hours since we'd made our escape from the flophouse. Our progress was slowed down by the frequent stops we had to make to avoid armed patrols. It was close to noon when we reached a small roadside park and then a number of evidently private villas, followed by a cluster of small, single-family homes, whose recent vintage and location could only mean that we had arrived at the city's farthest periphery. This was indeed the case. Ahead of us lay a snow-covered plain, with some small trees and a few bushes here and there and, in the very far distance, some buildings that looked like a farm. All the villas and houses we had passed were clearly deserted, and the signs of panicky departures were unmistakable.

Yakiv and I had gotten out of the city safely, but now we were in a different kind of danger. Moving in that flat, sun-drenched, blindingly white landscape with hardly any cover, we were quite visible from all directions. We hunkered down behind a small bush to figure out a way to proceed. We couldn't go back and hide in one of the deserted homes we'd passed — we would be found in no time and shot as deserters.

The only thing we could do was to continue running in the same westerly direction. Ideally, we would do this after the onset of darkness, but darkness was still several hours away. Moreover, waiting would mean sitting still in two-foot-deep snow until after sunset, but under the existing circumstances remaining motionless was out of the question: we would simply freeze to death. Approximately fifty to seventy-five metres ahead of us was a small copse with a couple of trimmed-down willow trees and some undergrowth, and we decided to make a dash for it, not only to be less visible, but also to find some shelter from the increasingly icy wind. Of course, we couldn't run through the snow, but we slogged through it as swiftly as we could, bending forward to try to diminish our silhouettes. What we encountered on arrival at the copse caught us totally unawares. I experienced a split second of heart-stopping terror, then instant relief. Hiding in the shade of those willow trees squatted a young Luftwaffe soldier who, judging by his expression, was undergoing exactly the same intense shift of emotions as he realized that we also represented no threat. None of us spoke as the soldier gathered up a bundle of large rags, nodded wordlessly at us, and ran down a slight incline. We followed him with our eyes and saw two things at the same time — the young soldier hastily wrapping those rags around his legs and, farther on, the dark glittering surface of a stream. The soldier waded into it, reaching its other bank in less than half a minute, then climbed out of the water, removed the rags, threw them away, and ran into the deep snow, eventually disappearing from sight.

It was instantly evident to us that he was a deserter unwilling to stick his neck out for Führer and Fatherland by defending the Fortress Breslau. But he had also shown us how and where to ford that shallow but rather swift-flowing stream to continue our urgent run to safety. We had no rags to wrap our legs with, but in our situation, this wasn't at all important. We stepped into the water without hesitation and headed for the other side, highly visible as we carried our belongings over our heads. This turned out to be a mistake, since in our haste to cross the stream, we hadn't bothered to look left or right. Had we done so, we would have noticed two bridges well over a kilometre apart, with the one on our left somewhat closer. We certainly became aware of them now, as uniformed figures on them gesticulated wildly and bullets came whistling at us — first, single shots from the right, and then, from the left, a series of shots clearly fired from an automatic weapon.

Yakiv yelled something in Ukrainian, I'm sure I yelled something in Polish, and I vividly remember moving forward ever faster, desperately ploughing the water toward the opposite riverbank, when the small suitcase I was carrying over my head almost fell out of my grasp. But I held on to it, even though I was totally disoriented by the suddenly erupting chaos around us, the strong cold wind, the icy water now seeping into my clothing, and the bullets zipping by or plunking into the water around us — all this over and above the overpowering need to get to the other side, dive into the snow, and disappear from view. It must have been a combination of fear and a powerful flow of adrenaline that drove us forward. I can't say how long it took us to wade across that stream, yet we did get to the other side and reached it at about the same spot as the Luftwaffe deserter had. The shooting continued briefly but then stopped, no doubt because we were no longer visible, hidden as we were in deep snowdrifts.

We crawled forward, pulling and dragging our belongings, Yakiv only a few feet behind me. Oddly, the urge to move ahead was so strong that we didn't even think about our clothes being wet and of the cold spreading through our entire bodies. With no sense of direction, the soft snow getting into our eyes, we inched on blindly but steadily, desperate to get as far away as we could from that stream — and forward to some sort of safety. Every few minutes, I looked back at Yakiv and asked if he was all right, to which he invariably replied with a smile and *"Izz gutt, ja!"* He was as happy as I was about our successful escape.

It was easily half an hour before we came to a slight incline in the landscape, and only then did I venture to raise my head above the snow to see where we were. The uneven terrain and the presence of some hedges helped to protect us from being shot at again. We hadn't come very far, but far enough for us to see that we were within a short distance of some buildings I'd noticed from the other side of the stream. Judging by the sun, they were northwest of where we stood, and since one of the three buildings appeared to be a barn, it was obvious that this was a farm. We couldn't detect any movement around it and had to assume that, like all the farms we had previously passed, it had been abandoned by its owners. After another half hour of trudging through the snow, we reached the first building, which had clearly served the dual function of horse stable and cattle barn. Everywhere we looked, there were signs of a hasty, and very recent, departure. Horse and tractor-tire tracks led westward, presumably toward the road we could see some distance away, identifiable by the presence of regularly spaced power poles.

There was nothing to prevent us from exploring the other buildings, primarily, of course, the house. Like all the others, it was built of red bricks, and although not large, looked sufficient to accommodate an average-sized family. The front door was locked, and we considered breaking in through a window; but when we walked around the house, we found that the back door was unlocked. Inside, there were further signs of a hasty departure, but we were not interested in leftover family mementos. We had neither had our clothes off nor washed properly since Katzberg. I was sure that Yakiv, like me, felt dirty, wet, and grimy, and here was a chance to take advantage of a break in our flight. Although the house had no bathroom — an outhouse served that purpose — we found a laundry tub we could wash in. Water came from an outdoor pump, but we couldn't risk heating it on the kitchen stove. Smoke from the chimney could bring trouble. Amazingly though, the electric power was still on, and, on a good-sized hot plate, we were able to heat enough water for a fairly thorough wash. As on previous occasions, we found food left over in the pantry, so we were able to cook a hefty meal of potatoes and blood sausage. We sat wrapped in sheets while our clothes dried near the hot plate, which gradually also warmed one of the house's bedrooms. There were a crib and two beds, both with eiderdown covers so comfortable that we managed to exchange only a few sentences before I fell asleep and Yakiv took over the watch.

We had established that we couldn't just walk forever and that we had to find some sort of transport to take us westward. Attaching ourselves to a refugee trek would be risky. Those endless lines of tractor- and horse-drawn wagons, sometimes even automobiles, filled with refugees were always accompanied by Nazi Party functionaries, ostensibly to keep order, but in reality to look out for "deserters" like us. It would be more sensible, we agreed, to get on board a train, preferably one with freight cars, where the controls would be less strict than along the roads with their endless streams of refugees and their possessions. We decided to head in a northwesterly direction, on the assumption that we'd eventually encounter railway tracks, then follow them and, taking care not to be seen, sneak onto a train wherever space was available.

Yakiv woke me up early in the morning. It was now January 20, and the sky was overcast, but it was warmer, and no snow was falling. Yakiv improvised some breakfast, and, with our clothes now more or less dry, we were ready to leave, except for the fact that the sole of my right boot had come away from the top and urgently needed repair. I had bought this pair of boots from someone as second-hand goods, knowing that they were of German wartime production quality, which had become progressively slipshod toward the end of the war. I was almost in despair, but then Yakiv began searching through the various nooks and crannies of the house and found a pair of well-worn but eminently serviceable boots, which had clearly been used for farm work — they still had bits of straw and manure clinging to their soles. I tried them on, and, except for some looseness in the width, they fitted perfectly.

By the time we set out, some of the clouds had cleared, and we managed to get out onto the narrow country road that I had previously noticed running parallel to the power lines. There was no traffic for miles in any direction, the air was still, and walking was, for a change, reasonably easy. We talked about the war and what it had done to our people, and as we talked, I discovered within myself a feeling of closeness with Yakiv. He was a Ukrainian completely unlike those who in this war, with Soviet or German blessings, had massacred many thousands of Poles in Tarnopol, Łuck, and other cities in eastern Poland. In my eyes, he was what the Jews call a *mensch*. Obviously, it was the ugly war that had brought us together, but I am sure that even if circumstances had been different and peaceful, and devoid of the malignant hate between our two nations, Yakiv and I would have become as close as we did. He and I shared oppression and misery, cold, and hunger, and the bond between us became stronger with every step we took together, as we tried to escape the insanity surrounding us. To this day, I think about the strange kind of logic that impelled us to flee toward Germany, in the direction of an enemy who was clearly losing the war. But Yakiv had told me what might happen to him if he returned to Ukraine, now again under Soviet rule. He could very well have ended up being shot or at least sent off to die in a Siberian labour camp for having volunteered to work in Germany. What drove me back to Dresden was, of course, the need to return to a place from which, after the war, I could go back to Poznań and my parents and once again live a normal life. Yakiv hoped that his wife and son would be spared a fate such as the one that possibly awaited him and that he, too, would some day return to his small hometown of Razdol in Ukraine.

I don't recall how far we walked. Around noon, we stopped to rest in a sort of roadside shack, and then continued, avoiding the highway on which a refugee trek was slowly moving in the same direction. We bypassed more abandoned farms and small villages, with deserted administrative buildings, post offices, schools, and the ubiquitous Nazi Party quarters. Late in the evening of that day we found a farm, off the main road and totally emptied of everything, except for two cows in the barn, restless and moo-ing mournfully. They clearly hadn't been milked since before their owners had left them to their fate. But Yakiv knew how to milk cows and helped them out of their misery. We slept on a kind of concrete walk that ran the length of the barn. The cows' body heat kept the barn — and the two of us — warm throughout the night. We didn't sleep.

15 RETURN TO DRESDEN

How many kilometres we had covered by then, I don't know and probably never will. But it didn't matter. We were making progress, even though the need for constant vigilance and the occasional stop to check for possible sources of trouble slowed us down. We judiciously avoided the wider, more-travelled roads and kept to those narrow, rutted country trails whose far-flung net connected farms and only sometimes joined the wider secondary arteries, now packed with refugee traffic. Here and there, it was necessary for us to cross those crowded roads, and we always waited behind some bush or a high mound of snow before walking across to the other side under the pretence of belonging to the mass of refugees. Naturally, we did this only after making sure that no armed SS or Nazi Party guards were around at that moment, because we certainly would have attracted their attention — two bedraggled-looking individuals, one speaking German with a thick Slavic accent, the other speaking that language a bit more fluently, and looking as if he could be a deserter. Given the tense atmosphere of that time and the unstable, hair-trigger temper of the Nazi escorts, now armed with Schmeisser MP38 guns, we could have been killed on the spot as spies or saboteurs behind the front line.

Nevertheless, and despite having to take all these precautions, we moved ahead, certain that we would eventually get to a railway line and some sort of station, and get on a train going westward. Somewhere along the way we found a child's sleigh, onto which we put our belongings. Now we could pull rather than carry them.

It was early afternoon when, following a country trail, we walked into an extensive grove of what I thought were poplars, rising from dense undergrowth. The narrow path we were on ended at a rutted road we could have crossed, had it not been for a *Kübelwagen* — that open vehicle used by the Wehrmacht — coming our way with three men in it. Behind the helmeted, uniformed driver, who wore the insignia of military police, sat a young man in officer's uniform with a prominent shoulder patch bearing the big letters *NSFO*. On the back seat next to him sat an individual in civilian clothes, hatless, and with a bloodied face. As we crouched behind a clump of evergreen bushes, the car went past us and stopped about ten paces farther down the road. The engine was running, so it was clear that their stop was to be brief. The two uniformed men dragged the civilian from the car, and it was obvious that he was unable to protest, let alone resist the blows and kicks meted out by the officer and accompanied by a stream of barracks-type obscenities. The man was pulled over to the side of the road and dropped there, where he received a few more kicks, this time from both the officer and the driver. Moments later the officer reached to his holster, drew out a pistol, moved back a pace, aimed at the man's head and pulled the trigger. The head exploded.

I find it emotionally difficult to describe that hideous moment. Such things can be seen in many films filled with violence and destruction. I prefer to remember only Yakiv saying under his breath *"Bozhe pomyluy"* ("God have mercy") and crossing himself, as if in a death rite for the man we had just seen killed.

The two Germans drove away. Knowing there was nothing we could do to bury the body, we crossed the road and went on our way in silence. It was only much later that we were finally able to talk about what we had witnessed. Among other things, Yakiv wondered about the young officer's uniform and the NSFO shoulder patch. I explained to him that those letters identified the man as a *Nazionalsozialistischer Führungsoffizier* (National Socialist Leadership Officer), one of a newly created rank of officers attached as political leaders and Nazi Party supervisors to every fighting unit of the Wehrmacht. "Oh," he said, "that's like a Soviet military commissar?" "Yes," I said, "Ironic, isn't it? The Nazis aping their enemies ..."

Shortly after this, having crossed a large, snow-covered field, we came to a country road bordered by some scraggly growth. This was more of a trail, too narrow to carry the kind of heavy refugee and military traffic we had encountered before. We could have crossed it easily, were it not for some sort of an indefinable crowd, a mass of humans approaching very slowly from a southeasterly direction. We could hear some shouts, obviously sharp commands, but other than that, nothing. This crowd moved in total silence. We decided not to risk crossing the road, but to wait, reasonably well (though only partly) concealed in a roadside ditch, until whatever was approaching us had passed. Yakiv insisted we use snow to give us some suitable camouflage, and we quickly threw as much of it as we could on one another, hopefully making ourselves well nigh undetectable. The indistinct mass of people coming toward us was still about a hundred metres away, but, as they moved ever closer, we could see that they were quite unlike the refugees we had encountered before. This was a ghostly trek of almost lifeless humanity, dragging itself not of its own volition, but driven by the snarling commands of SS guards walking alongside this macabre display of downtrodden human agony. With what one could only call rags — filthy and marked with dark, broad stripes — hanging on skeletal bodies, the sinister parade moved past us slowly and sluggishly, in a silence broken only by the screams of guards urging their prisoners to move faster, ever faster. Some of the wretches made a pitiful effort to speed up, but almost immediately fell back into the slow, lagging, mechanical forward motion. As this crowd passed mere metres in front of us, we could see that only a few of them had what might have passed as shoes, well worn and falling apart; others had wrapped their feet in odds and ends of cloth. And, then there were a few, quite a few, whose swollen and bleeding feet were almost bare. Some wore wooden clogs. How many prisoners were there in that terrifying march past? Possibly seventy-five or a hundred. But how can one put numbers to such suffering? The entire column gradually disappeared into a densely wooded area, and just as Yakiv and I got up and shook the snow off ourselves, we heard the unmistakable sound of sub-machine-gun fire and a few screams, followed by some pistol shots. As I recall, we didn't have to ask each other what that meant. We knew.

Only after the war did I learn that we had witnessed one of what came to be known as Death Marches, commanded by the SS. Still-surviving concentration camp inmates were marched from Auschwitz, Theresienstadt, and other such places of horror in eastern Europe to be placed in death camps well inside Germany itself, away from the rapidly westward-moving Soviet armies. Only a small percentage of these prisoners survived the Death Marches.

We had to bypass several farms because they were too close to highways already crowded with refugees and their wagon trains. It was getting dark when we came to a couple of modest buildings quite a distance from the nearest road and clearly part of a very small land holding. One of the buildings was residential, with two rooms and a kitchen, the other clearly a garage, now empty. We were hungry and began to look for food. In the pantry, we found some preserves and a loaf of home-baked bread, now stale. It was then that it occurred to me to reach into the opening in the kitchen's chimney, a place where I knew that many, if not most, country people stored smoked meat such as ham or homemade sausage. What I found was a treasure — a bundle of four sausages, each about seven inches long and two inches in diameter, with a looped piece of string at one end. No doubt the owners of the place had left in a great hurry and had forgotten, or didn't care, to take with them what for us was a prize find. We decided to share the sausages fifty-fifty, cut into halves, and save them for later as a kind of iron rations, rather than eating them right away. Instead, we had some of the bread and preserves, and drank cold water from the kitchen pump. As a precaution, we took turns sleeping in three-hour intervals, one sleeping while the other kept watch, ready to wake the sleeper in case of approaching danger. This time it was I who stayed awake, looking out the window attentively and probably beset by the kind of diverse thoughts that always flow into one another. I'm sure I thought about my parents. But there were so many other things on my mind as well, no doubt most of them anxieties, mixed perhaps with an awareness of the measure of luck that had helped me out of so many trouble spots over the past five years. I was no doubt also thinking back to what I had witnessed only hours before — the murder of a man and the misery of that shuffling mass of humanity. I remember pressing my coat sleeve against my face in an effort to somehow subdue the emotions that threatened to overwhelm me, and then going outside into the cold. The night sky had cleared, and I still have the distinct memory of moonlight brilliantly reflected on the snowy plain. I eventually calmed down and returned to resume my watch.

It was the morning of January 22 when we again set out in our chosen direction. But it was slow going, mainly because of the increased traffic of military units of various sizes moving both east and west, mixed with the seemingly ever-present refugee wagons inching their way forward. Crossing these crowded roads was difficult, not only because the breaks in the erratically crawling line of vehicles were so rare, but also because the presence of military police and armed SS was now more or less constant. However, we managed to get across on two occasions, both of them during traffic pile-ups. One of these was caused by a tank ploughing into a team of horses that was pulling a truck with a family of refugees in it. The mess was such that no one paid attention to two bedraggled civilians sauntering through the wreckage to the other side of the road and disappearing among the birch trees. Even so, we could move only with difficulty, since that morning's snowfall had added to the already existing snow cover, and we had to proceed with more than usual caution over the treacherously uneven ground. But we were spurred on by the virtual certainty that the smoke we saw on the horizon signified human habitation, maybe a town and — hopefully — of a railway line running through it. The smoke was dense and sooty, an indication, according to Yakiv, of the low-grade coal used at that time by German railways. I said it could just as well be coming from burning buildings, but Yakiv was certain it originated from locomotives. He'd seen it often enough back home in Ukraine.

He turned out to be right. An hour later, we reached the edge of the birch grove and soon found a clearing with a railway line running through it. We followed it for perhaps a kilometre, and there, just past a gentle curve, stood a train — a long line of boxcars and passenger carriages, all mixed up and evidently put together in a great hurry, but now standing with its locomotive near a tall water tower, no doubt replenishing its water supply. Some people were standing beside the train, and we approached them, asking if and where there might be space in the box or passenger cars, just for the two of us. But all the answers we got were negative and downright hostile. We met with the same sort of reception as we walked the entire length of the train, even though we could see that in some cases there was plainly enough room for two additional passengers.

By then, somewhat disheartened, we even thought about climbing onto the roof of a boxcar and lying flat on it while the train moved. But after walking past some twenty or so cars, we stopped, both struck by the same idea. There, attached to one end of a freight car, was a tiny brakeman's booth, in those days a common feature on all European freight trains. We decided to try it out. The booth was about three feet square and six feet high and contained a minute bench for the brakeman and, of course, the brake wheel. We managed to squeeze into this contraption and agreed to follow the system we'd used on the train ride eastward. One of us sat on the tiny bench while the other one stood, and after two hours, we changed places. Equipped with small windows front and back, the booth also had doors on either side. Of course, it wasn't heated, but at least we were protected from the snow and wind. The boxcar to which this brakeman's booth was attached was somewhere in the middle of the train, no doubt positioned there in a hurry, to accommodate yet another fifty or more refugees with their children and all the baggage.

It was late in the evening when we finally felt the jolt and heard the clanging of buffers as the train began to move. I'd already had an hour's sleep, and it was my turn to stand for the next two hours while Yakiv had his well-deserved rest. As the train crept across a snow-covered landscape, there was nothing to see except the sparks discharged by the locomotive. Even though we were protected from the wind, it was cold; my feet and hands felt icy. But that didn't matter — we were relatively free and moving away from danger. I was wide awake during my two-hour rest break, but that wasn't important, either. The train crawled along without stopping at any of the stations we passed through, leaving behind crowds of despairing people who were waiting for any kind of rail transport, even if it was only on flatcars. The tiny space I stood on while Yakiv dozed allowed for only a minimum of movement, but I was able to occasionally bend my wrists and elbows and twist my body a little to keep the blood circulation going. Somewhere along the way we stopped to take on coal and picked up the news that Breslau was already under siege. The Red Army was moving west faster than anyone had expected. I wondered if the Russians had reached Poznań, and the thought of my hometown under siege, with my parents in the midst of it, swept everything else from my mind.

On the following day, January 23, we were still under way. We had travelled right through the night, Yakiv and I changing places some five or six times. It was around ten in the morning when we entered what appeared to be the suburbs of a larger town. It turned out to be Görlitz,

My father with his sister, Helena Kamieńska (Mater Maria Bronisława) in July 1953 at Lubomierz, where she had remained since her evacuation from Breslau in January 1945.

a provincial city, and we reached it just as it was being hastily evacuated. Our train stopped at the eastern end of the station platform, and we got out of our brakeman's booth to find ourselves in the midst of total pandemonium. A passenger train standing ahead of ours seemed to have begun loading, and we made a run for it. A mass of humanity, a screaming mob of men, women and crying children, soldiers — among them also many wounded — was pushing and shoving, moving like a wave toward that passenger train, reaching it and now fighting to get aboard, hitting and screaming, climbing in through doors and up through open windows. I lost sight of Yakiv and looked around for him desperately, yelling his name, but to no avail. My voice couldn't possibly carry over the hellish din. As I attempted to climb the steps of a passenger car already filled beyond capacity, I realized that my belongings had fallen from my hand. Under the circumstances, this loss hardly mattered. What counted was getting on board that train. In this, I succeeded, just ahead of the last individual, an evidently well-fed Nazi official in Party uniform. I found myself wedged between him and some other people. All of us stood squeezed tightly together and unable to move. The space we occupied was next to the toilet, which also had two or three people in it, presumably with their belongings. Anyone who needed to use that facility would certainly have been out of luck. For some unknown reason, although the train was clearly full, it stood in the station for more than two hours. But then it finally started to move, gradually gaining speed until it was going only a little faster than the train Yakiv and I had been on.

We reached Dresden late in the afternoon. Being so near a door of the passenger car, I was one of the first to step out onto the still relatively empty platform under the great glass roof of the city's central railway station. As the train's passengers spilled out onto the platform, I searched for Yakiv, hoping that he had also been lucky enough to find a square foot of space on the train and would now be able to return to Pillnitz, where he worked. But Yakiv was nowhere to be seen. He had probably not succeeded in getting onto this train, I thought, and would try to get back to Dresden some other way. I practically ran out through the station's exit, which, to my amazement, was unguarded, and caught a streetcar that took me to Hellerau.

I had given Yakiv my Hellerau address, but never heard from him. I have only a picture of him in my memory, and sometimes wonder if he ever got to his hometown in Ukraine, to his wife and son.

Part 4

THE REICH COLLAPSES

16 WAITING FOR THE END

Old Frau Heinich had tears in her eyes at seeing me again, and cried when I presented her with half a sausage. I had carried two of them — my share of the treasure I'd found in the farmhouse chimney — tied to my belt, inside my old-fashioned knickerbocker knee breeches, even though this sometimes made walking difficult. I kept the other half and took the remaining sausage over to the Ulichs. There, I learned of an air raid that had hit Dresden in mid-January, just about the time that I was leaving Katzberg. But now I was moving with the last vestiges of energy. Having received the Ulichs' heartfelt welcome, I dragged myself home, somehow got out of my clothes, fell into bed, and slept until evening of the next day, with only a break for a thorough wash.

I learned from Franziska that, despite the now highly critical situation on the approaching front, Boehner Film Studios were still hard at work producing training films for the German Navy and Luftwaffe. This, although laughable, was pretty well in line with the Nazi Party guidelines, which allowed only one paramount belief, that in the *Endsieg* (Final Victory). But Franziska was also convinced that the studios' owner, even though a member of the Nazi Party, was aware of the coming debacle and that the reason he went on stubbornly producing the now useless films was because they were officially still designated as *kriegswichtig* (essential to the war effort). Those who worked on them were therefore *unabkömmlich* (indispensable) and not subject to the military draft. Two days later, on

January 26, I went back to the Ulichs' house. Listening to the BBC, whose signal was now jammed only intermittently, I began to gain a better understanding of the hopeless situation in which Nazi Germany found itself. I could safely speculate on the imminent end of the Third Reich. Hamburg, Cologne, Berlin, and most important industrial centres in Germany were being turned to ashes by Allied bombers. Yet Dresden remained naively calm in the assumption that its beauty and history were protecting it from the war's vicissitudes, despite the fact that, aside from the Goehlewerk factory, there was some significant industry worth the Allies' attention. Population numbers had been increasing with the influx of people fleeing the heavily bombed western parts of Germany and of refugees trying to escape the onslaught of the Red Army in the east. Conventional air defence measures applied in the big German cities had proven to be inadequate in the face of the Allied air superiority. In Dresden, this lesson was blithely disregarded by the Nazi Party which, led by its *Gauleiter* (district Nazi Party chief), Martin Mutschmann, was responsible for the civil air defence of the city. Only one project was carried out. A huge basin, maybe ten metres square and five metres deep, with inward-sloping walls and made of concrete, was constructed in Dresden's *Altmarkt* (old Market Square) and filled with water for fire brigades to use in fighting possible conflagrations — though only those in the basin's immediate vicinity. Within the city centre, cellars of apartment buildings were designated as bomb shelters, only to later become death traps for many thousands of victims of the coming Allied raids.

At work, the atmosphere had become downright grotesque. I believe there were about fourteen persons in the animation department, including a cameraman and the director. In this number were two ardent Nazis, who seemed to believe firmly in Germany's final victory, while the rest of the crew only silently pretended to agree. Now, the two Nazis had lost all their bombast, hardly speaking to anyone or even with one another. On the other hand, all of the others were now having feverishly whispered conversations, and from what I gathered, I wasn't the only one who listened to the BBC or to a Swiss radio station that aired neutral analyses of the war's progress. The ruins of Warsaw had finally been "liberated" by the Red Army, but I wondered how Poland would fare, now that it had once again been overrun by the Russians. I was horrified to hear that Poznań, like Breslau, had been declared a "fortress" and was to be defended to the last man. Now, my thoughts were with my parents. I fervently hoped they would find a place safer than our home in the city, perhaps in a small town or a village out in the countryside. The Red Army's ring around Poznań closed on January 26, and the battle for the city went on until early February. Soviet air bombardment and heavy artillery fire from both the Soviet and German sides virtually destoyed the beautiful Old Town, and the loss of human life, both civilian and military, was immense. My parents survived, but only to face another, personal, tragedy the following year.

In the POW camp located next to the film studio's terrain, the captive British and New Zealand soldiers and a few Americans who had recently been added to that contingent were all smiles. And no wonder: on the little pieces of paper thrown over the fence by some of us, they could read about the rapid progress of Allied forces into Germany and of an imminent end to the war.

"Defended to the last bullet" in 1945, Poznań lay in ruins.

Around the end of January or the beginning of February, I happened to be in the Ulichs' house when the phone rang and Franziska picked up the receiver. For a short while she listened, then, in a strange tone of voice said, "Oh, God" and wordlessly handed me the receiver. The mother of our dear and close friend, Jochen Arenhold, had called to tell us that he had been killed in battle at the Eastern Front near the small town of Stoczek. As I listened to her speak in an odd, obviously self-controlled way, I felt as if something had hit me so hard that at first I didn't know what to say. But then I reacted in a way that even now I find difficult to understand. I was overcome by an intense, unstoppable outbreak of hysterical giggles. I think it lasted only a short time, maybe a few seconds, but to this day, some sixty years later, I feel a kind of shame at having broken down in this strange, unexpected way. Frau Arenhold told me that Jochen had left a will, in which Franziska and I were among the beneficiaries, and she invited us to visit her in order to receive our inheritance. We went to see her on the following day, and I excused myself for my hard-to-explain breakdown the night before. She was gracious and understanding, while clearly holding back her grief over the loss of her only child.

Much later, after the war, I spoke to a psychologist friend about this strange and embarrassing outburst of laughter. He told me that upon receiving news sufficient to create a shock (regardless of whether the news is good or bad), the recipient's brain decides on an immediate reaction. The recipient undergoes momentary stress, and it can happen that bad news results in hysterical laughter (as happened in my case) or conversely, that good news causes the adverse reaction of a crying jag.

To Franziska and me, Jochen had been more than a friend: we saw him as a brother. Although only eighteen years old, he was an immensely talented artist, far ahead of us and brilliant in his use of colour, especially in portraiture. I forget what it was that he willed Franziska, but he left me all his art materials and two books of writings by Gauguin. To this day, two of his brushes, never used by me, have a place among my mementos, to stay there till I'm gone.

When I began working at Boehner Film Studios, Günther Nitzsche had already been there for over a year. Severely crippled by childhood polio, he could walk only with the help of a cane, dragging his legs. He was an intellectual, a connoisseur of classical music, an amateur painter, and, as I learned only after our friendship had deepened, a man beset with hatred of the Nazis. His wife, Anni, came from a Mormon family, but did not practise that faith. They had a little daughter named Bärbel, at that time still a baby. Franziska and I became close friends with the Nitzsches and visited them often at their tiny apartment in the old, densely built-up centre of the city. Thus, it so happened that we found ourselves in their home on the evening of Sunday, February 11, 1945, to spend a few hours over ersatz coffee, debating the fast-approaching demise of the Third Reich. I remember that occasion particularly well, since it preceded an event that has found a prominent place in the history of the Second World War. Dresden had already experienced many false air raid alerts and a couple of lesser bombing raids, but so far most of the city had escaped the tragic fate of other, much heavier populated centres all over Germany. I recall us talking about the evacuation of the priceless works of art from Dresden's world-famous Art Gallery: paintings such as the Sistine Madonna, and all the others by Titian, Rembrandt, Rubens, Botticelli, and virtually all the greatest artists of the past. Even though half convinced of Dresden's immunity from the ravages of war, I was relieved to know that works of art, which really belonged to the whole world, had been deposited in a safe place — deep sandstone caves near the small town of Meissen, a few miles northwest of Dresden. And I also remember us talking about a very close friend of theirs, a talented musician and composer, who had been taken by the police and had disappeared without a trace because his father was Jewish. Later, I think, we ran out of words and just sat in silence, Anni with tear-filled eyes, Franziska holding Anni's hands, Günther and I staring at the flame of a candle that stood on a small table between us. It's a memory of the kind one never loses. I carry it with me even now.

We went to work on Monday and Tuesday, more to show our presence than to do what the studio paid us for. The heavy influx of refugees from the East had begun several days before. The streets and squares were now crowded with tired, bewildered people of all ages and carts and

My friend Jochen Arenhold, a young and extremely talented artist, was killed in battle on the Eastern Front in 1945.

horse-drawn wagons piled high with household goods, a sight familiar to me from only weeks earlier, when Yakiv and I had tramped through snow to out-run the approaching front. Now, the front was in fact no more than a hundred kilometres from Dresden, and the numbers of refugees with all their belongings must have run into tens of thousands. The mood among the city's population had suddenly turned from mild optimism about its fate to fear and almost tangible panic.

News of the Red Army's rampaging through already-conquered German territories had reached Dresden not only by word of mouth, but also by way of Goebbels's propaganda machine, which spoke of rapes and killings in East Prussia.

On the evening of that Tuesday, February 13, Frau Troll, an immediate neighbour of the Ulichs, came to their door to invite them and me to her home for a quiet evening of good music. A spectacularly beautiful and cultured woman, she was an intimate friend of the famous conductor Joseph Keilberth and owned an extensive collection of recorded music, much of it in the Nazis' "verboten" category: Mendelssohn, Bruch, Ravel, Chopin, and Russian composers right down to Shostakovich. On this occasion, she decided to play for us Tchaikovsky's Symphony No. 6, the *Pathétique*, a work that to this day is indelibly etched in my memory, marking the most horrific event I have ever witnessed.

17 HADES

All of us knew the *Pathétique* by heart from the time when it was a standard work in every symphony orchestra's repertoire. But now we listened to it as a forbidden pleasure, beautiful but potentially lethal. After all, it had been banned by the Nazis, who severely punished anyone caught playing or listening to it.

Well into the symphony's "Allegro molto vivace," Frau Troll's mother came into the room to tell us that the air raid sirens were wailing alarm, and that it would be best if Frau Ulich, Franziska, and I went to our respective homes, to wait in the basements for what might, or might not, happen. But we remained until our hostess lifted the playing arm off the record, stopping the music just as the first notes of the symphony's "Adagio lamentoso" sounded. As the music abruptly ended, we could hear the steadily rising and falling howl of sirens. We went outside, expecting this to be a false alarm. But the sirens' wail faded into another sound, the mighty, escalating roar of a fast approaching aerial armada, heading directly for the city, over which parachute flares — harbingers of things to come — were already appearing against the black, starless sky. I recall Franziska saying, "Oh, *Christbäume!*" (Christmas trees), which was what Germans called the flares used by Allied bombers to mark and illuminate their targets. And then she said, "Oh, God, maybe this is really serious." Which indeed it was.

For me, the sudden end of the *Pathétique* exactly at the beginning of its last, "lamentoso" movement became emblematic not only of a burning Dresden, but of all war disasters and life's finality.

Franziska and I ran to a clearing several houses away, from where we could look down toward the Elbe Valley and over the undefended city, where explosions were beginning to appear, a great many of them as bright as those flares floating up in the air. Moments later, a huge wave of sound reached us as the explosions grew and multiplied, and we stood there, unable to say a word or even to believe that this was really happening. I am not sure what was going through my mind just then, but it's possible it had to do with fate exacting revenge for what Germany had done to Poland, Russia, England, and so many other nations.

I think it was Franziska who first said something about the people "down there" in the burning city. I immediately thought of our friends, Anni and Günther, and of Yakiv Hnizdovsky, a talented artist we had befriended at the Academy. I have no doubt that, for me, Franziska's words led to the forming of my idea to do something for them, to help them get out of the city and give them a refuge in the distant suburb of Hellerau. It was only much later that I realized how totally this idea defied all reason and how moonstruck I was to imagine I could be of any help. Franziska was a pragmatic person, and she would have talked me out of this purely emotional impulse — but I did not tell her about it. We walked back to our homes in shock and hardly able to speak. We parted without a word, both no doubt feeling that to wish each other a good night while Armageddon was raging in the city below would have been tragically grotesque.

Its mission completed, the bombing armada flew off. The raid had lasted no more than twenty or thirty minutes. Meanwhile, my idea to help my friends had become a firm resolve to get to Dresden as fast as I could. Using Franziska's bicycle, to which I had unrestricted access (and which I kept in Frau Heinich's garden shed), I was sure I could cover the seven kilometres from Hellerau down to the city's outskirts in less than half an hour. It was a cool night, and I was glad to be wearing a sweater under my jacket, a cap, and a well-worn pair of gloves. I was already quite familiar with the route leading into the Elbe valley and eventually got onto Königsbrücker Strasse, which led southwest into Dresden. But it wasn't

Top: *Anni Nitzsche.* **Bottom**: *Günther Nitzsche.*

an easy ride. The road was now teeming with vehicles all going in the same direction — fire trucks from the nearby suburbs and towns, Red Cross vans, military vehicles of all kinds, some carrying rescue equipment and personnel — all racing toward the burning city, rushing past me at breakneck speed and forcing me to ride on the sidewalk, where military and police motorcycles crowded me to the side and slowed me down. By the time I passed the great industrial zone on the other side of the road and reached a complex of military barracks, formations of soldiers had joined the moving mass of vehicles, and it became virtually impossible for me to get ahead on the bicycle. I put it behind a streetcar shelter, where it couldn't be seen, manoeuvred my way through the pandemonium, and leaped onto the running board of a huge military truck.

I can't remember much about my emotions in the total confusion that reigned. In that crazy melee of vehicles, driven by men looking insane in their desperation to get down into the city and bring help, my senses were dulled and my mind became a hellish carousel. Only when the truck I was hanging on to stopped near Albertplatz did I begin to smell the heavy, harsh smoke. It seemed to be coming from everywhere.

As we drove into the *Neustadt* (New Town) part of Dresden, separated from the *Altstadt* (Old Town) by the Elbe river, it was clear that most, if not all, of the fires that were burning were in the old city, while Neustadt had suffered only modest damage. Nonetheless, it now became difficult to breathe because of the acrid smoke wafting over from the old city. Also, the heat emanating from the fires was increasingly difficult to bear, the closer one came to the Neustadt market square and, from there, to the Augustus Bridge that led across the Elbe into the old city. Here, all vehicles were stopped, and rescue teams had to cross on foot. It was feared that the bridge, though still passable, had been weakened by the bombing and that the weight of the vehicles might cause its collapse. I took off my sweater, dipped a sleeve into some icy water in the fountain in front of the Albert Theatre, and held it against my face. Cautiously, I moved over the bridge along with the mob of soldiers and firemen, many wearing gas masks, others shielding their faces as well as they could with whatever they had at hand. But the closer one came to the other side of the river, the greater the heat became — radiating not only from the fires and smoke, but also from the pavement. The smoke was rising high, with flames flickering through it. I could plainly see that both the Royal Residence and its beautiful baroque church were burning fiercely and that the large, dark shapes flying through the fire-red smoke were heavy sheets of the church's copper roofing. Through the pandemonium of crackling fires, waves of sparks, and masonry breaking up and crashing to the ground, I could hear screams, high-pitched, but muted by the thick smoke. Yet all that noise was merely part of an all-pervasive, giant, massive roar — perhaps of pain, fury, madness, and despair, perhaps the death rattle of a great and beautiful city.

From that moment on, sucked into the chaos of fire and smoke, I let my mind give up on pure reason and let instinct take the lead. This is perhaps why, sixty years after the bombing of Dresden, a great deal of detail has escaped my memory, and I have retained only the most pertinent facts. Coming off the Augustus Bridge and seeing the Saxon Legislature Building on my left also beginning to burn, I turned right, into a somewhat less smoky area between the church and a row of small restaurants overlooking the Elbe. Many others were taking the same route to get to the city centre. A number of small fires were burning in the big square in front of the opera house, no doubt from incendiary bombs, and some fires were also evident on the opera house's roof. I could hardly see the great Art Gallery through the smoke, but the Cosel and Taschenberg Palais were burning fiercely on my left. Some people were running with me toward the centre of the Altstadt. A fireman coming from the other direction stopped and breathlessly told us that everything looked hopeless around the Postplatz, that the big Post and Telegraph Building was in flames, as were all houses in the streets leading from that square. Nothing could be saved, he told us, coughing constantly, his lungs no doubt affected by the smoke — bombs had put the water supply out of commission. He staggered off toward the bridge, and I headed into the Postplatz square.

It was not easy to get there. I fought my way through ever-heavier smoke, avoiding the flames that shot up from asphalt already boiling in the heat. Falling into a shallow bomb crater, I managed to get out, only to stumble over a body half-covered with rubble and fall again, recoiling as my gloved hands made contact with the almost sizzling-hot cobblestones. I couldn't see too far ahead, but was able to get my bearings as I saw one of the lovely Zwinger complex's pavilions on my right, eerily lit by the flames consuming the great Taschenberg Palais across the street. At a certain point, the heat became so intense that I had the momentary sensation of my clothes burning on my back. I was wearing the boots that my friend Yakiv had found for me. They had very heavy, double-thickness soles, but even through these I could feel the heat rising from the pavement.

I had a fleeting impression of the dark mass of St. Sophia church on my left, before the small group I was with — firemen, a few Red Cross workers, and a soldier or two — ran out onto the expanse of the Postplatz and into the ring of buildings surrounding it. Some of them were already burning, and on the roofs of others, small flames were beginning to take hold. There was clearly no way to enter any of the streets leading off the square. Looking down them, I could see only long corridors of four- and five-storey apartment buildings brightly lit by flames, all of them on fire. But "looking" is the wrong way to put it: I was in motion, and my eyes could record for mere fractions of seconds what I saw through the smoke and conflagration. Somehow, the motley group I found myself in was heading toward the centre of the square, running, tripping, falling, screaming incoherently, yet moving, as if driven by an unseen force, toward the large kiosk in the middle of the Postplatz. Once there, they almost trampled each other, tumbling down the steps leading into an underground public toilet already full of people squeezed into every corner — sobbing women with babies in their arms, old men trying to be brave but wide-eyed with panic, wounded soldiers obviously concealing fear under a pretense of stoicism.

Little did I know that just then, on the Altmarkt, people who had been set afire by exploding incendiaries were trying to extinguish the flames by jumping into the big water basin constructed there the year before. They succeeded, but as soon as they climbed out of the water, their hair and skin quickly dried in the hot air (which in places reportedly reached 2,000 degrees Celsius) and the phosphorus that had first set them on fire flared up again, turning them into living torches.

I was practically the last to reach the stairs leading down into this public facility turned bunker, and remained huddled on the topmost steps. Sticking my head out, I could see the big Post and Telegraph Building on my left, Schweriner Strasse straight ahead, and the beginning of Ostra Allee on the right. In the centre of the square, a streetcar was burning brightly. Just as in front of the opera house, there were small fires all over the Postplatz, obviously caused by fire-spitting incendiary bombs. So far, the kiosk above us seemed to have been spared these. But everything was wreathed in drifting smoke, sometimes close to the ground, other times rising into the air or blowing in from streets leading into the Postplatz square. I had covered my lower face with a handkerchief, and on top of that, with my sweater, but the smoke was making my eyes tear, so I had to blink repeatedly. All the while, I was desperately trying to assess my situation. There was no way I could reach Günther and Anni Nitzsche; they lived in Kleine Plauensche Gasse, a narrow street in the oldest part of Dresden, so densely built up that both getting there and getting out alive now appeared virtually impossible. To this day, I wonder about the quixotic notion that moved me to try to help my friends, and which could have turned out to be suicidal. Would I do the same thing today? I don't know, and there's no way to answer that question.

At that time, however, such doubts could only have flickered through my mind, obviously superseded by the sheer hell I faced wherever I looked — people throwing themselves to the ground, attempting to smother the flames devouring their clothes; women, children, old men, trying to find a way out of this ring of flame, running aimlessly, stumbling, falling, getting up to fall again and perish in a carnival-like shower of sparks cascading out of incendiaries; people giving up, kneeling on the burning hot pavement and praying; and those who screamed in despair, only to lose their voice and just stand there, mouth still open in a soundless cry. And the already dead, lying in grotesque poses, with little flames flaring up from their clothes.

I would have had to run into raging fires to help my friends, and certainly perish in the attempt, or abandon them and stay alive. It was, and still is, a terrible quid pro quo moral question that troubles me, even though the Nitzsches actually had managed to get out of their apartment and escape the area before it turned into a fiery inferno.

There I was then: forced to make that awful decision and, having made it, to look for a way out of the trap I'd run into. There were two directions I could take to escape. One was to risk a run along Ostra Allee, which seemed to have fewer fires than anywhere else. The other was to retrace the route by which I'd arrived at this extraordinary underground toilet bomb shelter. I wasn't at all familiar with Ostra Allee and clearly didn't know what to expect farther on in its reaches. However, I already knew the way back to the Augustus Bridge and across the Elbe into Neustadt where, I remembered, there had been fewer fires than in the centre of Dresden itself. I decided that this was the way back.

As I was about to climb out of the unusual shelter and make a dash for the bridge, I looked around. The streetcar in the centre of the square was now totally engulfed in flames, apartment buildings all around were

Dresden in Ruins, *painted from memory in 2003.*

burning even more furiously, and there were people running away from the flames, only to encounter other fiery pockets or run into banks of heavy smoke. Words fail me as I try to describe the sounds of a fire as all-consuming as that which was destroying Dresden. I can only recall that they carried something human in them, a *vox humana* that groaned, screamed, whined, hissed, and sobbed — all of this, and more, melding into an extraterrestrial, hellish howl. I looked to my left and saw a woman running past the now brightly burning Post and Telegraph Building. She was on fire, and as she passed the big, open entrance, she suddenly disappeared into it, swallowed by the flames.

I suppose I was predestined to survive in the relatively small window of time between the first bombing attack at 10:00 p.m., and the second one, which followed at 1:00 a.m. It must have been fate that moved me to leave the shelter at Postplatz exactly when I did and run toward the Augustus Bridge. I was thus saved from the firestorm that soon developed, consuming the greater part of the Altstadt and all that was still alive there. As my watch had stopped functioning, no doubt due to the excessive heat, I can't say when the firestorm began — it had to be shortly after the first wave of bombing stopped and the flames were getting a grip on the city, probably right after I'd run from Postplatz to head for the bridge. The raging storm not only incinerated everything in its path: it also fed the beacon that brightly illuminated the target for the next wave of bombing, one hour past midnight, to complete Dresden's hecatomb.

Just as I was climbing out of the stairwell, a woman appeared before me, her face covered with soot and blood and carrying a baby in her arms. Somehow, I managed to help her take my place before taking off in the direction of the Augustus Bridge. Although lit by the fires from the Cosel and Taschenberg Palais, the route had become much more difficult to traverse, not only because of craters and breaks in the pavement, but also because of the incendiaries that lay scattered about, still spitting sparks and flames. As well, the Taschenberg Palais, which weeks before had been turned into a military hospital, was being evacuated, and those patients who hadn't perished in the conflagration were now either hobbling or being carried on stretchers by nurses and doctors in the same direction I was going. This gruesome procession and I moved at a snail's pace, trying to avoid the pitfalls along the way, especially farther on, close to the Royal Residence church, an old, exquisite structure from whose upper parts huge chunks of masonry had fallen off. I was able to reach the bridge, while that grim parade moved on toward the Elbe River quays, probably in the assumption that they were safer there than in the built-up centre of the city — a tragic error, as the events of the next day would show.

I was not alone on the Augustus Bridge. What before had been a mere trickle was now a mass of frightened, bewildered people, clearly still unable to believe, let alone understand, the reality of what had befallen them — sobbing women pushing baby carriages or pulling children's play wagons loaded with whatever could be saved; old men walking unsteadily, some on crutches, trying to look brave, but not succeeding. I distinctly remember passing them and perceiving the distinct smell of acrid smoke coming from them every time a cold breeze blew upward from the water of the Elbe River. My clothes must have smelled like that too, maybe even more than theirs. Surely, these poor wretches had come from the very heart of the fiery hell. Many of these refugees, I found out soon afterwards, lost their voices through smoke inhalation, some of them permanently. As for me, although I did have difficulties with my voice, managing only a hoarse whisper, this passed after only a few days.

Once in Neustadt, the northern part of Dresden on the other side of the Elbe, I saw that quite a number of buildings, which had previously received only a few incendiaries, were now burning wildly. But it was possible, via the boulevard in the centre of the wide street traversing Neustadt to go on toward Königsbrücker Strasse. This was the very street I had taken into the city, and here, too, a mass of refugees now moved, slowly but steadily, seeking safety wherever they might find it. I walked on with them until I was about to collapse with exhaustion. There were fires on both sides of the wide street, though not as concentrated as those in the Altstadt. There, the firestorm had grown to apocalyptic proportions, and its unearthly howl drowned out the crashing sounds of buildings collapsing on either side of the broad Neustadt Avenue. Like all those refugees escaping from Dresden's inner city, I kept to the middle of the street. At a certain point, on my right and past the smouldering ruin of a multi-storied building, I saw an exceptionally large conflagration and knew right away that it was the big structure housing the famous Sarrasani Circus. It was burning like a torch, with probably hundreds of people inside and many exotic animals caged and unable to get out. I looked away and walked on, aware of being utterly helpless in the face of such a catastrophe with all its horrors and, ultimately, all-consuming death.

Fortunately, I was able to reach the streetcar shelter behind which I had parked Franziska's bicycle. To my amazement, I found the bicycle where I had left it, but I was too tired to cycle back to Hellerau. Instead, I took it into the shelter, put a leg through its tubing and sat on a bench to rest. For a while, I watched the steadily moving line of refugees, but then I dozed off. I was jolted from a deep sleep by the all-too-familiar, terrifying, wave-like sound of a clearly very large formation of heavy aircraft, still distant, but rapidly growing louder as it neared the brightly burning city. After no more than a minute, the first aircraft of this armada passed high overhead. It flashed through my mind that bombs would fall onto the large Luftwaffe airfield at Klotzsche and that the Polish workers in the nearby camp would be in mortal danger. However, the huge formation did not drop any bombs until it reached the hapless city, only seven kilometres away. It seemed that the last aircraft of that force were now directly over the road along which the mass of fleeing humanity was trudging. But only a few, I among them, ran off the road to hug the ground and instinctively seek safety in this desperate but futile way. When I eventually got to my feet, I saw that the long column of refugees was still inching along. Shaking with fear, I could hardly believe that yet another death-bearing bombing raid was taking place only a few hours after the first one had set the city on fire. It was as if a monster had merely paused, returning to again breathe flames on the witches' Sabbath down below.

Now, recalling the ghastly image of hundreds upon hundreds of people vaguely illuminated by the fires of Dresden, dragging themselves, as if sleepwalking, into the unknown, I see before me a scene that Hieronymus Bosch could have created in his vision of the Apocalypse. Maybe even their fear was gone, left behind in the burning city, and now they had nothing more to lose. They seemed numb, a ghastly, silent crowd of the almost-dead.

As for me, I wasn't any worse for the wear. My eyes were stinging, my throat was painfully sore, and there were burn holes in my clothes. They had been scorched in several places by sparks from the incendiaries, and I had extinguished the fire with my gloved hands. Most conveniently though, I was mobile. The bicycle was in good working order, and I decided to get home as fast as I could. I was exhausted, but Hellerau was now only a few, perhaps two or at most three, kilometres away, and I was certain I could get there in a matter of minutes if I went on the paved shoulder, not interfering with the creeping column of refugees.

I pedalled furiously, on pure adrenaline, not even thinking of being tired, until I reached the top of an incline in the road. I stopped to look back, and there it was again, down in the Elbe valley: a sea of flame and smoke, and huge blockbuster bomb explosions ploughing over and over through a city already in its death throes. The sounds of bomb bursts reached me

Collateral Damage Dresden, 1945.

several seconds later, just as thunder follows lightning. I thought of my friends down there and felt deeply ashamed at having escaped their possible fate. When I got home, a tearful Frau Heinich greeted me, clutching my hands, wailing in her old, reedy voice, *"Mein Gott ... mein Gott ... "* and blubbering about "The End," whatever she meant by that. I calmed her down somehow and climbed upstairs to my room. I happened to glance at my little alarm clock: it was around three in the morning. I'd been away for close to five hours. Suddenly all the energy I had mustered to escape from the horrors of Dresden was gone. I managed to take off most of my clothes before collapsing on the bed and closing my eyes to shut out reality.

18 AFTERMATH

I forget what time it was when I woke up. Franziska was standing by my bedside, looking absolutely furious and holding up the short, heavy jacket I had worn the night before. Our exchange consisted of blistering anger on her part, countered by feeble, though sincere, scratchy-voiced explanations and excuses on mine. She pointed to the jacket and, more specifically, to the holes burnt into its sleeves and back. "You went there, didn't you?" she shrieked, waving her arm, as if to show where "there" was, and followed this by calling me several choice names of which "idiot" was but one. Yet she soon calmed down sufficiently to listen to my excuses, though she still hurled a salty epithet at me before she left, slamming the door.

Only then did I realize how much I needed to wash. A look in the mirror showed me a face blackened by smoke, hair dirty with dark ash and dust, hands looking as if I'd dipped them in tar; I looked like a runaway from a blazing Hades, which in a way I was. I spent quite some time cleaning myself up to resemble a human being, all the while thinking of the many thousands who had perished in the flames and of the wretched survivors dragging themselves out of the burning city. Even today, so many years later, I keep wondering why my own escape from that hell should have made me feel guilty for having survived.

Maybe it was morbid curiosity, or perhaps the need to reaffirm in my mind that which I'd lived through the night before. Around noon, I took a short walk to the clearing from which Franziska and I had watched the first bombing attack only hours before. I stood in awe of the horrific panorama spread out where Dresden used to be. A thick, dirty, grey cloud of smoke covered the Elbe Valley, with fires flickering through it and fingers of flame shooting skyward where the city's graceful spires, topped with lovely verdigris, had once punctuated the landscape. In places, the columns of smoke reached high into the sky, and a strong wind blew it along the valley and up its slopes. Once again I could smell the smoke that had gotten into my lungs and permeated my clothes earlier, but this time there was something else in it … an odour I remembered from childhood when, together with a playmate, I had set fire to a little pile of hair and fingernail clippings. It now hit me: this was the stench of human flesh. With the smoke came ashes from the fiercely burning city — paper, fragments of incinerated wood, and vegetation — and with all that came the sudden thought that this happened to be Ash Wednesday, and that the previous night's inferno was the last, macabre joke of a truly ultimate Carnival.

And yet, the Carnival wasn't quite over. The city's corpse was about to receive one last kick, to make sure it was really dead. As I stood in that clearing, with the wind blowing the smell of smoke and the stench of death toward tranquil Hellerau, the deafening sound of massed, low-flying aircraft bore down on me in hellish cacophony. The even, fast-rising growl of planes seemed like an echo of the previous night as they rapidly closed in on the city. It appeared to me that I was almost in their flight path, and I cowered in fear as they flew overhead. But the wooded heights of Hellerau were of no interest to the bombardiers. In a matter of minutes, which seemed endless, they had flown past and were over the city. The attack itself was amazingly short, lasting no more than ten or fifteen minutes. Then the whole formation turned northward and gradually disappeared from sight and hearing. To stage a third air attack as a kind of curtain call to a tragedy that had already played itself out twice mere hours ago was, of course, devoid of any sense or reason. The first attack had lighted the fires so that the second could better do its deadly work. The third bombing assault merely raked through the ruins.

I walked back home as fast as I could, to wash again, this time more thoroughly. The water supply system in Frau Heinich's house provided cold water only, and there was no real bath either. If you wanted to wash in warm water, you first had to heat it on either a wood or coal stove. A cake of quite useless wartime soap barely lasted for one wash, and after that, you used only a stiff-bristled brush and hot water. Afterwards, feeling a little more human, I went over to the Ulichs' house, where I met with a mixed reception. Franziska was over her anger. Frau Ulich put her arms around me, kissed me on both cheeks and called me a "foolish young man." Dr. Ulich only shook his head as if in disbelief, but then wanted to know what damages I had seen. It was clear that these decent, proud, and civilized people kept their sorrow inside them. They mourned their beloved Dresden just as we Poles mourned our country. However, to me it was significant to hear Dr. Ulich say in a quiet, sad voice, "We are paying for what we've done to others."

Dr. Ulich's foresight in holding some radio batteries in reserve proved to be wise: we were able to listen to the radio even though the city's power supply no longer functioned. The BBC delivered a dispassionate, matter-of-fact report, telling its audiences simply that the Royal Air Force had attacked industrial targets and railway installations in the German city of Dresden. From Wehrmacht reports, we learned that the first two air raids had been conducted by the RAF and the third one by the American Air Force. German reports seemed to be strangely subdued, stressing the usual (and correct) aspect of terror against the civilian population, but appearing reluctant to divulge the whole, awful truth. Subsequent reports included expressions of outrage at the destruction of one of the world's most beautiful cities, but shied back from giving an estimate of human losses, obviously in an effort not to further panic the rest of an already demoralized German populace. In later, sporadic reports, it was announced, among other things, that the many thousands of victims included refugees from the east of Germany, encamped with their horse-drawn vehicles and their possessions on the wide, grassy banks of the Elbe River. Hearing this, I remembered with anguish the grim procession of military hospital evacuees I had seen trudging down to the riverbank.

Other announcements dealt with emergency measures. Among these figured most prominently a prohibition to enter the city unless specifically
permitted by the authorities.

In those first few days following the attacks, most of the city centre
was still in flames, and few would venture to enter that area. It took more
than a week for the fires to die down, but still no one was allowed to cross
the security lines guarding access to the city, not even those who desperately wanted to find their families and learn about their fate. The number
of dead was now floated as 300,000 and up by Dresden's Nazi Party officials and the Goebbels Propaganda Ministry, but no one could possibly
know a final number with any certainty. Not until a few years later was the
final, official number of the raids' victims announced as just under 35,000.
The gruesome task of identifying and disposing of the victims' bodies was
quickly organized, and the smoke of burning buildings was now replaced
by that wafting up from thousands of identified bodies stacked like cord-
wood, doused with gasoline, and cremated in Dresden's Altmarkt square.
Unidentified remains were buried in mass graves outside the city.

Those who, after the bombings of Dresden, maintained that the city
was virtually undefended were only partly right. With the Allies launch-
ing massive air offensives against major German cities and industry in the
West and the Red Army relentlessly pushing the Eastern Front westward,
German military authorities sought to reinforce their air and ground
defences in those parts of the Reich that they considered most liable to
be attacked. To this end — and possibly also led by a commonly held
but totally unwarranted belief in Dresden's immunity from air raids —
they had withdrawn most of the big ack-ack anti-aircraft weapons from
Dresden. Deprived of heavy flak, Dresden was now protected by a weak
system of low-calibre flak artillery, manned partly by teenaged boys drawn
from the ranks of the Hitler Youth. Apart from this hardly effective shield,
a squadron of eighteen Messerschmitt fighter aircraft sat on the airfield at
Klotzsche, fuelled and ready for takeoff should a truly massive air attack
threaten Dresden. But when the attack came, the squadron remained
on the ground, and it was only well after the war ended that I learned
the reason for this bizarre situation. The authority of the Dresden area

Fighter Command had recently been transferred to the Central Fighter Headquarters, near Berlin. This meant that the Messerschmitt fighter squadron could be sent up to defend Dresden only by command from Berlin. But, since communication lines between Berlin and the Klotzsche airfield had been destroyed, the command never reached its destination and the Luftwaffe pilots were left sitting idly in their machines, forced to watch, from afar, the horrible end of a dying city.

And yet, not all of Dresden perished during that tragic night. While most of the bombing force's attention was given to the city's densely populated centre, much of the surrounding area received less serious damage or escaped it altogether. Dresden's industry was predominantly located on its periphery, and great complexes such as Goehlewerk, Seidel & Neumann or the *Industriegelände* (industrial area) were almost untouched by the bombing. On the other hand, many smaller factories — also involved in war-related production but situated closer to the city's centre — were virtually annihilated. Railway lines leading into and out of Dresden were also destroyed, but German engineer troops restored the whole system within mere days, to facilitate the transport of troops and weapons eastward and strengthen an almost collapsing front, now only a couple hundred kilometres away.

Needless to say, I was anxious to find out the fate of the Polish labourers and their camps. Rumour had it that even bucolic Bad Schandau had received a few stray bombs, though I was fairly certain that the Klotzsche camp had escaped undamaged. But I worried that some of the inmates might have been working night shifts in the inner city and perished in the two initial night bombings. It was now February 17, and I made up my mind to find out what had become of them. The Klotzsche camp was within walking distance, and I discovered that it had been completely abandoned. The main gate was open and so were all doors to the now empty barracks. For the time being, my curiosity was satisfied. As I later learned, the inmates of the camp had merely fled to the *Industriegelände*, where their workplaces were located; some would later return to Klotzsche.

I felt strange, realizing that the task that had been given to me back in 1941 — to keep up the spirits of my hapless compatriots in their labour camps — had been overtaken by events and was no longer relevant. I had no way of knowing if my efforts had had any positive effect on those captives of the Third Reich. I now felt as if I were abandoning them, just as I had felt about having to leave my friends, Anni and Günther, to their fate in the hell of Dresden.

At that time, too, Franziska and I found ourselves wondering if the Boehner Film Studios had been affected by the air raids and where we stood in regard to our employment there. Telephone inquiries were, for obvious reasons, out of the question: the central exchange had been destroyed. Public transit had been largely wiped out, and the city was still not accessible. But there was a good chance that the studios, located in Gorbitz, a practically rural suburb several kilometres away from the city centre, had escaped Armageddon, and we agreed that I would try to get there by bicycle, using a circuitous route around the city. It would lead me to the undamaged Autobahn, across the Elbe, and on to Gorbitz.

I left early the next day, and it took me roughly three hours to get to the studio, which, as we expected, had not suffered any damage. But once inside, I encountered a grim crowd of studio personnel, almost all of them bombed out, wearing torn and burnt clothes, pale-faced and with inflamed, still fear-filled eyes. Quite a few were missing. Herr Best had lost his voice to smoke inhalation and answered my questions by writing on a scrap of paper, almost illegibly, "Have nothing left." Others had found their way to the studio because it could offer them a roof over their heads. And some, like me, had come to see if there was still a future for them, a life after so much death. The answer was "not now" and "not here," because all the studio equipment — cameras, lights, miles of cable, editing facilities, raw film and film archives, and especially all precious stereo opticals — was to be taken away to the West in two large trucks before the Wehrmacht, or what was left of it, collapsed and the Russians moved in. The whispers no longer expressed doubts about the war's outcome; utter and complete defeat was now seen as certain. Still, conversations were cautious, since everyone knew that a careless, loudly spoken word could be overheard by an unsuspected snitch and lead to an arrest. Having recovered from the shock of the air attacks, the Nazi Party was functioning again, as was the Dresden radio station, triumphantly broadcasting news from the Western and Eastern fronts, announcing clearly fictitious victories even as the front lines were tightening their grip on the Reich day by day. But the radio also broadcast news of looters caught in the ruins of Dresden and shot on the spot and of "defeatists," those who spread fears of Germany's imminent collapse and were just as swiftly executed. Many defectors were hanged from street lampposts.

The destruction of Dresden had left most of the city's surviving population in a kind of inner paralysis. Their world was irretrievably lost, and the city had become a great gaping wound. They wandered off into the suburbs and farther yet, to outlying towns and villages, anywhere a roof over one's head could be found. They survived somehow and ever so gradually began to think about a future. The war was still raging, but only somewhere else, and memories of the disaster were displaced by a fear of the victorious Russians. When spring came, wildflowers and all sorts of other growth began to appear amidst the mass of rubble left from the bombing raids.

The POW camp next to the studio property was deserted, and I was told that the prisoners had been marched off to look for and recover the decaying bodies of those who had been killed in the Allied air attacks. Judging by clandestinely photographed evidence I saw some time later, this must have been one of the ghastliest, most horrifying kinds of work a human being could be forced to perform.

Around mid-March, the authorities lifted the ban on entering Dresden. Franziska didn't want to come with me to see for herself what a dead city looked like. Miraculously, some of the public transit had been restored, and even though it operated only sporadically, I was able to at least get to Albertplatz by coal-gas bus, and, from there, on foot, to the only slightly damaged Augustus Bridge. Dresden's Neustadt side looked even more severely damaged than before, when I had seen it after that first attack, although, unlike most of the Altstadt, it wasn't totally destroyed.

I remember that it was a lovely, sunny spring day without a cloud in the sky. And, save for the strangely subdued voices of passersby, an eerie stillness prevailed. As I walked over the bridge, I encountered probably only five or six people going either away from, or toward, the city centre. On my left, I saw the large, seemingly undamaged building that housed the Fine Arts Academy, but next to it, the ruin of the exquisite Palais Brühl. Bright sunrays shone into the devastated Royal Residence church. I walked along the very same route I'd taken on my mad dash of February 13. The Taschenberg and Cosel Palais, then burning, were now mostly huge mounds of rubble. In front of one ruin, I saw an abandoned stretcher stained darkly, apparently with blood. It must have been there since the military hospital had been evacuated from the Taschenberg Palais. I could only imagine what a story that mute, blood-spattered witness might tell. A few steps farther, on my right, stood what was left of the once elegant Pavillion of the Chimes, part of the early eighteenth-century Zwinger complex. Once an example of beauty and grace, it had been turned into a testimonial to the hideous present.

I came out onto Postplatz to face almost total devastation. Only the burnt-out mass of the Post and Telegraph Building still stood, its windows blind-eyed and the clock blackened with smoke and missing its hands. The buildings surrounding the square had collapsed into themselves, with only a few of their chimneys pointing like dirty, sooty fingers up to the clear blue sky. The round kiosk on top of the public toilet had been damaged by fire, caused no doubt by phosphorus incendiaries and the firestorm, but still huddled in its old place. I looked down the stairs leading to the toilets, but then retreated, aware I couldn't expect to see or find anything there. The burnt-out streetcar still stood where I'd seen it weeks before. Two people, a man and a woman, were crossing the square, carefully avoiding bomb craters and chunks of sandstone. Their heads down, they walked silently, holding hands to support one another. The only sound I could hear was their footfalls on the dangerously uneven surface. Then they disappeared among the ruins, and I stood alone, trying to detect some other sound, any kind of sound, but there was only total silence. Nothing stirred. It was as if the stillness had a voice of its own.

It was such a beautiful, warm day. I remember walking off in the direction of Kleine Plauensche Gasse. To this day, I wonder what made me want to go there, since there was no hope of my friends, the Nitzsches, having survived over fifteen hours of merciless bombings. But I went. I climbed over huge piles of rubble. I fell a couple of times, but went on until I could see the doorway of the house they had lived in. It was some distance away — the only part of the building that was left. The entire narrow street was made impassable by collapsed walls, and in places the rubble was over two metres high.

I began my slow climb back, more or less the same way I had come. But after a while I decided to stop and catch my breath, resting on a very large block of fire-blackened sandstone. Looking around, I could see into a sort of gap between what was left of two narrow buildings. This space was relatively free of fallen bricks and stones, and in it I could see four completely burnt and twisted, short pieces of wood. It would have been quite natural in this neighbourhood, where the old buildings had been constructed with a lot of lumber. But there was something odd about these logs — forms that looked like branches sticking out of them, but couldn't possibly belong to any building material. I climbed off the stone I was perched on to get a closer look at what had caught my interest. I stared down in horror. What I had thought were burnt and broken pieces of wooden logs were completely incinerated human bodies, and what I imagined to be branches were the grotesquely twisted arms and legs of what appeared to be have been three adults and a small child. Years before, I had seen men who were wounded, some who were dying, and quite a few who were dead. I had seen a man shot only months before. But I had never before seen human bodies so utterly destroyed by fire. No, I didn't have to be sick, even though what I saw was so repulsive. I turned away and began a hasty scramble over the stony rubble toward home.

As I reached Postplatz, two policemen stopped me and demanded to know what I was doing climbing around in the ruins. I answered truthfully that I was trying to find out what might have happened to my friends who had lived in Kleine Plauensche Gasse, but all I had found was total destruction, so I now assumed they were dead, along with their little girl. What was their name, the elder policeman wanted to know, and I said, "Günther and Anni Nitzsche, and the little girl's name was Bärbel." He wanted to see my papers; I handed him my stateless passport. He looked at it thoroughly, and then handed it back to me, evidently satisfied with what he'd seen. Then, to my surprise, he barked, *"Hände hoch!"* ("Hands up!") I raised my arms, asking, "Why? I haven't done anything wrong." To this he said, "We'll see about that" and, turning to the younger cop, said, *"Absuchen!"* ("Search!") I was searched and patted down, but the procedure yielded only a photo of my parents and, I believe, a pencil stub and the key to Frau Heinich's house in Hellerau. I asked again why I was being searched, and was told that theft from bombed-out homes brought with it immediate execution by shooting.

This, of course, I already knew, but I wasn't aware that it still applied after so much time had gone by since the February air raids. Then it occurred to me to mention the four charred bodies I had seen just a short time before. Could they have been forgotten in the search for and disposal of the bombings' dead victims? "Oh," he said, "we still find those burnt corpses now and then. They'll get picked up eventually. The decaying bodies had to be dealt with first because of epidemics. The burnt cases aren't dangerous anymore." He shrugged and turned on his heel.

19 INTERLUDE

I t took me a long time to get back to Hellerau. There was no bus. The badly damaged streetcar line ran only part of the way, and I had to walk the remaining few kilometres. That evening at the Ulichs', I heard that Käthe Kollwitz, a great artist and champion of the downtrodden, was now living in Moritzburg, only an hour's walk from Hellerau. Either right then or some time later, Franziska and I decided to pay our respects to the famous artist, whose work had been banned by the Nazi regime, removed from public collections, and destroyed. The temptation to exchange even a few words with the grande dame of the arts was irresistible. More than that, brash young artist I was at that time, I thought it might be exciting to present her with one of my own woodcuts, and maybe elicit some kind of judgment of my artistic potential. Franziska expressed doubts about this idea, but finally said, "Well, nothing dared, nothing won." The next day we set out for Moritzburg.

Käthe Kollwitz was staying with a friend in a two-storey house, one of the very few in the village. I don't remember how Franziska had found the right address (or, for that matter, even discovered the artist's presence in the area), but there we were, knocking on the door and being received, somewhat suspiciously, by an elderly lady, to whom we submitted our request to exchange a few words with Frau Kollwitz. That the lady was suspicious was only natural: we could have been unfriendly Nazis with some nefarious purpose in mind. I unrolled my woodcut for her to see

Das Grauen (Horror), *1941 — the woodcut that I gave to Käthe Kollwitz when Franziska and I visited her.*

and said I very much wanted to give it to Frau Kollwitz, as a present from an admiring young artist. She asked us to wait outside while she found out if her friend would receive us and came back a short while later to let us in and show us into a small salon. Near a window and with a book in her lap sat a white-haired old lady, who looked at us unsmilingly and asked who we were. Of course, we recognized her from the various self-portraits we'd seen in publications from the pre-Nazi era. Mustering all my courage, I introduced us both and, stumbling over words, asked if she would accept a woodcut as a gift from me. At that, her facial expression showed interest, and she said, "Let me see it first." I handed her the print, and she put on her glasses to see it better, holding it well in front of her.

The woodcut was executed in the very rough surface of a piece of lumber, with no attempt at finesse in line or texture. It showed only a face, with hands covering the mouth and eyes wide open, as if witnessing something unspeakably hideous. She looked at it for what to me felt like an eternity. I waited for some sort of comment, good or bad, but none was forthcoming. Finally, she put the print aside, waved her friend to come closer, and whispered something in her ear; the lady left the room. Käthe Kollwitz asked us about our ages, our studies at the Dresden Academy, and specifically asked me if I preferred graphics to painting. I don't recall what I said, but then her friend was back with a sheaf of what looked like graphics and carefully put them into the old lady's hands. We looked on as she leafed through them, stopping at one point to tell us that these prints were a small part of what had been saved from her bombed-out studio apartment in Berlin just a few months before. Finally, she took one print from the stack, put it on top of the rest, and asked her friend for a pencil. She then signed the print and handed it to me. "Thank you for your woodcut," she said with a little smile, "and here's something in return."

Whatever my reply was, it had to be a jumble of words of gratitude for such a privilege and honour. I felt like kissing her hand, but shied back from such a surfeit of admiration. I had been judged and not found wanting by one of the greatest living artists of that era. Her gift to me is entitled *Hunger* — a stark depiction of a mother grieving over the body of her dead child, a theme which Kollwitz pursued for much of her working life. Her son, an only child, had been killed in Flanders in the First World War. We ran home, and the next thing I remember was proudly showing my prize to Franziska's parents and receiving enthusiastic congratulations from both of them.

Käthe Kollwitz died on April 22, about five weeks after Franziska and I visited her. A few days later, we went to her funeral in a small cemetery in Moritzburg. It was a grey, cloudy day, and no more than a dozen people attended the interment. A young man gave a short eulogy, carefully omitting her fight for social justice and against war. There was no religious ceremony as the simple, modest casket was lowered into the ground. Franziska and I returned to Hellerau in complete silence.

The final Soviet offensive began on April 16, 1945, and German radio changed its tune from being certain of an "eventual" victory to "holding

Hunger *by Käthe Kollwitz — the woodcut that Frau Kollwitz gave me.*

out to the last bullet and the last drop of blood." To all this, a downright ludicrous postscript was added in the claim that the Kurland Armee, a few battered Wehrmacht divisions trapped in Latvia and completely cut off from the German Reich, were able and ready to rush to the aid of the Fatherland in its hour of need. It didn't seem to matter to Goebbels's propaganda scriptwriters that these divisions would have to fight their way across several hundred kilometres of territory already in Soviet hands and be annihilated in the process.

The last letter I had received from my parents had reached me at the beginning of January 1945. Among other things, and in a way that allowed me to read between the lines, my father wrote that quite a number of German officials and their families had been transferred back to the Reich and that many offices established by them in Poznań in 1939 had been closed indefinitely. This, of course, told me that the Germans were finally on the run to save their skins. The few lines my mother added to that letter were filled with worry and deep love. I promptly wrote a reply, but never found out if it reached my parents. We were nearing the end of April. The Red Army had pushed the Wehrmacht out of Poland and East Prussia and stood at the Oder. After five and a half years of brutal occupation, Poznań was once again free, but the war was still on, and my thoughts were constantly with my parents. With that, I also realized that being with them again was possible only when the killing was over, once and for all.

Following Käthe Kollwitz's death I made a woodcut, attempting to fix her in my memory and honour her as an artist and a great human being. Toiling on this project made me think of the Academy, and I began planning to go into the city to find out how much that magnificent, if eclectic, building had suffered under the Allied air attacks. I had already seen it from afar, when I'd ventured into Dresden to try and discover the fate of the Nitzsches. From a distance, the Academy building seemed hardly touched by the conflagration, and only the huge studio windows gaped with dark emptiness, their glass either blown out by the air pressure of explosions or melted in the heat sprayed by incendiaries.

The partly restored streetcar service still moved quite capriciously, and I walked most of the way. Once across the Elbe, I climbed the wide expanse of steps leading to the Brühlsche Terrasse, on which the Academy was located. Named after an eighteenth-century royal minister, Count Brühl, this once-exquisite palais was now just a pile of rubble. The terrace itself was a very large, wide expanse, high above the river level, with a magnificent view that eventually gave it the grandiose name, "The Balcony of Europe." Now, its surface was pitted where bomb splinters had hit. In many places the asphalt had melted or buckled from the heat of incendiaries, some of which still lay around, burnt-out octagonal tubes of metal, about half a metre long. The Academy's massive building loomed over this dismal sight, but as I approached its main entrance, I saw that parts of the huge windows had been filled in with sheets of plywood and cardboard. Clearly, some desperate care was being taken to protect the building's interior from the elements. The great entrance door stood open, and I walked in, unimpeded. As I expected, there was interior damage: cracks in the walls and marble floors, and a noticeable shift in the stairs leading up to the classroom studios. But there was life too. Walking down a long corridor, I met Herr Lehmann, who had been Professor Sauerstein's anatomy assistant. Lehmann was now in charge of securing the building and, having been bombed out of his home, was ensconced in the Academy's basement. He was not the only person taking shelter here. Herr Eckhardt, the graphics printer who had given me the printing equipment for my bulletins, was living in the subterranean printing shop. Neither of them knew what had become of Professor Dietze, my former teacher. Lehmann had no objection to my wandering around the building. "Go ahead," he said. "There's nothing interesting left to see."

He was only partly right. Walking from studio to studio, I found mostly desolation — floors covered with shards of glass, some hopelessly damaged paintings, and a good many students' drawings, now sopping wet with rain that had come through the blown-out windows. However, in one of the master students' studios, that of my highly talented friend Yakiv (later Jacques) Hnizdovsky, I saw amongst all the wreckage a shelf with several sheets of paper, evidently still dry. They turned out to be signed prints of his woodcuts, first-rate examples of this gifted artist's work that I could not simply leave to disintegrate or be thrown away by someone unaware of their true value. I gathered them up and took them with me, Lehmann agreeing with me that this was certainly the best way to save them. For years, neither Yakiv nor I knew if the other was still alive and where in the world he might be living. As it turned out, Yakiv eventually settled in New York, where he became a successful freelance artist and book illustrator, faithful as ever to his chosen medium of woodcut. Thirty years after the bombing of Dresden, when Yakiv had an exhibition in Winnipeg, I was finally able to return his prints to him. In gratitude, he presented me with a few of them.

20 FINAL DAYS

On April 30, to the accompaniment of some dreary Wagnerian dirge, the German radio announced that the Führer and Supreme Commander of the German Wehrmacht had met the death of a hero "while leading his troops against the barbarian enemies." The announcement added that Admiral Doenitz had been appointed Hitler's successor and that the fight would go on. Only a day later did it become known that the Führer had actually committed suicide.

The next day a rumbling of tanks could be heard, leading some of Hellerau's citizens to assume that the Soviets had arrived. The panic grew in its intensity when word got out that the tanks belonged to a small, combat-weary detachment of an SS Panzer division. Four Tiger tanks were dug in next to a stretch of the Moritzburg highway, right near a cluster of attractive and well-maintained family homes. It soon became obvious that the SS hadn't parked its tanks there just to have a picnic, but rather to do some shooting, should the enemy dare to approach what, if anything, was left of Dresden — and in the process shoot Hellerau to pieces.

In the meantime, the BBC broadcast the news of the surrender of all German forces in Italy. A tense situation lasted four days, after which, to everybody's relief, the SS took its tanks and disappeared in the dead of night. Another, more peaceful, disappearing act took place in Hellerau at the former, once world-famous Jacques Dalcroze School of Dance, which was later turned into some sort of social sciences institute. Finally, in the dying months of the war, it became barracks for Caucasian, Uzbek, and Kazakh troops, Soviet deserters mustered in desperation by the Germans to provide last-ditch resistance to the Red Army. The building was within sight of the Ulich home, only a few minutes away by foot. I was in my room at Frau Heinich's house when Franziska came running up the stairs with news that the *Osttruppen* (Eastern Troops) were gone and that quite a number of civilians, probably residents of Hellerau, were crowding into the now abandoned building. She invited me to come along with her to look at what might have been left by the runaways, and we set out right away.

Inside the building, we encountered an indescribably chaotic and bizarre scene. The great central hall was almost completely filled with huge mounds of German-type military gear, all separated according to category. None of it was stacked up in an orderly fashion, but had been thrown — obviously in great haste — into piles, some of which easily exceeded six feet in height. There were uniform jackets, coats, pants and underwear, belts and backpacks, gas masks still in their containers, food utensils, shoes, socks, forage caps and dress caps, fatigue uniforms, boots, steel helmets — everything but weapons and ammunition. Clearly, the Eastern Troops had bolted in panic, most likely westward.

Leading off the central hall were the usual barracks facilities — a big kitchen and a very large dining room, washrooms, toilets, showers, some offices with everything still intact (except for the open safe doors), and big washbasins full of ashes, no doubt of hastily burnt documents. All over — on top, around and inside this chaos — a horde of usually ever-so-genteel Hellerau residents, most of them women, but also a few men, crawled, climbed, dug, selected, tried things on, threw them away, tore them from each other's grasp, cried out in triumph, swore and yelled at one another, creating a hellish kind of din.

Franziska disappeared into the kitchen, and I headed for a huge pile of boots. My footwear, found for me so many weeks ago by Yakiv, my Ukrainian friend, had, ever so sadly, outlived its usefulness, and was in dire need of replacement. What I was looking for were not the typical German hobnailed infantry clompers, but a pair of those well-made, knee-high officers' riding boots that I had already noticed in the big mound of assorted military footwear. Unfortunately, these handsome boots were not lying around in pairs. So, if you got hold of, say, a left boot, you had to rummage around to find its right match. Still, there was nothing for it: I had to search to make up a pair that would fit me. Given the literally dozens of boots I had to look through, this was a difficult job, and it became more discouraging as time went on. At one point, I became frustrated and cursed in Polish: *"Psiakrew!"* ("dog's blood!"), at which a man standing nearby chuckled and asked if I was a Pole. I said yes, and we chatted in Polish for a few minutes before I succeeded in finding a matching pair of practically new boots. The man had already found what he wanted and departed, saying that he hoped we might run into each other again. Franziska still seemed to be busy somewhere else, so I took my priceless find and went off to take a look at other parts of the building.

After peering into a few office rooms with their standard desks, chairs, and filing cabinets as well as the equally standard large photographs of the late Führer, I found myself in what must have been a conference room. A long table with several chairs on each side took up most of the space and was presided over by a huge, gold-framed, life-sized, mass-produced colour portrait of Hitler. So many thoughts went through my mind as I stared at that picture. I returned to a corridor in which I had seen some firefighting equipment, found an axe, went back to the conference room and, with one furious whack, imbedded the blade in that hated face. Then I threw the axe onto the conference table and left, thinking how strange it felt to be able to do something for which, only a few days earlier, I'd have been sent to the guillotine.

Years of being in an almost constant state of fear and apprehension, of hiding my thoughts and emotions, skulking in the dark, living two separate yet parallel lives, and thus having to lie even to my friends — all this was suddenly over, gone, finished. No authority threatened me. Germany was defeated, even if the war was still on. This was an interregnum in the true sense of that word. And clearly, a kind of anarchy, too.

Obviously, there was no way for me to tell my friends and benefactors, the Ulich family, that for years I had been active in the Polish

Resistance, fully aware that, had my activities been uncovered, their lives might have been in danger. Yes, the Nazi nightmare had been lifted, and soon no one would have to fear the Gestapo. But I had learned from one of the last couriers passing through Dresden in November 1944 that the Soviets, who by then already occupied half of Poland, were dealing with the former Polish Underground as mercilessly as the Germans had done. It was therefore incumbent upon me to keep my mouth shut and be wary of anybody I spoke with, be they German or (in the near future) Russian. Even as I write this, I still feel a twinge of guilt toward those decent people who helped me so much, not knowing how terribly dangerous it was for them to befriend me.

Franziska and I returned in triumph to our respective homes, she dragging a great load of food, mostly canned meat, in an improvised bag made up from a military greatcoat, and I wearing my newly liberated boots. I recall carrying with me the old clompers that had served me so faithfully. Maybe I thought of having them repaired, or perhaps giving them a suitable burial? In those days, one respected and hung on to such mundane, yet important, objects.

It was now May 5. Berlin had surrendered three days before. The German radio had gone off the airwaves, but according to BBC reports — now entirely free of jamming — the Red Army had succeeded in tightening a noose around Berlin, and German resistance was rapidly collapsing. Yet another BBC report announced the British government's official recognition of a newly formed Polish government in Lublin. I listened to this, stunned and confused, but it was Dr. Ulich who right away understood the meaning of this piece of news. "The British have withdrawn recognition from the Polish government in London," he said and left it at that. I could only nod in agreement, trying to hide my despair. It wasn't enough for Britain and especially the United States to betray Poland at Tehran and hand my country over to the Soviet Union; they now gave their betrayal the final, official confirmation! This meant that Poland, the West's first and most faithful of all allies in the struggle against Hitler's Germany, had shed the blood of tens of thousands of its young men in vain, in battles on land, in the air, and at sea. The Poles had defended Britain, and this was how Britain was paying them back. Now I understood the meaning of the expression "perfidious Albion."

On the day following this tragic news, Frau Heinich knocked on my door and said there was a man to see me. In the days past, I would have braced myself for an unannounced visit, perhaps by police or even the Gestapo, but all that fear was now gone, and I went downstairs to see who this visitor might be. It turned out to be the man I'd spoken with in Polish while digging around in the pile of boots. I let him in, we shook hands, and he introduced himself as Konstanty Baum. He knew my name already, he said, so introducing myself wouldn't be necessary. Although somewhat startled by this, I accepted his explanation, assuming that his information had come from one of "our" (meaning Resistance) sources. He made a trustworthy impression and spoke excellent Polish, but, ever mindful of the underground's strict rules, I kept mum and let him do the talking until I felt more confident of his credibility. His story was colourful and exciting.

Konstanty Baum ("Call me Kostek," he said) was born well before the First World War, in Łódź, an important textile-manufacturing centre, then still under czarist Russian rule. His father, a textile businessman, had been transferred to the Russian city of Kharkov, where Kostek received his high school education. After the First World War, the family had returned to newly liberated Poland, and he, too, entered the textile trade as a travelling salesman. In the early 1930s, he had worked at the Alexandria Cotton Exchange and became very successful, partly because of his complete fluency in the Polish, Russian, and German languages, not to mention a fairly good knowledge of French. As well, his endeavours were furthered by his salesmanship and a personal charm, which, as I later found out, also made him quite successful with the ladies.

After Poland's 1939 defeat and under the subsequent German rule, he joined the Resistance movement, at the same time maintaining his contact with the textile trade in Łódź, now run by the German occupiers. His knowledge of the textile market and his competence, combined with linguistic skills, made him an ideal candidate for keeping the trade successful in countries friendly to Germany, including Vichy France, and supposedly neutral ones, such as Spain and Portugal. He acted as a salesman, at the same time functioning as a contact between the Polish underground and the West. Armed with genuine identity papers and documents showing him to be a representative of Łódź's textile manufacturers, he travelled several times to Sweden, a few times to Italy, Vichy France, and Spain. He was on his way to Switzerland in the spring of 1943 when relations between the British government and the Polish government-in-exile became strained to the breaking point following the discovery in Katyń of the mass graves of several thousand Polish officers. Courier traffic became virtually non-existent and was only partially revived prior to the August–October 1944 Warsaw Uprising. The tragic end of that uprising caught Kostek in the town of Cottbus, en route to Dresden, from where he was to travel westward, in the direction of France or Holland.

By now, however, the fronts had moved so quickly toward and even into Germany that all attempts to reach the goal of his journey were proving to be utterly futile. But he did come close to Dresden, reaching the village of Willsdruff, only a relatively short walk from Hellerau. Carrying with him a good supply of Reichsmarks, he rented a room in which to wait for the grand finale of the war, which by then was pretty well certain to end in a complete German defeat. He befriended his landlady and her daughter, cementing that friendship with an impressive number of food coupons and other personal favours. He witnessed the destruction of Dresden from afar, but preferred not to visit the city after it was mortally wounded. Some time in March, he moved from Willsdruff to Hellerau, to live with a newly met lady friend, a divorcee who looked to be in her late forties or fifties and owned a rather nice villa. So now he lived nearby and, entrpreneurial as ever, had begun to establish ties to the black market. He visited me not only to make my acquaintance but also to offer me help in those very humgry days. Eventually we became very close friends.

May 6 was a sunny and warm spring day. I found it hard to believe that the war was still going on and the Red Army hadn't yet moved into what had been Dresden and its seemingly still intact environs. From time to time, one could hear a distant, rumbling sound of artillery, but the fearfully awaited Soviet troops hadn't yet shown up. Looking through my window, I could see that most of the houses up the street had blossomed out with homemade white flags of surrender: bedsheets, pillowcases, table napkins, anything short of white underwear. Especially prominent in this manifestation of defenceless innocence seemed to be the houses of those who, in days just past, had festooned their flagstaffs, walls, and windows with swastika banners. Now, even my landlady, Frau Heinich, untouched by any kind of politics, felt moved to declare herself a noncombatant by nailing to the front door a table napkin. To underline the sincerity of her surrender, she sacrificed one from her trousseau, a lovely item of damask cloth, with a border of fine lace. Interestingly, neither the Ulichs nor Frau Troll bothered to hang out a white flag. Maybe they felt it wasn't necessary and that the Russians wouldn't be impressed anyway. And since a white flag had never helped to protect a population from the barbarities of war, it hardly mattered whether you displayed one or not.

As the day wore on, the tension became almost palpable, although looting of the deserted barracks continued. Franziska and I made a quick repeat foray into that building, to find that most of the uniforms, boots, forage caps, and other such equipment were gone, but that a few odds and ends still lay around. Among them, I discovered some brand-new officers' riding breeches, with a leather-reinforced seat, that I thought might fit me. I appropriated two pairs made of grey cloth, found some suitable braces, and departed for home to try on this whole ensemble. Together with the previously obtained boots, they turned out to be an almost perfect fit. Unfortunately, my civilian jacket, made of some scratchy material of war-time production quality and beginning to show signs of intensive wear, introduced a note of haphazardness to my new sartorial combination.

But in those days one didn't think much, or at all, about elegant attire. They were days of tragedy, death, and triumphant victories. Throughout Europe, Germans surrendered en masse, and my country was finally free of them, too. The Ulich family celebrated, in lieu of wine, with herbal tea, and now listened to the BBC's evening broadcasts without a blanket over the living room window. Electric power was only sporadic, but no one cared about the blackouts anymore. Yet the tension was still there, even though the activity of Soviet artillery had slackened somewhat. Nerve-racking anticipation of barbarous behaviour by what the Germans came to call "Mongolian" Soviet troops made the population quiver in fear. These probably justified anxieties were supported by the steady stream of horror stories which, over the previous years, had emanated from the Goebbels propaganda machine and were still believed. Much of it turned out to be true.

It was some time in mid-afternoon that the already familiar sound of a rapidly approaching heavy aircraft formation could be heard. I happened to be standing with Dr. Ulich on the front steps of his home, when we saw five or six bombers marked with red stars coming at great speed from the east. They were less than a kilometre north of Hellerau when they turned toward the Klotzsche airfield and released their bombs, presumably onto the still-parked, abandoned, and now useless German fighter aircraft. This action lasted hardly more than half a minute, after which the bombers made a wide turn and flew off eastward, leaving behind them a huge column of black smoke. There wasn't any need for us to take cover.

Later that afternoon, as we were listening to the BBC reports of Nazi Germany's last gasps, we heard a brief item that dealt with the presence of Polish troops approximately twenty kilometres northwest of Dresden. They were dug in on the Elbe riverbanks and attacking the old, historic town of Meissen. Naturally, this was of interest to me, though I viewed it with mixed feelings. I explained to the Ulichs that this Polish formation was no doubt part of a division composed of Polish soldiers imprisoned by the Soviets in 1939. Many of them had been released in the summer of 1943, but only if they agreed to serve in a newly formed Polish division under Soviet command. The BBC news item also mentioned very active Polish participation in the battle for Berlin. This, as I recall, led Frau Ulich to say that she hoped the Poles would kill as many Nazis as possible — strange words coming from this German lady, yet a sincere sentiment expressed by a war-hating socialist.

On May 7, there was not a cloud in the sky. It was very warm, and Frau Heinich was puttering in her tiny garden patch. Up and down the street, the white bed sheets and pillowcases were proclaiming peace and political innocence, although there wasn't a single Russian in sight. Still, one could hear some distant artillery fire — just irregular little pops, presumably to let everyone know that the war wasn't over yet. In whichever direction I looked from my window, not a soul could be seen out on the street, most people evidently feeling more secure inside their homes. This, of course, was completely illusory since, as everyone knows, a soldier's boot, when applied with some force, can kick in any average door.

I went downstairs and then outside, chatting with Frau Heinich before setting out toward the Ulichs' house, only to meet Franziska, who was just coming in my direction. We strolled down the street, discussing what might happen once the Russians arrived, and she said that she looked forward to greeting them as liberators. All Germans, she said, should receive them with flowers and as friends. Hardly able to believe my ears, I was sure she was joking — but then I realized that she actually meant what she said. Clearly, it was time to enlighten her about what frontline troops and those who followed them could, and possibly would, do to the enemy's civilian population. This, I pointed out, might particularly apply to soldiers who were out to avenge themselves for the devastation of their country and for the millions of dead killed by the Nazi enemy. I was sorry to destroy her illusions, idealistic though they were. She saw the Russians (a generic name given by the Germans to the Soviets and to the Red Army) as heroes straight out of Tolstoy's *War and Peace* or from the the poetry of Pushkin, Lermontov, and Nekrassov. The music of Tchaikovsky or Borodin made her think of the Russians as romantic idealists, now arriving to slay the Nazi's militarist monster. In my argument, I didn't mention any of that, but gave her examples of the Russians' customary brutality in the 1920 Polish-Bolshevik war and in their occupation of eastern Poland in 1939. Still, not wanting to destroy all her ideals, I added that there were always exceptions to any rule, and there would surely be many Russians who would behave like good and decent human beings.

In the late afternoon, it became very hot, and we sat in the Ulichs' living room, whose large window was shaded by an apple tree. We were talking, probably about the Russians, who were expected to march in at any moment. But whatever the subject, our conversation ended abruptly. I had heard the sounds of artillery fire, the screams of Stuka bombers, the whistling of bombs falling and of bullets zipping by me, but never before had I heard such a high-pitched, mournful wail, like that of banshees flying past and warning of incipient death. It began so unexpectedly and had such a paralyzing impact that any reaction or response was out of the question. The sound was deafening, but I had retained a shred of sensory perception. I felt the whole house shake, and when a small pane of glass cracked and popped out of the window, I felt a strange sensation of the air momentarily becoming denser and closing in on me. We were huddled together, yet each was unto himself, trying not to think of the unthinkable.

But, all of a sudden it was all over, with only the howling screams still ringing in our ears. We speculated that since no nearby explosions could be heard, it meant that whatever had made this horrifying noise had simply flown overhead and was probably aimed at a faraway target. "Not even at Verdun have I heard anything quite as frightening," Dr. Ulich said, and added, "those must have been their Katyushas." He had been a German officer in the First World War and had served during the battle of Verdun, one of the bloodiest in the annals of warfare. Now, in the Second World War, it was common knowledge in Germany that the Red Army possessed the Katyushas, multiple rocket launchers that could fire salvos of several missiles simultaneously, devastating approximately a square kilometre of enemy territory. The Germans aptly called it the "Stalin Organ." Our experience was merely with the screaming sound this weapon made, and it had lasted mere seconds. But following the air raid on Klotzsche's airfield, this was yet another notice by the Red Army that it was ready to enter and occupy the now completely undefended territory around Dresden, as well as take possession of what was left of a mostly ruined city. As I found out after the war, the Katyushas were the Soviet equivalent of the German *Nebelwerfer* (smoke mortars), both capable of firing clusters of up to forty-eight rockets propelled by solid fuel and eliminating everything as far away as eight kilometres.

The sun was setting that evening as I went home after the meagre evening meal at the Ulichs'. On my way, a neighbour whom I knew only by sight stopped to tell me that he'd just been out on a stroll. "You'll never guess what I just saw when I was passing the Hellerau community offices."

"What?" I asked.

"A fellow was taking down his swastika flag and replacing it with a red cloth! What do you think of that?" he said.

I chuckled at the news. "Comes as no surprise to me," I said. "It seems that a lot of people are losing their Party badges these days, judging by how many of them I've seen lying on the ground lately. Odd, isn't it?"

"Oh, indeed!" he said with a snort. "All of a sudden, nobody around here ever had anything to do with the Nazis, did they?"

We exchanged a few more remarks about those ever-so-swiftly changing times and went our respective ways.

Just then, I heard Franziska calling my name, turned, and saw her hurrying toward me. Breathlessly triumphant, she told me that, according to a BBC broadcast she had just heard, the Wehrmacht had officially surrendered to the Allies and that the act of Germany's capitulation had been signed the previous night, somewhere in France. In her excitement, she had missed the name of the place where it happened (it was Reims), but that didn't matter anymore. What counted at this point was the ultimate defeat of the worst scourge under which Europe had suffered since the Thirty Years' War (1618–1648).

I realized, of course, that this was a great historic moment, and that along with many millions of others, I was fortunate to witness it. What also went through my mind was the fate of my compatriots who had died, because they were of either Polish nationality or the Jewish faith. The images of what I'd seen while still in Poznań were firmly embedded in my memory. There were people who had paid with their lives for being who they were, but I had survived, and ever since then have felt both fortunate and uneasy about it. Did they have to die so that I could stay alive? It's a question that haunts me still.

These days, when I think back to the moment when Franziska told me about the end of the Third Reich, I recall acknowledging her news in only a vague, almost routine manner, with maybe a nod or a grunted "hmmmm …" She was surprised at my response, saying it was, after all, an earth-shaking event, and she had thought that upon hearing such news, I'd be dancing for joy. In reply, I said that the event had long been predictable and was now anticlimactic. This, of course, was true. The writing on the wall had begun to appear in the fall and winter of 1941, with the Wehrmacht's defeat by snow and frost only a few kilometres from the walls of Moscow. From then on, and despite a number of notable German victories, the Wehrmacht had begun to suffer endless debacles on land, at sea, and in the air. With America's entry into the war and the German catastrophe at Stalingrad, the writing on the wall had become much clearer, and following the Normandy landings it was plainly readable. The end of the Third Reich was inevitable. Yet another empire had ceased to exist. We watched the sun go down, and I remember saying to Franziska that all the happenings of that day made me think of a Wagnerian *Twilight of the Gods*. She gave out a short laugh and said: "The Nazis would have liked that." We said good night and went off to our respective homes.

The events of the morning of May 8, 1945, are etched in my memory with exceptional clarity. I woke up just past six o'clock. The sun was up and the night air coming through the open window had kept the room pleasantly cool. A couple of days before, Kostek, already well into the black market, had let me have part of a loaf of bread he'd obtained from one of his mysterious sources, and I now breakfasted on a slice of it. The liquid part of this morning meal was, as usual, water. On my little table lay a work-in-progress: a wood block I planned to finish and proof-print later that day. I got dressed. I dawdled. I thought about closing the window to keep the room cool. But just as I was about to do this, I heard sounds coming from outside, not very far away. Although they seemed familiar, I couldn't quite make out what they were. Suddenly it hit me: what I was hearing was the creaking of badly oiled farm wagon wheels, along with the clacking of horseshoes on a hard surface. The sounds were accompanied by loud voices, but the language wasn't German. There were a lot of wagons, a lot of horses, and a lot of voices. And then I knew: the victorious Red Army had arrived, not in T-34 tanks, but on rickety farm vehicles pulled by tired horses!

I ran downstairs and was standing outside on the front steps as a soldier in a strange, dust-covered, khaki-coloured uniform and an odd forage cap on the back of his head walked up to Frau Heinich's fence, grinned and said, *"Eh! Vodka yest?"* ("Hey! You have any vodka?") To me, the question about vodka was perfectly clear, and I remembered the Russian word *nyet*. It was that word that made him smile even wider, then shrug, and ask if I were Russian. This, too, I understood, and told him I was a "Polack," to which he nodded and stretched out his hand. I grasped it, and we shook hands. *"Druzya,"* he said. "Friends."

The war was over.

Part 5

THE RUSSIAN OCCUPATION

21 NEW BEGINNINGS

T he name of that first Russian soldier was Vanya. He looked to be in his mid-forties or even older, but later he told me by gesturing that he was only thirty-something. Everything about him seemed to be dust-covered: his somewhat tattered uniform, the well-worn boots, his face, and even the drum-magazine-equipped gun he carried strapped over his back. He was unshaven, and his red-star-adorned forage cap sat rakishly on his head, only partly covering a rich, and of course dusty, crop of dark blond hair. Two medals dangled over the pocket of his uniform, and he also had some sort of kit bag slung over his shoulder.

He paid absolutely no attention to the long line of horse-drawn carts and wagons rolling down Moritzburger Weg toward Dresden, carrying troops and their weapons. Nonchalantly, he reached into the kit bag and took from it a piece of newspaper and a little packet of something that looked like chopped grain stalks. He rolled this into a crude sort of cigarette, lit it with a match, inhaled, and blew the smoke in my direction. I recoiled. It had the nauseating smell of carbide and was my very first whiff of the Russian soldier's cigarette: a tobacco by-product called Makhorka and consisting of the crushed stalks, midribs, and veins of the plant, rolled into a bit of *Pravda* or *Izvestia*, and strong enough to explode the lungs of any non-Russian.

Vanya and I set out together for a walk along the street, he anxious to scour the neighbourhood for vodka, wine, or even eau de cologne — basically anything with which to celebrate the end of the war — and I trying to keep him from discovering any such liquid treasures. That I steered him away from the Ulich house was only natural. My brief friendship with Vanya ended abruptly when we encountered a Red Army patrol, which had already collected a handful of marauders and now added him to their number. I was left alone, apparently the only non-Russian who dared to show himself out on the street.

Eventually other civilians began to muster their courage and venture outside their homes, for whatever reasons. Some complained bitterly that Russian soldiers had robbed them of their rings or watches. Others, however, reminded the complaining victims of much nastier German activities in parts of Europe occupied by the Third Reich. So now it was Germany that found itself occupied! As yet, only little was known of what was going on in the British, American, and French zones of occupation, but it was clear that the newly established Soviet Military Administration was not about to harm the German population as a whole, but rather, seemed to be turning its occupation zone into a socialist (read: communist) state and a part of the Soviet bloc. All this became clear within days. The German language, culture, and customs were to be left intact, unless they had fascist or capitalist connotations. Billboards displayed Stalin's declaration that while Hitlers might come and go, the German nation would outlive them. History was to be rewritten, former Nazi Party members kicked out of office, and streets renamed. Whatever was left of industry would be either taken as war booty and, with all its machinery, transported to the Soviet Union, or nationalized. Trains would no longer run regularly or in both directions. Wherever the conventional, double-track rail system existed, only one track would remain, the other to be disassembled and shipped to the USSR.

But there wasn't much left for the Russians to plunder when they stormed into Germany proper. Hitler's idiocy in trying to defend every centimetre of the Reich's territory already ploughed under by the Allies had left much of the country in ruins. Its industrial West had been largely flattened by bombings, and major cities and centres of culture and civilization such as Hamburg, Cologne, Munich, and Berlin — not to forget

Dresden — had been devastated, often beyond recognition. To the Russians such devastation was a familiar sight: they'd seen it in Leningrad, Stalingrad, Kharkov, and Kiev, and so many other towns and villages left in ruins by the invaders.

And yet, despite all the urban devastation, a few vestiges of culture and civilization remained in some peripheral areas that had partly or wholly escaped the ravages of war. In abandoned homes, apartments, or farms, the Russians marvelled at ice chests and refrigerators, fine furniture and fancy dishes, and happily availed themselves of anything of value that the owners had left lying around. But admiration played no role in the Russians' feelings toward what they found in postwar Germany; instead, there was envy and the satisfaction of revenge, plain and simple.

It's true that some drunken Russian soldiers perpetrated horrendous rapes, this being as much part of any war as fire, plunder, or death by starvation. But when (and if) found out, the rapist was severely punished by his superiors — or so, post factum, the German population was told. As has so often been proven, by and large it was not the frontline troops who committed these crimes. Having been in possibly heavy battle, they were only too anxious to leave behind them the violence, with its blood and gore. The outrages were perpetrated mainly by troops of the second echelon, those who as reserves had been lucky enough to miss the bloodshed.

Not that I wish to be partial to the Soviet forces occupying the eastern part of Germany, but in all fairness I must say that I later met many Russians, of most ranks, who were decent and honest individuals. True, a lot of them seemed to live according to their own idea of wild laissez-faire. They never talked politics with a non-Russian like me. And yes, they liked their vodka, but I hardly ever saw any Russian soldier keel over dead drunk; apparently, staying upright was for them a point of honour. They taught me to drink vodka in their own sto-gram (one hundred grams, or the contents of an average water glass) manner, by disposing of it with one single draught. You just tossed it down your open throat, the way you drink from a wineskin.

But these hard-drinking, trophy-hunting Russian warriors would turn mushy-sentimental at the sight of young children. Walking past a former

German barracks, I saw a Red Army soldier, ostensibly on guard duty at the gate, seated on an old wooden box, his Thompson automatic weapon leaning against a post. He was holding a little German girl on his knee, both of them laughing happily while the girl's mother stood by, beaming down at them.

Shortly after the Russians marched into Dresden, the wife of my friend, art teacher and sculptor Walter Fleming, gave birth to their first child, a boy. One afternoon, as the baby slept peacefully in his crib, crashing sounds were heard on the stairs leading to the family's second floor apartment. Moments later, a Russian soldier, armed and wearing hefty boots, clomped in — obviously a marauder in search of loot. Frozen with fear, Walter and his wife could merely watch as the man looked around the apartment. Eventually, though, he spotted the crib and bent over it to look at the baby. Straightening up with a smile, he put a finger to his lips, uttered a soft "Shhhh ..." and clattered in those heavy boots out of the apartment. Once back on the stairs, the soldier's ponderous steps were heard diminishing, until the downstairs door closed behind him.

These were but a few instances among many I saw or heard about that illustrated the gentleness of the average Russian soldier toward the children of the former enemy. It stood in direct contrast to the inhumane treatment the Germans had accorded the children of their enemies. On the other hand, the Russians dealt with captured Nazi Party functionaries — who had usually been denounced by their neighbours or even their own families — roughly, even brutally.

Looking at the friendly, smiling faces of those young Russian and Ukrainian soldiers, I found it hard to believe that they came from the same stock as their Red Army and paramilitary NKVD predecessors who, in concord with the Wehrmacht, had invaded eastern Poland and committed unspeakable crimes of genocide, oppression, robbery, wanton destruction, and carried out the forcible deportation of over a million Polish civilians — men, women, and children — to Siberian labour camps. While in the presence of these usually amiable warriors, I couldn't help thinking that maybe the fathers or brothers of some of them had pulled the triggers of machine guns that killed thousands of Polish Army officers in Katyń and places like it. Still, to someone like me, who during the war had witnessed and experienced German treatment of the Polish population, the behaviour of the Soviet occupants of East Germany — except, of course, for the very ugly cases of rape and robbery — could be looked upon as almost polite. The Russians were not at all racist. To them, the Nazi concept of *Übermensch* (superhuman) versus the *Untermensch* (subhuman) seemed incomprehensible.

Considering themselves infinitely superior to Poles or Russians, Germans used to openly call them *kulturloses Gesindel* (uncultured riff-raff) or *Polacken Dreckschweine* (filthy Polack pigs), while the targets of these insults had to endure them calmly, even as they seethed with thoughts of revenge. As the German conquerors rode victoriously into Russia in 1941, they surely used similar epithets to characterize the enemy. Yet four years later, the population of the defeated Third Reich displayed an astonishing, virtually boot-licking docility in the face of the Russian victors who, surprisingly, had only one jocular name for their former enemies: they called them *Fritzes*. It was probably some time in the summer of 1947 that I stood on the rear platform of a streetcar packed with passengers, when two Russian soldiers came aboard, clearly expecting to get seats inside the car. Finding that they were all taken, one of them said *"Tam wsio Fritzi"* ("It's filled with Germans"), meaning there would be no room for his friend and himself. By then I had learned enough Russian to understand the other's reply: "Shh! It's not polite to call them *Fritzes*," he said. "They are now called *Germantsy!*"

This small episode, among others, taught me a bit more about the difference between Germans and Russians. It must be added, however, that seen from a purely linguistic point of view, the power of Russian curses exceeds that of any other nation. It is both crude and sophisticated, rich in colour, picturesque, realistically illustrative, and capable of ornamental variants on the single theme of insulting an opponent and his family, possibly several generations back. By comparison, German-language insults are downright primitive and often carry with them the unmistakable scent of the barnyard.

Several days after the war ended, I walked over to the Klotzsche camp, which I'd found deserted after the February bombings. The guards had disappeared, and I got a look at the miserable conditions in which my compatriots had been housed. A handful of former inmates, now free, stood around, debating ways of returning to their homes in Poland. From them I learned that the camp had been temporarily abandoned in the night of the bombings. From the slight elevation on which Klotzsche was situated, the camp's inmates had had a clear view of the first air attack on Dresden. Horrified by the sight of the city in flames and in panic that the approach of yet another bombing force might mean an attack on the nearby Luftwaffe airfield, the inmates had fled, embarking on an arduous trek to the *Industriegelände*, a complex of factories including the one in which they worked. There they had remained in ghetto-like conditions for some time before returning to the camp. (The airfield, of course, had not been bombed until May 6, and it was the Russians, not the British or Americans, who performed that brief operation.) I also finally learned more about the SS raid on the camp that I had witnessed the previous summer. It had been, I was told, only one in a general *Aktion* in all labour and POW camps. While no one had been arrested or taken away from this camp, executions had been carried out in others, most notably in Freital. But no one could tell me why.

A few days later, I borrowed Franziska's bicycle, rode out to Radebeul, and walked through the now wide open and unguarded camp gate, hoping to find Halina. The situation in this camp was pretty well the same as in Klotzsche, though many of the freed Poles had already left for home. I found Halina in a group of Ukrainian girls, her friends and campmates. Obviously glad to see each other again, we discussed the previous year's SS raid on the camps, and she told me that much to the SS men's chagrin, they had found nothing in the Radebeul camp but a few packages of smuggled-in cigarettes, not enough to justify arrests. But the disappointed SS had needed some form of satisfaction, and several camp inmates, both male and female, had been severely beaten. Halina herself had had some teeth knocked out, but wasn't too concerned, saying it could have been worse. I asked her about the bulletins, whether they had been read and what had happened to them afterwards. She said yes, they'd been read and then burnt in the small stoves that had been installed in every hut for occasional cooking and to provide a little warmth in the winter. Once the risky reading material was destroyed, the news from it had been transmitted orally from one inmate to the next. Only on a few occasions was such a news bulletin left lying around before someone noticed the danger that it presented. It was then either burnt or torn into tiny pieces, which were then disposed of in the latrine.

Sometime in the summer or autumn of 1945, the Academy, although still in need of extensive repairs, opened its doors, albeit unofficially. The fifty-one-year-old building had miraculously survived all three successive Allied bombing raids, and structural damages were caused mostly by the vibrations resulting from "blockbuster" bombs exploding even at quite some distance away. This created cracks, through which moisture would later seep. Materials, such as lumber, glass, and cement, were scarce. Quite a few volunteers turned up to help with the repairs, work which entitled them to a modest paycheck and a few grams more in food allotment.

I was one of the first to register as a student in the class of Professor Wilhelm Rudolph. On the basis of the work I submitted, I was judged to be sufficiently talented and technically advanced to be rated a *Meisterschüler* (master student) and awarded my own studio in the Academy's building. Not long after this, to my infinite joy and relief, I received greetings from the Nitzsches through a mutual friend, Otto Griebel, an older artist colleague. He was able to tell me that, only hours before the sirens had begun howling on February 13, the Nitzsches had left their apartment to stay with some acquaintances in Kaditz, a suburb several kilometres from the city centre. Thus, during the first bombing raid, which had so completely devastated the heavily populated core of Dresden, they were already on their way to the relative safety of Kaditz. When Anni learned from Griebel that I was at the Academy, she came with little Bärbel to visit me in my studio. As we had not seen each other since just before the bombing raid, it was understandably quite an emotional reunion. And it was with obvious concern that I asked about Günther. Anni hesitated for a second before replying. He had gone to live with his family in Chemnitz, she told me, leaving Bärbel with her. As far as the decision to leave Dresden for Kaditz was concerned, it had evidently been planned for some time and was realized abruptly after discussing the Allied bombing raids which were moving ever closer into the eastern and southern parts of what was left of Germany. Anni believed that the decision to leave Dresden had come from the Almighty; in spite of her professed agnosticism, her Mormon upbringing helped her when needed. The last I heard of Anni was a brief note, along with a photo of herself and Bärbel, sent from some small town in Bavaria. I wrote back, but never received a reply.

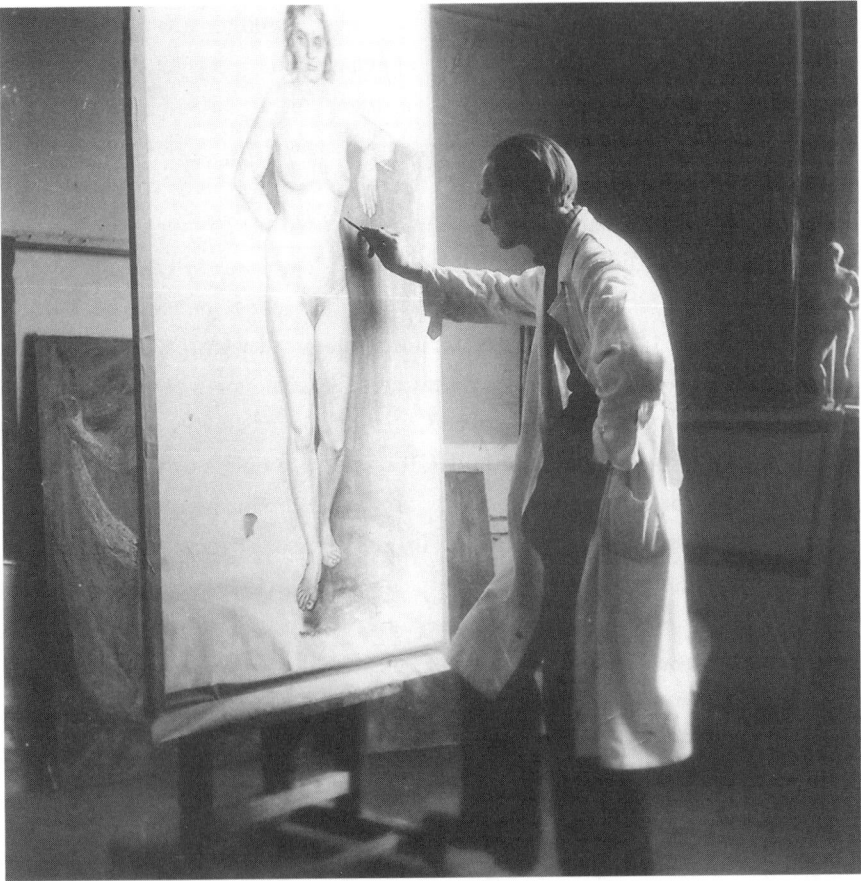

In my master student's studio around 1946.

At the Academy, I devoted my time to painting and graphics. In the latter, my chosen mentor, Professor Rudolph, and I certainly saw eye to eye. He was not only a painter of quite some renown, but also the creator of a memorable series of woodcuts depicting a destroyed Dresden, probably the most poignant European graphic work of the postwar era. However, what I resented in him was his way of commenting on his students' work. Instead of giving a verbal opinion, he'd grab the palette and brushes and "correct" by painting into our work in his own style. He was, of course, a marvellous painter of the realist school, but the pervasive forcefulness of his teaching methods resulted in producing mini-Rudolphs, rather than artists with their own way of seeing the world. He had held a professorship at the Academy in the early 1930s, but was fired by the Nazis for refusing to join their party. Like Käthe Kollwitz and so many others, he was forbidden to exhibit his work and was subjected to other Nazi chicaneries. Reinstated as Academy professor in 1945, he was once again dismissed in 1949, this time by the Communist regime, for political nonconformism. I own one of his woodcuts as part of my small, but wide-ranging, collection.

March 1946 was sunny, but cool. The Academy had had its worst wounds more or less healed, although repairs continued unabated. Classes were held regularly, and some of us were thinking of higher things, such as celebrating spring with a costume party. Not outdoors though, since there was still a fair layer of snow in the Academy's large and shady courtyard. Instead, we planned to stage the party in a number of classrooms. These we decorated with vistas of faraway cities, perhaps as a discreet statement of our Western orientation in a Soviet-occupied land: the Eiffel Tower was unmistakable, as were the Leaning Tower of Pisa and a wild interpretation of New York's skyscrapers. Lastly, one classroom became an underwater scene with blue and green lighting (electricity was back again), and fantastic sea fauna, sharks, octopi, and other monsters, cut from cardboard and richly painted, suspended from the ceiling.

Wine, such as it was, had been bought on the black market and paid for by the guests' entrance fees. Music came from scratchy records played on an ancient gramophone. The event was called *Musentümpel* (puddle of

At the Musentümpel *Costume Ball in March 1946. A fellow student (left)
and I are dressed as Pat and Patachon, a popular Danish comedy duo.*

the Muses), a pun on the word *Musentempel* (temple of the Muses), with invitations featuring a drawing of the nine Muses, naked and up to their knees in water.

As parties go, it became a bacchanal, with dancers filling the classrooms, corridors and staircases, and eventually spilling out into the courtyard to begin a snowball contest. This was attended by the best of our life (i.e., nude) models, Else Hoffman, who, no doubt animated by wine, appeared in her costume, in other words without a stitch. Throwing snowballs and getting pelted in turn, she was untroubled by the cold; two days later, she came back to work and told the class that despite all the snow, she hadn't even gotten the sniffles.

Watching these goings-on from the sidelines, Walter Fleming wondered if after many years of darkness we, the young, were opening a door into the light. Then he corrected himself to say it wasn't light at all, but an absence of blackness — in other words, only shade. He meant, of course, that the war had moved us from one dictatorship into the clutches of another. "And yet," he said, pointing to a girl with a flower in her hair, dancing joyously by herself, "there's your picture of hope." Some weeks later, he began work on restoring the rich statuary of cherubs, amourettes, and all the rich ornamentation that had once adorned the exquisite pavilions of the baroque Zwinger, so recently bombed into ruins. Of course, Fleming was only one of many who worked at recovering the city's beauty; the rebuilding of Dresden took thousands of willing hands and lasted many decades. Today, evidence of the catastrophe of February 13, 1945 and its deadly harvest can be found only in history books.

22 THE TROPHY BRIGADE

As a *Meisterschüler* with my own studio, I was not obligated to attend classes and could come and go as I pleased. This meant that I was free to find employment to support myself, and I was soon able to find work as a translator. Having kept an ear open to the sound of the Russian language, which could now be heard everywhere on and off the streets, I decided to get better acquainted with it. What made it easier for me was, naturally, a certain affinity between Russian and Polish, especially the similarity of many words. Grammar presented no difficulty, nor did the usually melodious Russian inflection. My ear was able to catch all the nuances of Russian speech, and with the help of Kostek Baum, by now my close friend, I even became fluent in reading texts printed in the Russian Cyrillic alphabet. Here I must add that my acquiring that language was partly a result of Kostek's urging. He spoke it effortlessly, and after the Red Army marched in, his multilingual skill became a greatly sought-after commodity. He became a translator, unofficially, but fairly well paid by the Russians for his services.

After more than a month of concentrated study, partly under his tutelage, but still in need of practice, I was introduced by Kostek to Lieutenant Agashvili, a junior Russian officer commanding a unit pompously named the Trophy Brigade and charged with finding and confiscating everything and anything automotive and German-owned, from new and used parts to cars, trucks, motorcycles, and even lubricants. I became their translator, working two or three days a week, depending on how far afield we travelled. The four-man unit was made up of the lieutenant, a driver named Pyotr (known to all as Pietya), an enlisted man named Dmitri (known as Dima), and the somewhat dreamy Vladimir (known as Volodia), who also wrote quite passable poetry and used to visit me, both at home and at the Academy.

They were all veterans of the war, proud of their medals and anxious to return home. When facing the ruins of Dresden they'd only shrug and say, "You should see Leningrad or Stalingrad and count *our* dead." Conveniently, the Brigade was housed in the same building which had earlier been ransacked by the usually law-abiding population of Hellerau, including Franziska and me. The building's close proximity to Frau Heinich's little house made it possible for my Russian friends to visit me, either as bearers of much-needed victuals such as grits or potatoes or, every now and again, a bottle (sometimes two) of vodka, which we would drain while discussing life and death and fate in general. It was on such an occasion that the poet Volodia described being in the second wave of an infantry attack and seeing the first wave mowed down by German machine guns, so that the dead Russians fell on top of one another, creating a barrier of corpses between which he and the others could aim their weapons and return fire. Speaking slowly, he drew for me a picture I could hardly have replicated on canvas. He also stressed the fact that the attacking infantry was followed by NKVD troops ready to shoot and kill from behind any laggards fearful of facing the enemy or running away from the line of attack. Any representation of such an attack could only turn in my mind into a static illustration depicting fast and furious action as frozen motionless in time and place and lacking the true essence of deadly combat: the horror of it. Volodia's description was that of a sensitive witness who survived that murderous assault and painted it for me with the words of a budding poet.

As if by an unspoken agreement, we avoided talking about politics. This wasn't easy for me as I very much wanted to discuss the fate of Poland, which again found itself under the Russian aegis and subject to Communist rule. Talking with these relatively young veterans, I found signs of genuine hero worship — surprisingly not so much of the "Great Leader" Stalin as of Lenin, now long dead and embalmed. Only once, I think, did I hear the word *Apparat* mentioned in passing, and referring to the high echelons of the Communist Party, also known officially as WKP(B), the "All-Union Communist Party" (Bolsheviki). Other than that, all our conversations were on the higher planes of music and literature. Not surprisingly, my friends were well acquainted with the works of Dostoevsky, Tolstoy, and Sholokhov, but had only heard of Shakespeare. Volodia, of course, excelled in his knowledge of Pushkin, Gorki's stories, and Mayakovski's stormy poetry. It also went without saying that music, always a supreme part of Russian culture, played an important role in the lives of those soldiers. I recall asking one of them if it mattered to him that a composition titled "Träumerei" and so widely played in the Soviet Union, was written by Robert Schumann, a German. In answer, he shrugged and said, "It wasn't music that brought war to my country."

My conversations with Red Army officers and non-coms were, of course, conducted in Russian. This involved a form of address in which the family name of the addressee, even if known, was omitted, and the so-called patronymic form was applied, in which one used a person's first name in conjunction with his or her father's first name. So, since my first name is Jan (or Ivan, in Russian), and my father's first name was Lucian (Lukian in Russian), I was mostly addressed as Ivan Lukianovich, meaning "Ivan, son of Lukian." In cases of closer acquaintance, such as my friendship with the soldier-poet Volodia, the name "Ivan" acquired the diminutive form of "Vanya." The old Russian form of address *Gospodin* (Mister) had been abolished during the October Revolution of 1917 and replaced with *Tovarishch* (Comrade), which then became universally applicable.

In my role as translator, it was unavoidable that I met all kinds of Russians, aside from the few who constituted the Trophy Brigade. Among them, I encountered a captain who appeared to have an eye on all aspects of the larger unit, a tank regiment, to which the Trophy Brigade was attached. I was told that apart from his rank he functioned as a *Zampolit*, an officer in charge of political awareness within the unit. He was, in effect, a ranking deputy of the regiment's commanding officer, even empowered to veto any and all of that superior's decisions. In times past, such a deputy had been called a "commissar," but some time in 1942 or 1943, a decision was made in the highest echelons of the Soviet command to change the title "commissar" to "Deputy in Charge of Political Matters," abbreviated as the acronym *Zampolit.*

There were other changes too, some visible and obvious, others representing a political about-face vis-à-vis Russia's past history and decorating Communist ideology with a great many trappings of Russian patriotism. The Red Army's crushing 1941 defeat by the German Wehrmacht, caused mostly by Stalin's total decimation of the army's high echelons between 1931 and 1938, had led to a rethinking of ways to strengthen the Soviet Union's defences. Repairs were urgently needed. A Russian's patriotism is always close to the surface of his psyche — it had worked supremely well in 1812 against Napoleon, and, it was reasoned, ought to work just as well against the German invaders. Accordingly, the Politburo (i.e., Stalin) banned the playing and singing of the "Internationale" and replaced it with a new, purely Russian patriotic anthem. This served the additional purpose of mitigating the fears of Communism harboured by the Soviet Union's new Western allies. Some, though not all, Russian Orthodox churches were reopened, and ancient Russian heroes began to be once again publicly celebrated. Patriotism was also spread by way of pop music ("Katyusha," "Kalinka," et cetera), motion pictures, public mass meetings, literature, and by the mass media such as radio.

Changes were also carried out within the Red Army. It had regained most of its power in the grim winter of 1941–42, as the Wehrmacht's drive toward Moscow collapsed in the deep frost and endless snow. The Red Army's transition into a successor of the former tsarist military force was carried out simply by bringing back the old-style rank distinctions. Officers' stars, once displayed on Soviet-style uniform collars, were now placed on equally old-fashioned epaulettes. Lesser ranks' and subalterns' Tsarist-dated stripes were also reinstated. The once demoralized Red Army seemed to have acquired the look and spirit of the former Russian military, the drubbing it once got from the Germans in 1914 notwithstanding. The

Russian soldiers I met were almost all imbued with patriotism bordering on chauvinism. Only my friend, Volodia the poet, appeared to realize that these emotions grew as a result of clever manipulations by Soviet leaders. In the end Stalin won this war, perhaps confirming Dr. Johnson's famous quip: "Patriotism is the last refuge of a scoundrel."

Financially, the translating work wasn't very rewarding, but once a week I received a box of food, mostly of the kind that constituted the Russian soldier's diet: primarily barley "kasha" and also a few kilos of potatoes. I was able to share this modest bonanza with Frau Heinich and, of course, with the Ulich family. Even so, we were only a little better off than the rest of the population, among whom death by starvation was becoming more and more frequent. Whenever that Russian food ran out, I would spend the occasional day living on only one or two of my saved-up potatoes. On a few dark nights I sneaked over to a nearby potato field to dig with bare hands for that precious commodity, speedily fill my coat pockets, and scurry back home. Stealing food was severely punished, as was cutting down trees for heating and stovetop cooking — something a neighbour and I also did at night, always running the risk of a very long stay in a labour camp or, worse yet, a penitentiary.

At around this time, both pairs of socks I owned were turning into shreds. They had begun to unravel during the flight from Breslau and now urgently needed replacing. I happened to mention this to Volodia, who told me that many Red Army soldiers didn't wear socks, but protected their feet with what were known as *laptye*, strips of cotton, each maybe a yard long and about three inches wide, wrapped in a special way around the foot, though only partly covering the toes. The system, which I adopted, worked quite well, and its lack of chic was fully hidden by my newly acquired riding boots.

To the detriment of my health, I had started smoking at about the age of fifteen, and the habit stayed with me for more years than I care to count. Thankfully, the war interfered with that addiction. Cigarettes were rationed and after the war were obtainable only on the black market, at horrendous prices. Nevertheless, the old longing for the odd whiff came back as I watched my poet friend Volodia roll his cigarettes and smoke them, while rhapsodizing about Mother Russia's endless birch forests or the majesty of her great rivers. Like Vanya, the Russian soldier I had met on the day the war ended, he smoked Makhorka. Every Soviet soldier received a daily ration of it in a little packet, whether he was a smoker or not. As for the cigarette paper, the soldier had to resort to using the readily available newsprint of journals such as *Izvestia* or *Pravda*, presumably — as Volodia put it — to emit a tiny amount of Marxism-Leninism in each puff of smoke. It was only fitting that under those circumstances Volodia, a committed lyricist, preferred to roll his Makhorka in the less political *Liternaturnaya Gazeta*. I managed to overcome my aversion to that vile kind of smoke, and still marvel at my lungs' staying (touch wood) in a reasonably acceptable condition.

Volodia, a gifted raconteur with a keen eye for the absurd, told me about an apparently true event that occurred as many thousands of Red Army soldiers were being withdrawn from the Soviet-occupied zone of Germany to be replaced by fresh troops from the USSR. The soldiers now going home were veterans of the final stages of a long war and, as victors, followed the time-honoured tradition of taking with them as many trophies as they could carry. Watches, rings and other jewellery were "liberated" from East Germany's civilian population, as were other portables such as musical instruments, silverware, household articles, clothing — in short, anything that the conqueror's eye found attractive. Among these trophy collectors were also some who kept an eye on the future. In the crowds of returning warriors crossing into their homeland at the Brest Litovsk border station, a young but bemedalled soldier lost track of his luggage, which consisted of only an average briefcase. He reported his loss to the military authority in charge of regulating the troop transports crossing into the Soviet Union and was asked about the contents of this case. He declared it with only one word: "Needles." This was received with gales of laughter, but evidently accepted as being true. It appears that the border authorities no longer even blinked an eye at the strangest objects the returning heroes brought with them from conquered Germany. The soldier's briefcase was found and discovered to be extraordinarily heavy — small wonder, as it was completely filled with sewing needles. And since in wartime Soviet Union all steel went into making tanks, artillery guns, and other war *matériel*, sewing needles had become a black market item, each fetching a price that could range from excessive to preposterous. There was wonder in Volodia's eyes as he painted a verbal image of the clever owner of the briefcase with a whole fortune inside it. But then he doubted if "they" — the Soviet state — would let the lucky soldier keep his trophy. "With them, you never know," Volodia said.

Like most Russians, Volodia delighted in satirical anecdotes that poked fun at the legendary Soviet inefficiency. One of these dealt with the postwar mess in the USSR as innumerable shipments from dismantled East German industries arrived as trophies on Russian soil. Three disassembled Luftwaffe hangars were to be delivered and put in place to serve the victorious Soviet air force. Their delivery and full readiness were to be reported to the force's high command in Moscow. Regrettably, only two such hangars arrived, causing great consternation among the recipients. But since the order from above called for three such facilities, some fast thinking had to be done to satisfy Moscow's mighty authorities. Two hangars were reported to be in service, with only a little more work to be done on the third one. Then, one of the existing hangars was dismantled, carried in sections to its allotted space, and reassembled, with a big number "3" painted on its door. The story made the rounds of the Red Army, but no heads rolled, since everybody had a good laugh. The Good Soldier Schweik might have had a chuckle, too.

The wartime system of food rationing was now inherited by the new German regime, but what had been severe austerity in the Nazi era now became a state of semi-starvation affecting most of Soviet-occupied Germany's urban population. The food coupons allowed only minuscule rations per person. I recall, for example, the monthly allotment of 1200 grams of bread of highly questionable content and of maybe fifty grams of what was laughingly called "marmalade," made from rather mysterious ingredients and sweetened with a mere touch of saccharin. Potatoes were rationed annually at a scant fifty kilos per person, as was coal, which was used for both cooking and heating. Some people who lived in the suburbs and perhaps had a little garden were able to augment the ridiculously low official rations by growing a few vegetables, but often lost them to hungry marauders raiding those garden plots at night. The main reason for the desperate food situation was, of course, the presence of the Soviet occupation forces, which, under the terms of German surrender, had to be housed and maintained by the defeated state. Food that under normal circumstances would have been available to the civilian population was now, first and foremost, feeding the very large Red Army garrison. If anything was left after that, it was divided into minute rations among the German civilians. The situation would have been much worse if many thousands of Dresden's inhabitants hadn't left the city after it was destroyed.

On May 16, 1945, the Red Army distributed 30,000 tons of potatoes, 95,000 tons of grain, and 1,100 tons of meat, and other provisions from "its own" resources. Possibly meant as an apology for rapes and robberies committed by its troops, this was more likely calculated to reveal the Red Army as a humane force rushing to help Dresden's starving population, in contrast to its Western allies, who had ruthlessly destroyed the city. I don't recall what criteria applied in this distribution, but it was commonly assumed that those worst affected by the catastrophe were most eligible to receive help from the feared former enemy.

I had written to my parents in the summer and fall of 1945, but received no answer. Neither was there a reply to two letters I sent at the beginning of 1946. I was ready to pack a few things and go to Poznań to find out what had happened to my parents, but a friend of Kostek's, who had just arrived from Poland, strongly advised against it, saying it would be better to wait a few more months until the conditions in Poland became normalized. He described the chaos in Germany as a kindergarten — and the downright anarchic mess in Poland as a veritable university of total confusion.

I was sorry to see the Trophy Brigade transferred to some other, probably more profitable, part of the Soviet zone. They'd always been friendly toward me, half drunk most of the time, gaily sloppy in carrying out their duties, and positively ecstatic to travel in a magnificent, convertible Maybach car — shiny black with red leather upholstery and a two-way radio. Lieutenant Agashvili personally "liberated" this car, which, he said, had once belonged to Joseph Goebbels himself.

23 DISASTROUS NEWS

After the Trophy Brigade left, my future looked bleak. I was broke, and the Brigade's departure meant that I no longer received their help in the form of kasha and potatoes. It was Kostek, that skillful black market operator, who came to my aid by bartering some of my landscape paintings for a few kilos of grain obtained from farmers who — often out of reach of the Soviet and now also the new East German regulatory authorities — managed to hide part of their crops to barter or sell privately.

Around that time I also painted a few portraits, among them one of Kostek, which is still in my possession. I had a lot of free time, so Franziska and I spent many hours wandering in the countryside around Dresden, areas that were untouched by the war, such as the enormous forest preserve called Dresdener Heide, the lovely suburb of Loschwitz, and the early eighteenth-century royal summer palace of Pillnitz. This palace housed a more contemporary collection of art, which, along with the great Dresden Art Gallery's truly priceless possessions, had been providentially moved out of the city before it was destroyed. After the war's end, the Soviet Administration declared the State Art Gallery's most important works to be war trophies and shipped paintings by Raphael, Titian, Rembrandt, Rubens, and a host of other old masters to Moscow and Leningrad. What the Soviets left was mostly German nineteenth-century art and a few twentieth-century works. It was this relatively modest collection that Franziska and I used to visit.

But on one occasion I went out to Pillnitz alone, and, as I wandered slowly from painting to painting, stopping now and then at some I particularly appreciated, I saw a Red Army non-com standing in front of a male portrait by Oscar Kokoschka, painted on raw sacking and in his free-wheeling, wild style. The soldier was examining it, I thought, to better see the signature, and curiosity made me move closer. We stood side by side, looking at Kokoschka's usual "OK" signature scribble, but there was also something else under that: it was the Russian word *khaltura* (garbage or trash), scrawled in Cyrillic letters with a so-called chemical and indelible pencil. We looked at each other, and the soldier, clearly embarrassed, pointed at the offending scribble, saying, "*Otchen nyekulturno,*" which is a Russian expression of deeply felt disapproval. (Translated literally, it means "very uncultured.") I nodded and said, in Russian, that I fully agreed with him. Naturally, he was astonished to hear a clearly non-Russian individual speak his language, and we began a conversation in which we exchanged names, places of origin, and so on. In further chit-chat we talked about art, so my telling him that I was an artist myself became inevitable. He wanted to know if I had a studio, and I said yes, to which he expressed the desire to see some of my work. I agreed, and about an hour later, more or less, began one of the most amazing and amusing episodes in my artistic career.

My newly acquired friend's taste in art was rather uncertain, but his enthusiasm for it was undeniable. While I was showing him my paintings one by one, he pulled from his shoulder bag a bottle of vodka and offered me a drink. It would have been an insult to refuse that offer, so I took a hefty swig. After that, the bottle passed back and forth between us, until I got sufficiently animated to say I wanted to paint his portrait. When? Right then and there, I felt the creative spirits urging me on. My visitor, clearly flattered, settled into the studio's ratty-looking armchair. I put a canvas on the easel, got the palette and brushes, and started right in. I can't describe whatever it was that moved my hand while I painted stroke after unfailing stroke. In fact, I have no exact recollection at all of that hour — maybe even somewhat longer — in which I worked on that portrait. The several snorts of Russian vodka had done it. I was blissfully drunk, and those creative spirits, straight from the bottle, banished any inhibitions I may have had. The result was a success in all respects, and the sitter was happy beyond measure. He had a camera, a (probably "liberated") Leica, no less, and took some pictures of the painting, promising to have the film processed and to give me a print or two, which he did a few days later. Along with other works, I regrettably had to leave this one behind when I departed from Dresden forever in June 1948. The memory of that episode, however, stayed with me, and some time later I painted someone else's portrait after deliberately consuming a fair quantity of Moselle wine. The results were … well, unfit to write about, and my model felt insulted, too.

I decided to stay in Dresden, and wrote a letter to the International Red Cross in Geneva, hoping for help in contacting my parents. Once again, I received no reply. Further letters, sent to my parents throughout the summer of 1946, also remained unanswered. In December, when I was about to give up altogether, I received a brief message from Poznań, sent to me in Hellerau and written by the daughter of a former cook of ours, Jadwiga Jakubowska. I learned that my parents had been imprisoned early in February of that year, that my mother had died in prison in July, and that my father had been released, but had recently suffered an accident and was now in hospital, convalescing after an operation. This was terrible news, but at least I had the young woman's return address and would finally be able to find out more about what had happened to my parents.

The message included the address of the hospital in which my father lay. Of course, I was overjoyed to finally have news about him — he was alive, even if incapacitated and clearly unable to write me himself. But then, there were those few terse words about my mother's death. How, under what circumstances she had died, the writer of the letter neglected to say. My emotions a melee of thoughts about death and survival, I found myself in shock and, for several days, unable to write to my father. But write I finally did, and the letter reached him a few weeks later. It elicited a prompt reply, in which I found all the answers to questions that had troubled me since losing touch with my parents in January 1945. While

Creative spirits, straight from the bottle, helped me paint this portrait of a Russian soldier.

I was already aware of the essential facts of their tragedy, it was only now that I learned its true and full background.

On January 25, 1946, the office of the Special Court Prosecutor in Poznań received a denunciation of Lucjan and Linda Kamieński, written by one Dr. Felix Marian Nowowiejski, a former student of my father's. In it, the informer stated that Lucjan Kamieński had worked against Poland during the German occupation; that even before the war, he had been active in Germanizing the Polish territory separating the Third Reich from East Prussia; that he had brought up his son as a Hitlerite; that he had worked as a translator for the Gestapo; that he had collaborated with Dr. Kurt Lück; and finally, that he had signed his name in the *Volksliste* (Register of German Nationals). Of all the accusations, only the last two were based on fact. While it was true that my father had done research work for Dr. Lück in February 1940, this was not unusual; collaboration among academics often crossed the Nazis' artificially created boundaries of ethnicity. As for my father's signing the *Volksliste*, this event had occurred under threats, violent pressure, and torture that virtually crippled his left hand. The court accepted the defence's argument that my father's was not an isolated case, as close to 150,000 Polish families had been similarly forced to sign the Register.

The rest of Nowowiejski's denunciation consisted of second- and third-hand unsubstantiated accounts — for which, interestingly, no witnesses could be found — and of outright lies so preposterous that the prosecution in my father's subsequent show trial didn't even dare to present them as evidence. Not surprisingly, the denunciator, Nowowiejski, shied away from appearing at the trial and taking the witness stand.

The reason for Nowowiejski's denunciatory calumnies was purely personal. His father, also named Felix, was a longtime colleague and acquaintance of my father's and a composer who, among other things, wrote an opera entitled *Baltic Legend*, which was premiered in 1924 in Poznań's Grand Opera Theatre. My father reviewed it in the magazine *MUZYKA*, with a critique that was as crushing as it was accurate in calling it a failure. It was this critique that, twenty-three years later, led the composer's son to take revenge, not only on my father but also on my mother, falsely accusing her of anti-Polish activities before the war, even though ample documentation proved exactly the opposite.

Aside from dealing with this opera's musical aspects and its shaky story outline, my father's review also brought to light the fact that this work, now trumpeted to be a "Polish national opera," was in fact a remake of the composer's much earlier German operatic effort entitled *Der Kompass* and written well before the First World War, when all of western Poland was still under the hated German rule. In 1918, after the German defeat and the simultaneous rebirth of the Polish state, the composer found it opportune to follow the spirit of the times and transform what used to be proudly German into something fiercely Polish.

I now come to a most difficult part of this narrative. It is a tragic story that could take place only at that particular time, in that specific place, and under those extraordinary circumstances. On the basis of Nowowiejski's denunciation, my parents were arrested on February 5, 1946, and held imprisoned by the State Security Office until February 22, when they were transferred to the Młyńska Street jail in Poznań. My mother died on July 27 of tuberculosis of the lungs, bones, and intestines, aggravated by malnutrition and maltreatment by prison personnel. My father, who was held in a different part of the prison, learned of her death only when guards led him to the cell where her body already lay in a plain wooden box.

My father's trial began on September 27, 1946, and ended the next day. The court acquitted him of the charges of collaboration with the German occupiers and of having acted to the detriment of the Polish state. He was, however, sentenced to three years in prison and the confiscation of his entire estate for having signed the Register of German Nationals. At the same time, the court expressed itself positively in regard to granting a full reprieve. Based on that opinion, the President of the Republic signed the appropriate document only a few days later.

He left prison on October 23, 1946, a lonely, homeless, broken man, with no means of survival and no possessions other than his well-worn clothes. On December 3, weakened by the abuse he had suffered both physically and mentally, he stumbled and fell on some uneven pavement, breaking his thighbone in the critical "neck" where it joined the hip.

Luckily, he was found by some well-meaning passersby and delivered to the municipal hospital, where he was operated on by an old friend and former university colleague. Unfortunately, his leg had to be shortened by a few centimetres. When word of his plight spread, many of his former students did whatever they could to help their teacher and mentor, so that after his release from hospital he was able to find a place to live. Meanwhile, contact had been established between my father and myself, as well as with his brother, Czesław Kamieński in Canada. Later, my uncle and I combined forces and began sending him a monthly stipend and, at regular intervals, parcels with all sorts of necessities. As his health improved, he began to compose again, and in 1957 he came to visit me and his brother in Winnipeg. Yet, despite finding comfort in being with his family, he felt increasingly uneasy in the mostly English-speaking Canadian environment. He spoke several languages fluently — Polish, German, French, Latin, and even classic Greek — but at the age of seventy-two found it almost impossible to add English to that polyglot collection. Regrettably, he left Winnipeg in 1958, saying that an old tree can't be uprooted, let alone transplanted. Back in Poland, he went on composing and teaching. Our correspondence resumed immediately. We wrote to each other frequently and regularly until his death in 1964. In 1960 the County Court in Poznań reviewed my father's case and ordered both case and sentence erased from the court records. This meant that they were to be regarded in every sense as having never existed. My father was now completely exonerated, his honour and dignity — as well as his books and manuscripts — finally restored to him.

In 1993, I travelled to Poznań, specifically to visit my mother's grave, but inquiries made at the court and jail archives, as well as a search of the burial records of various cemeteries yielded no information as to where she may have been buried. Finally, an official at the city's Hall of Records told me that in those turbulent postwar times, prisoners whose remains were not claimed by family were usually buried in either mass graves or in unmarked plots in cemeteries outside the city. As to the approximate location of these graves, no records existed. The man only shrugged, adding that they might have been ploughed under, perhaps to make room for a housing project.

24 ART FOR THE RUSSIANS

M y breakup with Franziska took place in the summer of 1946. It was sudden, painful, and irrevocable. Fortunately, our parting did not affect my close and friendly relationship with the rest of the Ulich family, who appeared to respect the distance that had grown between Franziska and me.

No doubt certain of their role in the occupation of what was now called the Soviet Zone, the Red Army and the Soviet Military Administration began settling in for a long stay. What was to become East Germany (the German Democratic Republic) had in fact become the Red Army's satellite domicile, a fact that quite naturally spawned its own offshoot of domesticity. Formerly German army barracks and other installations became home to Soviet state organs as well as quarters for officers and their families. The paramilitary NKVD (later called KGB), the civilian MVD (Ministry of Internal Affairs), and the GRU (the Red Army's intelligence arm) were housed in facilities that needed more of a real, homey Soviet look. This was achieved by the introduction of eye-catching posters glorifying the Soviet armed forces, the Communist Party and its achievements, the Economic Five-Year Plan, and whatever else was in need of promotion. Most such posters came ready-made from the USSR, but there was also a demand for other decorative art, such as huge banners with political slogans painted in big white letters on red cloth, for display on the outsides of buildings, or series of portraits of all ten or eleven members of the Politburo. Some of the Academy's studios became veritable hives of activity. We produced paintings of Kalinin, Khrushchev, Mikoyan, Beria, Kaganovitch, and the rest of that lot, which fetched anywhere from fifty to one hundred marks apiece, depending on the size of the painting. Portraits of Lenin, Marx, and Engels were also painted in considerable numbers, but none came off that production line in such quantities as likenesses of Stalin himself. I remember travelling by streetcar past a large, pompous building called the Albrechtschloss, on whose exterior and facing the street an enormous, four-storey-high portrait of Stalin was displayed. It had been painted in brown on some sort of beige textile, with the great man's head measuring about fifteen feet from chin to hairline. It was taken down later that day, when a strong and sustained wind made the monumental piece of art flap around, folding and buckling, so that The Leader's face snapped, grinned, twitched, and grimaced at the passing pedestrians. I was told that no one dared to laugh. The presence of armed soldiers in front of the building precluded any expressions of mirth.

On one occasion, a junior Soviet officer brought me a considerable length of yellow parachute silk and commissioned me to paint on it a battle scene representing Red Army troops storming Berlin's Reichstag building, which, quite mistakenly, was always regarded by the Russians as the centre of the German state. This was a big job, since I'd have to paint dozens of figures in action and do it on a surface about three metres in height and nine in length. I pointed out that creating a multicoloured painting on silk was out of the question and that the best anyone could do would be to produce a monumental monochrome picture. The problem of colour and quantity of paint needed to do this work was solved easily: a short time later, the officer brought me several large cans of reddish-brown floor paint, which, as it happened, perfectly complemented the silk's bright colouring. Working alone, I would have needed more than a month of sustained effort to complete the job, so I got a fellow artist, Werner Haenel, to help me. He, too, needed money, and was glad to join me in that undertaking. No studio in the Academy was large enough to accommodate this battalistic project, so we got permission to work in one of the long hallways. We were finished with it in about two weeks. When he arrived to inspect and claim this masterpiece, the officer told us that it would grace the wall of an officer's mess somewhere in a Dresden suburb, which had escaped the 1945 bombing raids. I never could imagine what it would be like to enjoy a sumptuous dinner face to face with a huge battle scene and all its attendant gore. Be that as it may, we were paid fairly well, though the money didn't buy as much as it had only a short time before. A loaf of bread of questionable quality and content was up to seventy-five percent more expensive than it had been on the black market at the end of the war.

The situation was the same in all other areas of the daily life, though for myself there was some personal compensation. My own "real" art was receiving recognition, and I was invited to have my first solo exhibition in the small but reputable Eisner-Bellak Gallery, located in one of Dresden's mostly undamaged outer residential districts. At the opening of that exhibition, I had my first personal encounter with art censorship. A Soviet "cultural" officer attending the opening ordered the removal of a pen-and-ink drawing of mine, showing a male figure wearing a military coat (free of any national characteristics and distinctions), with one leg missing and the head down, hanging on a cross, hands tied to the crossbar. Naturally, the invited guests and I, not to mention the gallery owners, were deeply shocked by this act of intolerance, reminiscent of the Nazi era that had just ended. The drawing was an expression of my anti-militarism, but the reason for its removal became clear to me only a year or so later, when Moscow-directed East Germany created the *Volksarmee* (People's Army), in answer to West Germany's rearmament under the aegis of the United States.

Other exhibitions followed, some solo shows and others in which I shared the space with other artists. A prize or two also came my way, but sales were few and far between, so, like many other artists, I had to make a living by painting the quickly and routinely produced and unsigned junk one sees all over the world, bought only to complement the colour of the wallpaper or of the chenille spread on a sofa. Completely fabricated from imagination, gloriously happy landscapes of the Swiss Alps, sunny Italy, or the sun-drenched Riviera came off our easels to dispel the public's dark memories of the recent past. By now, people had begun to earn some money again, but there was little that it could buy, and black market prices were going up by the day. Sunny pictures diverted people's thoughts from their gloomy life and could be bought legally as merchandise outside the State's all-encompassing coupon system.

In front of one of the many gory masterpieces I helped create for the Red Army Museum in Kamenz in the summer of 1947.

It was only natural that some smugly self-righteous critics would label such attempts to survive amidst general starvation as "art prostitution." They were right, and they would be right today, given the amount of second-rate art currently produced worldwide to satisfy equally questionable public taste. Except for the farmers, everyone in postwar East Germany was almost permanently hungry, including the art critics, and everyone tried to survive as well as they could. Artists had to produce marketable junk, and critics had to write the reviews.

Some time in 1946, I was lucky enough to get a somewhat larger commission: I negotiated the handsome fee of 1,000 marks to paint the portaits of all members of the Soviet Politburo. The portraits were to be identical in size, to eventually be displayed side by side along the wall of a large conference room in a building that housed a newly established section of the Soviet Military Administration. I was allowed to inspect that room, so that I could establish the ultimate width of the planned portrait display, which, I believe, came to something like three-quarters of a metre per painting, with about thirty centimetres in between them. When I had finished measuring, a young officer handed me a number of black-and-white portrait photographs of the Soviet potentates whom I was to paint in full colour. Of course, I began looking them over one by one, and since I already had some knowledge of the Cyrillic alphabet, quite automatically turned the photos over and read the names out loud. There were the usual personages: Stalin, Mikojan, Molotov, Kaganovitch, Beria, Khrushchev, Malenkov, Voroshilov, Zhdanov, and some others. But when I came to the name Voznesenski, the officer literally tore the photo out of my hand, saying, "No! Not this one, it's a mistake, this man is not in the Politburo anymore!" I shrugged and simply accepted this as necessary information pertaining to the project at hand. Many years later, I learned that Voznesenski and other Leningrad Communist leaders had been arrested on Stalin's orders and executed shortly after the end of war, ostensibly for treason (or so it was officially phrased).

In the summer of 1947, I received an unexpected visit in my Academy studio from a Red Army captain. He did not give me his name, but merely took a brief look at my paintings and then asked me if I would help create the decor of a small museum devoted to recording and honouring the war history of his unit. I wanted to know why I'd been chosen for this kind of work. He'd heard of a Polish artist who spoke passable Russian, he said, and it had taken only a few inquiries to find me. Having already learned quite a bit about Russian secretiveness and suspicion toward those who asked too many questions, I knew better than to ask about his sources of information. I stuck to a safer question: what kind of decor did he have in mind? He told me that he was thinking of maps showing the many places in the Soviet Union, Poland, and Germany where his tank division had fought, as well as paintings depicting various important battles in which his division had emerged victorious. He also envisaged a scaled-down replica of his unit's main battle tank, the T-34, to be placed prominently in the centre of the hall. This proposed museum, he told me, was to be installed in a small, disused school auditorium in the town of Kamenz, forty kilometres northeast of Dresden and easily reached by rail. I could do it, I said, but I would need help with such a large project — a sculptor to create the tank replica and another painter to assist me with the images of tank battles. The captain agreed right away, promising that we would be provided with separate rooms in the local hotel, given three meals a day from the divisional kitchen, and paid 1,000 marks each upon completing the work to the satisfaction of the divisional commander. It went without saying that all necessary materials would be provided by the unit's command.

Trying to disguise my eagerness at what amounted to a lifesaver for me and my fellow artists, I agreed to all points of his proposal. The officer and I discussed some final details, and after he left, I immediately contacted a talented art student named Manfred Grünert and a young sculptor whose name I have forgotten. Like me, they were living hand-to-mouth, and such a commission was akin to a gift from heaven.

A few days later, we reported for work at the Kamenz *Kommendatura*, and the same officer who had hired us to create the museum took us to see its proposed location. The school's auditorium was set apart from the main building containing the classrooms, and was well chosen for the size and proportion of its interior. Relatively small, it nonetheless could accommodate a good number of exhibits, including the tank replica and our paintings. The necessary materials, such as lumber, canvas, paint, brushes, and turpentine were in place, and all that was missing was an ample supply of clay for our sculptor to make the T-34 tank replica. A local carpenter was to build a display case for the many decorations and honours the division had received in its history.

Our hotel rooms were tiny, high-ceilinged, dark, and musty, but the beds were almost comfortable and the bedding clean. I was already familiar with the kind of food cooked in Red Army kitchens, and I told my artist friends not to expect any gourmet fare. But none of us really cared about the Red Army's monotonous menu as long as the food was more or less tasty and there was plenty of it. We had been starving for a long time, and it didn't matter that we got barley soup three times a day. It was enriched with well-sized chunks of meat and came with freshly baked bread, dark, substantial, and heavenly tasting.

Once the supply of clay arrived, our sculptor began work on the tank replica, while Manfred and I started on a huge map chronicling the progress of the division, which had gone into battle in 1942 at a place called Staraya Russa. After fighting at the constantly shifting front and taking heavy losses in the famous Battle of Kursk, the division was reconstituted and incorporated into Marshal Konev's so-called First Ukrainian Front, which in 1945 stormed into Germany and, together with Zhukov's armies, took Berlin and, en route, also Dresden. I asked Manfred and the young sculptor how they felt about working for the conquerors. After all, they'd been in the Wehrmacht and seen action — surely they must have some feelings in that regard. But they both only shrugged and gave me the same, pragmatic answer: "The war is over, we've survived. Why worry whom we're working for, as long as the work is there?"

To make things easier for us, we were given a helper, a simple enlisted man by the name of Misha. As "our" captain told us, this was done to relieve us of tasks that someone else could carry out, which would give us more time to do our real work. Sure enough, Misha turned out to be quite useful in helping us to put up structures, fetch things, get our meals from the army kitchen, and perform myriad other small jobs. Although we were not slowed down by these tasks, we took care not to work too quickly, not wishing to finish too soon and have to leave our cozy situation. Misha was a delight to have around. A native of Siberia, he was short, strong, on the chubby side, with straw-blond hair, an open, laughing face, and twinkling blue eyes. He had a repertoire of several songs, which he performed in true Russian manner, almost sobbing while singing the nostalgic ones, or bursting with verve as he sang the jolly, sometimes cheerfully obscene ones from back home. Like all Soviet soldiers, Misha wore his campaign medals permanently fixed on his tunic. There must have been six or eight of them, in all colours of the rainbow, and they clinked merrily every time he moved.

We had to paint ten fairly large pictures, each two and a half metres high and one and a half metres wide. Manfred and I divided our work in such a way that I roughed out the entire scene and painted the figures of infantry either charging or riding on top of tanks (which, of course, had to be T-34s), and Manfred painted the backgrounds, ruins, smoke and fire, explosions, and so on. This system worked very well, and during his frequent inspection visits "our" captain, sometimes in the company of other officers, spoke enthusiastically of our painterly work, though he occasionally criticized our colleague, the sculptor, for omitting seemingly unimportant details on the T-34 replica. But our friend had an easy excuse, since he had only a few amateurish photographs to work from. By and large, though, our relations with the captain were quite pleasant.

A single discordant note marred the agreeable atmosphere. At one point, our mentor, the captain, told me to report to a certain room in the divisional headquarters. Typically secretive, he didn't divulge the reason for the summons, and, of course, I didn't ask. I found the right door easily enough and, noting that the very small sign on the door of the room gave only the occupant's rank — *Leytyenant* — but not his name, I knocked. A man's voice told me to come in, and I found myself facing a swarthy, black-eyed, dark-haired officer of unmistakably Caucasian origin. From behind his desk, he gestured for me to have a seat across from him, and then, unsmiling, interrogated me about my past, my parents, my education and, most importantly, about how, when, and where I had learned to speak Russian. I had nothing to hide, and almost two hours later, he let me go. Back at work, when I told Misha about that experience, he simply shrugged and said, "*Smersh.*" I'd never heard the word before, but eventually learned that it was an acronym for "*Smert Shpionam*" (death to spies). The lieutenant was an investigator for that counter-espionage organization, and he must have accepted my story, since after our session together I never heard from him again.

I've come to think of that episode in terms of "having gotten away with it." The explanation of my relative fluency in Russian was easy. Being Polish by birth, I found a great similarity between the two languages, and coming from a musical family, I had no trouble in adapting to the particular sound of Russian speech. The *Smersh* officer seemed to accept that without any further comment. Making copious notes, he also accepted the story of my previous employment at Boehner Film, though I had to explain to him — in general terms, of course — the principal features of stereo film technology. This story also made my presence in Dresden believable, and neatly camouflaged the other essential reason for my being there rather than back in Poland. Any — even the slightest — mention of the Polish Resistance would have gotten me into more than just hot water. The Soviets dealt severely with members of the Polish Underground.

Now, thinking of those times from the perspective of more than sixty years, I find myself harbouring persistent doubts about some of the individuals I encountered. I honed my Russian skills with Volodia and learned its vernacular from Misha, in long soul-baring debates. But it soon became clear to me that there were hidden dangers in our discussions on art, literature and — most certainly — politics. When, for example, Misha came up with an innocent remark praising Zoshchenko's satirical writings, I kept my mouth shut, already knowing from Volodia that this writer had been heavily criticized by the Communist Party. Was Misha, ostensibly there to help create a little divisional museum, in reality an agent provocateur placed by the *Smersh* to keep an ear open for any — even the slightest — remark opposing the policies of the Soviet state? If so, then his report to the *Smersh* lieutenant must have been disappointing: I simply didn't bite. Obviously, I had no proof of either Misha or Volodia being an informer. But the misgivings remain: Why, I wonder, did an officer of the dreaded secret service release me after such a short time?

After work and back in our hotel, we sometimes spent time fraternizing with other occupants of that establishment, but mostly with a corporal by the name of Anatol (Tolya for short) Miller, who, in spite of his German name was an epitome of the Russian soul. A professional musician, he was a virtuoso accordion player who had also earned his campaign decorations as a tank driver, and now entertained the division's officers at their frequent revels. But classical music was his true love, and he often played for us his own transcriptions of works by Mozart, Schumann, Chopin, Brahms, and Dvořák.

Inevitably though, our work came to an end, and the division's commander, General Babadjinian, came to inspect the *muzey* he had commissioned. A swarthy Armenian, slender and elegant in his long greatcoat, he entered the hall smiling, but exuding authority just the same. After he had handed his coat and gold-braided cap to his aide, the three of us were introduced to him. We shook hands, and, since I could speak Russian, it was only natural that I would show him around and explain what had been done to honour his division. He admired everything unstintingly, but demanded one change: the ten paintings had been framed using natural, light-coloured wood; the general, however, wanted the frames to be painted gold. Fortunately there was a modest supply of imitation gold powder among our art supplies, and after the general left, we spent the rest of the day painting the frames, muttering to ourselves all the while about the general's hopelessly bourgeois taste. In the end, though, each of us received the promised 1,000 marks and left for Dresden on the evening train.

It seemed that word of my skill in portraiture was spreading. A day or two after returning to my studio in the Academy, I was visited there by a Russian *polkovnik* (colonel), who wanted me to paint a portrait of him. Before I could answer, he pulled out a black-and-white photo of himself in gala uniform, bedecked with decorations, and held it in front of me. "You paint from this?" he asked, and of course I said yes. We bargained about the price until I won. "It will be ready in a week's time," I told him, "but it has to dry for a month." Disappointed, he sighed and asked if putting

A portrait of Kostek Baum around 1947.

it near a source of heat would dry it faster. "*Nyet,*" I replied, to which he shrugged, promising to return in *tchetiri nedyeli* (four Sundays') time. I got to work and found it easy going. Having painted the whole Politburo made this one almost effortless — or so I thought. When the colonel turned up a month later, he took one look at his portrait and exploded in a flow of invective. I had committed a grave sin in painting a blue stripe instead of a green one onto the silk-like ribbon that held the medal fastened to the officer's uniform. "But it's impossible to tell colour differences from a black-and-white photo," I explained and eventually he understood my problem. "I'll repair the damage," I promised. Some time later, he returned to get his portrait and, now satisfied, paid me the agreed-upon fee. But he was still grumbling as he left my studio.

25 FAKE ART

As time wore on, even the Russians' art commissions dwindled to nothing, and exhibitions became an exercise in hopelessness. So it was with quite some alacrity that I accepted a proposal to paint a portrait from a photograph. A well-to-do man, the former owner of a huge grain-milling complex which was about to be nationalized, with him remaining as pro tem general manager, came to my studio in the Academy and asked if I would paint the likeness of his father. He showed me an old, sepia-coloured photo of a stern-looking, mustachioed man in a dark suit, wearing a stiff, high collar and dark tie. The photograph had been taken in the late 1870s, and its subject would be easy to reproduce on canvas. I promptly agreed to undertake the work and even quoted a price. We shook hands, the man left, and I immediately began to prepare a canvas for painting the portrait. It took me only a couple of days to finish the work, but the paint was still wet and had to dry before I could deliver the picture to my customer's home. Since it was the height of summer and the days were hot, I simply put the portrait out to face the sun, and it was dry in something like a week's time. I took it to the address the man gave me and found a veritable mansion with three floors. My customer lived in the top floor apartment, while the main and second floors had been requisitioned by the Soviets to house some of their military administration offices.

The man liked the painting very much and paid me for it on the spot. Then he asked if I could paint portraits from a daguerreotype, an early form of photography showing the likeness on glass. I said I probably could, providing the image contained enough contrast to work from. He showed me the object in question and, tilting it into the light, I found that it was nice and clear. It was a picture of a man and a woman, both looking to be well past middle age and dressed in what appeared to be the fashion of the mid-nineteenth century. My client said that they were his grandparents and that he would like to hang their portrait in his study, next to that of his father. Painting from that ancient glass photograph was far more difficult than working from a print on paper. But I did the best I could, and this double portrait, too, found full acceptance by the couple's grandson. I didn't see him until a few weeks later, when he once again came to my studio to engage my services. This time, however, the project was quite different, though it still involved portraiture.

He seemed to be having difficulty explaining what he wanted, talking at great length about his family, past and present, before coming to the point. He wanted me to paint several portraits of his ancestors, dating back to the second half of the seventeenth century, when one of those personages, a citizen of Dresden and a miller by trade, had been appointed supplier of flour to the court of August II, Duke of Saxony, and elected King of Poland. This portrait was to be followed by likenesses of the miller's descendants, right down to those I had already painted. The last painting in the entire collection was to be one of my patron himself. He looked rather embarrassed when I asked about some visual material to work from. He shook his head and said there was none, but that be could give me all names and dates pertaining to his ancestry. I said this would be helpful, and that I could try using his father's and grandparents' features to establish a family likeness going back those several generations. I could see he was relieved to get so much cooperation from me, although he couldn't know what I really thought of that sort of commission. I was being asked to create a gallery of fictitious ancestral portraits to help this elderly, clearly intelligent man lessen, or even overcome, the totally unwarranted complexes he had about his social background. In a way I felt sorry for him, but I was also glad to accept the work. I had bought art materials at black market prices to paint the double portrait from daguerreotype and could hardly pay for the vastly overpriced potatoes that kept me from starvation. I asked the man for an advance, and he willingly handed me a few hundred marks. He also left me a sheet of paper with a sketch of his family tree, including names and dates. As I recall, he underlined the names of personages whose portraits he wanted me to paint, and they all turned out to be men. The only woman in that whole collection would be my patron's already depicted grandmother, of the daguerreotype provenance.

The first thing I did was to borrow the painting of the man's father to copy his face in several drawings and memorize it, so that I'd be able to show it from more than just one angle. Since the quantity of materials I had to get was considerable, a major portion of the advance the man had given me went toward obtaining them. The amount of work involved appeared monumental, so I began painting as soon as I had finished my notes on the variety of seventeenth- and eighteenth-century dress that I'd be introducing in the portrait series. This was, of course, quite different and far more interesting than producing (and I use that word advisedly) endless portraits of Stalin, Lenin, and all the members of the Soviet Politburo. It required all the skill and attention to detail I possessed. In the first painting I followed my original intent to show the subject as an elegant gentleman, with just a bit of toughness showing in his facial expression and in the way he was positioned in the picture. He was to be a well-to-do tradesman from the post-Napoleonic era, though the milling trade would not be referred to in this painting. As was usual in those days, he wore black with a white collar, and I showed him leaning on a little round table, holding a rolled-up sheet of paper in his hand. The background was of the colour we students derisively called "brown sauce," a totally neutral, darkish hue against which you could place any colour and make it stand out. Naturally, I had no model to pose for me, but I actually didn't need one. To paint hands, always a tricky part in any portrait, I worked from the rich variety of plaster cast hands found in the Academy's sculpture collection. These were used for drawing and study, particularly by beginner students, and were shown in many expressive attitudes: fisted, cupped, finger-pointing, warding off, inviting, waving, writing, grasping, saluting — in short, doing everything that hands ordinarily do.

The first portrait took me a week or so, and I started the next one right away. I decided to work going back in time, so my next subject wore his hair in a little pigtail at the back. His face was turned to partial profile, and he wore a light-coloured coat of the sort fashionable among German gentry around 1790 or thereabouts, according to my notes from that time. The gentleman was leaning on a walking stick, and I showed him against a rustic background. The picture's mood was downright romantic.

My scribbled notes, their paper now yellowed and brittle, tell me what went into the remaining eight portraits. Suffice it to say that working my way back in time not only involved depicting a variety of fashions, but also necessitated painting facial features that changed ever so slightly from one picture to the next, always retaining a little something reminiscent of past generations: the shape of a nose, the chin, cheekbones, or the setting of the eyes. I remembered the genetics of the Hapsburgs, whose bulging lower lip was always prominently visible in portraits of practically every member of that inbred family, which for five centuries ruled much of Europe and overseas colonies.

But in addition to all the above, I had to give each painting an appearance in keeping with its supposed date of origin. I was creating fakes, and my patron was fully aware of it. Fakes of "old" paintings require "ageing" to make them look genuine. For the first few of the eight fakes, I needed only to cover the dried surface with some vegetable oil mixed with a little soot, and gently rub it into the texture created by the brushwork. If vegetable oil was unavailable, crankcase oil also worked quite well. I also used that method to age the next few paintings, applying a little more force and a tad more soot. It was, however, the last of the fake portraits that I aged with special care. It was supposed to be the oldest of the lot, dated 1690. In it, I painted a man with a somewhat rough face, penetrating eyes, wearing a large wig à la Louis XIV, and with a type of dark fur cape partly thrown over his shoulders, but arranged to reveal some of his arm, which was encased in shiny armour. The latter touch was intended to suggest the man's possible (but just possible) ties to nobility.

Ageing a painting requires some skill. The canvas on which an oil painting is to be executed is always first covered with a special substance called a primer, which prevents the paint from being absorbed by the fabric of the canvas. In my days at the Dresden Academy, we art students primed our own canvasses with a carefully measured mixture of water, kaolin (a finely ground white clay used in making china and porcelain), and rabbit-skin glue. If there is not enough glue in that mixture, the oil paint will seep into the canvas. Conversely, if there is too much glue, the layer of paint will remain on the canvas, but forms cracks when dry. It was exactly the latter effect that I was after when I painted the "oldest" fake portrait. Once the paint was dry, I rubbed the back of the painting with sufficient, though gentle, pressure to produce a generous number of small cracks, of precisely the kind you find in very old oil paintings that have not been well taken care of. The next step was to hold it, image facing down, a safe distance over a lighted candle, and move it about carefully so that its entire surface became covered with a thin, even layer of soot. In the final step, I used a soft cloth to rub the soot all over the picture and into the newly formed cracks. Voilà — my just-off-the-easel antique was ready for a fake antique frame.

My patron was ecstatic, and so was I. He had paid me royally for immortalizing several generations of Dresden millers and possibly making other people believe that they really had existed. Eventually, I also painted his portrait. My earnings enabled me to pay my debts, survive the best part of the year 1947 almost worry-free, and be able to work on my own art while developing a personal style. I had toiled for over three months to produce those fake portraits, and the time had come for me to be myself once again.

Part 6

TO THE WEST

26 ESCAPE TO FREEDOM

Late that year I met Christine Bollerhoff, a young and talented artist studying at the Academy under the tutelage of the well-known illustrator Joseph Hegenbarth. Our friendship eventually led to marriage, and our wedding took place in March 1948. Almost immediately, we began planning to leave East Germany and cross over to the British zone of occupation. There were very good reasons for our decision to leave. First, there was the constant, unabating hunger that dominated practically everything one thought or did. Then there was also the huge wave of Soviet-motivated political thought that began suppressing any new artistic ideas and in effect led us back to the super-realist style, ordered and enforced by the Nazis, which we artists had been so happy to be rid of. My unnerving experience of having had an anti-war drawing confiscated by a Soviet censor found an echo in the Academy's classrooms, a bit milder maybe, but pervasive nevertheless. In the public domain, there was was an opening of an exhibition of paintings rescued from the infamous 1934 Nazi-staged travelling show of what they called "Degenerate Art." In it you could find the works of progressive artists from the first thirty or thirty-five years of the twentieth century: paintings, sculpture, and graphics of which the Nazis disapproved for reasons of ideology and their own petty bourgeois tastes. Among the rescued works now on display in two great rooms of the Academy was the once well-known, large triptych by Otto Dix, titled *The Trench*, a masterfully executed, realistic, and most gruesome work, depicting a First World War trench filled with the gore of dead, mangled bodies, replete with bloody guts, maggots, and other such shocking details. This brilliant work of art and powerful tool of anti-war propaganda drew great crowds, including many Germans who only recently had themselves experienced horrors of this kind. The painting stayed on display for only two days, after which, on orders of the Soviet Military Administration, it was taken away to an unknown location, along with all the other progressive art to which, for ideological reasons, the Russians, like the Nazis, objected.

The Cold War was now with us on every level, replete with the Berlin blockade and airlift, so Christine and I finalized our plan of escape to the West. She had crossed the East-West border before and knew the right routes, as well as the necessary stops along the way. These included staying overnight with friends of hers in Quedlinburg (which was still in East Germany) and Hanover (which was in the British-occupied zone of Germany). Our ultimate goal was, of course, Canada. My Uncle Czesław, with whom I'd been corresponding since late 1946, had been urging me to move to West Germany and to wait there until he could facilitate our voyage to Canada.

We left Dresden in July with mixed feelings, but generally glad to be on our way. We carried only a minimum of luggage, and this proved to be the right decision. In Quedlinburg we stayed overnight with Christine's friends, leaving the next morning for Halberstadt, a town not far from the border between the Soviet and British zones. From there we had to make our way to the modest house of a youngish man who had been recommended by the Quedlinburg friends as a reliable guide across the border, for an appropriate fee, of course. As it turned out, he was available, and we set out on foot through some dense forest in a northwesterly direction. This walk lasted well over an hour and led us to the forest's edge, from which an open, grassy plateau led down toward a line of small bushes and a little creek.

From among the trees, our guide pointed to those bushes and said, "There, that's the border." As he turned to go back home, he advised us to run for the bushes as fast as we could. The East German border patrols, armed with live ammunition, generally passed by every ten to twenty minutes. "But then, you never know," he added, before disappearing among the trees. I was sure the advice he gave us was worth every penny of the 200 marks I had paid him.

In fact, a patrol came by a few minutes later and, walking slowly along the edge of the forest, passed about ten metres from the thicket where we were waiting. As soon as he was out of sight, we took off. Our dash to freedom lasted no more than perhaps half a minute. We stopped at what we had been told was the border between two important military powers, once allied in a common struggle, but now enemies ready to fight each other. There was no sign to indicate that the scraggy bushes and the wee rivulet, less than a metre wide, was what separated freedom from oppression. And that an old wooden board, perhaps thirty centimetres wide, was actually a bridge between two Cold War enemies. In any case, Christine walked across it, while I made it to freedom with one big leap, yelling, "God Save the King!" — fitting words, I thought, with which to enter the British-occupied zone, and the few words of English that I knew.

We thumbed our way to Braunschweig, where, as I already knew, there was still a Polish DP (Displaced Persons) camp. This was a transit point for Polish forced-labour workers wishing to return to Poland and a leftover from the immediate postwar period. But now that the war had been over for three years, this facility, once run by the UN's International Refugee Organization, held only a handful of those who for various reasons didn't wish to return to their country. The camp's manager told me that he was no longer authorized to accept Polish fugitives from either Poland or any of the Soviet-dominated countries, including East Germany. To obtain refugee status, we needed to report to a Polish reception centre in Quakenbrück, a small town some sixty kilometres east of the border with Holland. I asked about the need for such a long trip and was told it was for purposes of "verification." All I could do was shrug my shoulders and accept this typical, immutably bureaucratic verdict. But there was a complication. Only a couple of weeks before, a monetary reform had taken place in all of West Germany's occupation zones, and the brand-new Deutschmarks had become the official currency. However, I had only the old Reichsmarks still used in Soviet-occupied Germany, which were now officially worth less than the new West German money. To my amazement, the man offered me an at par exchange of his new money for my old currency. Deeply grateful, I thanked him profusely. We now had sufficient funds to pay our fare to Quakenbrück and promptly went off to find the railway station.

After we'd figured out the complicated schedules of trains and transfers that would take us to our destination, we still had to wait a few hours for a train to Hanover. We settled in the station's bleak waiting room, where for the first time I saw British soldiers who were not POWs, a jolly, raucous lot, toting their belongings in large bags, probably off on leave. It had been a long time since I'd heard English spoken, aside from the occasional phrase that had drifted over from the POW camp next to Boehner Studios. Before the war, I'd heard it in a variety of American and British movies. I had also occasionally heard my mother converse in English with a lady friend, but it was only the sound of the language, rather than the spoken words, that I could now recall. It was Christine's working knowledge of English that enabled her to translate the odd word spoken or shouted by these soldiers.

However, we needed to discuss and update the plans we had made before leaving Dresden, taking into account our current situation. In Braunschweig, the Polish refugee camp manager had told me that only I had to report to the Quakenbrück reception centre for Polish refugees, while Christine could go wherever she wished. This brought us back to our original idea of finding a temporary place to stay with the Middings, friends of Christine's parents, on their farm at Muckum, a village near the town of Bünde in Westphalia. In fact, Christine had written to them prior to our departure from Dresden, asking if they'd take us in, and they had written back saying we were most welcome. We decided that Christine would proceed to Muckum, while I made my way to Quakenbrück, and that I'd join her after being "verified."

The train ride to Hanover was quite short. There, we found out that Christine would have to wait some time for a train connection to Bünde, but that a bus to Quakenbrück, with only one transfer along the way, would be leaving from a nearby depot within a half-hour. We parted in a hurry, and I made a dash for the bus. As it turned out, there were still more passengers getting on board, so that departure was delayed for quite some time. I don't recall much of that trip. I know I wasn't hungry, since we'd eaten some bread and sausage in Braunschweig, but I was totally exhausted, and the gentle rocking of the bus put me to sleep. I woke up only when the bus driver shook me by the shoulder, telling me that we'd arrived at the stop where I had to transfer and that the bus to Quakenbrück was already waiting. Half an hour later, along with two or three other people, I stepped off the bus into the hot July evening.

27 "VERIFICATION"

Following the directions one of the passengers had given me, I soon found myself at the Polish reception centre, an indistinct-looking, small-ish building only a short distance from the bus stop. A moment after I rang the bell, the door was opened by a short and somewhat dishevelled man, to whom I spoke in Polish, giving my name and stating my business. In reply, he merely grunted and ushered me inside, directing me to walk ahead along a short corridor.

Then, unexpectedly and without warning, he pushed me through an open door into a room. I found myself facing a well-dressed man, seated behind a desk and looking at me absolutely deadpan. Frantically trying to find out what was going on, I asked why I, a refugee, was being treated in such a rough, uncivilized way? To this, I received no answer. Instead, the man turned to the individual who had let me into the building, pointed to the briefcase I was carrying with me, and barked out, in Polish, a one-word command: "Search!" The briefcase was made of heavy tent-cloth and lined with some lighter textile. In it, I carried personal things, various papers, and a couple of Polish books. The bully yanked it from my grasp and proceeded to literally rip it apart, evidently looking for some sort of contraband. I protested, but the man behind the desk only stared at me impassively. When all the contents of my briefcase were put before him, he riffled through them quickly, then turned to the bully and told him to search me. By then I had stopped protesting, and watched helplessly as everything I carried on me was taken and placed onto the desk. This included the few Deutschmarks I had received in Braunschweig, my stateless passport, a letter from my father, an ID card with my picture, identifying me as a student at the Dresden Academy of Fine Arts, and my birth certificate. While the man behind the desk was busy examining those few papers, my attention was drawn to a little sign with his name on it: Dr. R. Gawenda — a name I am sure I will never forget as long as I live. He was the first of the inquisitors it was my misfortune to encounter. Although he didn't say much to me, every word felt like a threat. All my possessions were going to he kept in his office, he told me, and for the time being, I was going to stay in Quakenbrück. I started to ask why all this was happening, but he waved me off and ordered his assistant to take me away.

By then it was dark, so I couldn't see much of the surroundings as we walked to our destination. It turned out to be a modest, small-town hotel, two stories high and, as I found out the following morning, overlooking a market square. I was shown upstairs to a well-sized room containing several beds. Five or six young men sat playing cards at a table near a window. My guiding thug left, and I found myself in the company of young Poles who, like myself, had escaped from the East for a variety of reasons. Some had fled because of ideological conflicts with the Polish Communist regime, others to live a better life in the West. There was even one individual running from the law. He freely admitted to me that he had beaten a Communist Party functionary to a pulp, but then managed to get out of a police station's holding cell and make a dash for the border. They were all awaiting "verification."

They were a friendly bunch, and we all got along fine, especially since every one of us had a history of running away from something, and was now impatiently waiting to be released from what was de facto a kind of imprisonment, or quarantine. Yes, we were fed three modest meals a day, we played bridge and endlessly told each other our stories of woe. But any money we had and all identifying documents had been taken from us. Without the latter, the most important of our personal papers, we did not exist, at least not in the eyes of the law. We were Orwellian non-persons, suspected of perhaps serving the enemy, no matter how fictitious that charge may have been, and not entitled to a normal life. We were confined to this particular area only, although we could move freely in and around Quakenbrück. On particularly hot days, we'd troop out to the banks of the small Hase River, just outside of town, to cool off in the water or lie around and get a tan.

Despite all these distractions that made life bearable, we were constantly beset by fears of the interrogations, the outcome of which would decide whether we were set free or sent back whence we came. Even today I shudder inwardly, thinking of the times when, right after breakfast, one or two, sometimes three of us, were herded into a Volkswagen and driven at great speed to Cloppenburg, a small town no more than half an hour away. There, in an elegant requisitioned villa, we were called, one by one, for what the questioners euphemistically called a "chat," but which in reality was a grilling that could be friendly or rough, suave or brutal, civilized or merciless and insulting. Occasionally, the interrogator would force his subject into a physically painful position to soften his resistance to questioning or to make him divulge even more details of an already provided piece of information. There were three interrogators, two Poles and an Englishman, and we never knew which one would examine us or how long such a session would last. I had already been forewarned of all this when I first joined my fellow detainees.

A couple of days after my arrival, I found myself in that Cloppenburg villa, waiting to be called into the presence of an examiner. He turned out to be a Pole, middle-aged, pleasant and well mannered. His questions were of the elementary kind: when and where I had been born, who my parents were, what schools I had attended, what I had been doing in East Germany, and what had made me cross over to the West. There were also some questions concerning Christine, but they were not as incisive as those regarding me. Throughout the interrogation, he was making notes, to which he occasionally referred, in order to have me clarify some date or other detail. This session lasted maybe an hour or an hour and a half, after which I was released with a thank-you. Contrary to what I had been told by the other detainees, this experience was quite pleasant, and I said so upon being returned to the reception centre in Quakenbrück. My fellow refugees actually laughed and told me to prepare myself for much more rigorous, even quite rough, questioning in the days to come. Sure enough, only two days later, another Polish investigator told me right from the start that he wouldn't brook any falsehoods in my testimony, and if I insisted on lying, I would be promptly sent back to East Germany. This time the grilling lasted over three hours, during which I was required to tell my life story twice from beginning to end, but this time in considerable detail. It was, of course, impossible to repeat everything without forgetting a point or two given in the previous account. This made the investigator accuse me of distorting the truth, again threaten me with deportation, and force me to tell my story again from the beginning. After being released from this interrogation, I returned to the Quakenbrück hotel shaking, frightened, and confused. I didn't want to speak to anyone, and my fellow detainees, having themselves been subjected to these grillings, left me alone.

About three days later, I was back in Cloppenburg for interrogation by the friendly Polish examiner who had questioned me on the first occasion. This time, however, I was not asked to recite my whole life story, but only to relate certain periods in it. I described my first encounter with Zenek and my subsequent joining the Resistance, also living in Hellerau and providing a stop-off for couriers travelling west. The man wanted to know about the rest of my time in East Germany, and I told him about the Dresden air raid, my work as a translator for the Russians, and making a living painting Politburo portraits and other Soviet glory pieces. At his request, I elaborated on the Russians' attitudes toward the German population, on the black market, and the people's desperate plight regarding food and food distribution. In my mind, I was sure that the Western intelligence agencies were fully aware of what I was describing and that this sort of questioning was designed only to test my credibility. I had sent off a brief letter to Christine, telling her that the process of "verification" was dragging on and that there was no telling when I would be released from what amounted to custody. I was able to buy postage stamps only through the courtesy of a fellow refugee who had managed to hide some coins on his person.

The next interrogation was not as amiable as the previous one. It was conducted by the Englishman, a man in his thirties who, to my amazement, spoke impeccable Polish, though with the distinct trace of an English accent. Like the others, he began with a warning that I would be sent back east the moment he caught me at prevarications. And, like the others, he started making notes in shorthand, when, on demand, I commenced to tell the story of my life. Perhaps ten minutes later, just as I was describing the September 10, 1939 German air raid on Kutno and my being wounded, he leaned across the desk and screamed: "Thanks for giving me your little fairy tale! You had better watch yourself, unless you want to end up back in the workers' paradise!" I tried to remonstrate and was even willing to show him the scar left after the shrapnel was taken out, but he kept shouting me down, using language that was not only abusive and maligning, but richly larded with the coarsest of profanities. Wherever he had learned to use that sort of Polish billingsgate, it was not Eton or Harrow. But after he stopped yelling, he calmly told me to get on with my story, demanding to hear the "absolute truth," and once again start at the beginning.

I went on with it, but he interrupted me constantly, always referring to his predecessors' notes and demanding that I change or repudiate what I had said before. He did this in ways varying from ironic to threatening to abusive, gradually intensifying in hostility, until he ordered me to get up off the chair on which I was sitting and stand with my back to him, my arms raised high and facing the wall of the glassed-in veranda in which the interrogation was taking place. It was a sizzling hot July afternoon, and the sun shone in through the veranda's large windows and its glass roof. So now I stood in the bright light, arms up, while the interrogator remained in the shade and out of my sight. The questioning went on unabated, and so did the interruptions by which he usually succeeded in confusing me, turning my truthful testimony into a web of contradictions. He also continued his verbal abuse, but my attention was gradually turning toward the growing difficulty of having to stand motionless in the heat of the bright sun. Whenever I moved or dropped my arms, he screamed at me to stand as ordered. The same happened if, in order to steady myself, I leaned with my forehead against the wall, or tried to relieve the growing stress in one leg by putting all my weight on the other one. I vividly remember the sun beating down through the transparent roof into the veranda, and the fact that my face and body were wet with perspiration. Beyond that, the memory becomes a blur — heat, physical pain, the man's screams, my confused mumbles — before fading into nothing. I passed out.

When I came to, I found myself sitting in a chair in the corridor where we usually waited to be called in for questioning. I was given a drink of cold water by a fellow detainee who, having already finished testifying to another investigator, had been ordered to drag me out of the veranda and bring me back to consciousness. Shortly afterwards we were driven back to Quakenbrück, and it was only then that I fully understood why these Polish detainees called my most recent interrogator "the Basilisk." According to an English-Polish pocket dictionary that one of us possessed, it was the name of a mythological vicious reptile that killed with its poisonous breath and the lethal look in its eyes. As a description of the Polish-speaking Englishman, this was dead accurate.

It was another week before I was called up for interrogation once again. Understandably, my apprehension was constant, and I mentioned this to Jurek Rudzki, a fellow inmate who had befriended me as soon as I arrived in Quakenbrück. He was a young man about my age, blond, rather short, and, unlike the rest of us, fairly well dressed. He said hardly anything about himself, except that he had been born near Kraków and escaped from Poland for ideological reasons. I had already told him my story. Like most of the other detainees, I felt a natural desire to talk and communicate with those who shared the same fate and similar circumstances. Just as natural was our need to talk about our own life experiences, memories of childhood, adolescence, the war with all its horrors, as well as whatever it was that moved us to seek a better life in the West. All those memories and thoughts — essentially the same ones that I had told the investigators — I spilled to Jurek Rudzki. Now, looking back, I am convinced that he was a "plant" in the reception centre, placed there by British-Polish intelligence to make sure that the probably true-life stories offered him freely by the detainees corresponded to those made under duress.

The friend who resuscitated me after my session with the Basilisk told me that my interrogation had lasted almost four hours. It was a miracle I hadn't suffered from sunstroke. On the following Saturday, I was again taken to Cloppenburg. Fearing a repetition of the Basilisk's kind of interrogation, I was braced for the worst. But, as I sat in the hallway with two other detainees, waiting to be grilled, it occurred to me that it was July 27, the anniversary of my mother's death. I thought of her and remembered being a child, reaching out to hold her hand. The memory was so strong that I almost felt her presence near me. It probably lasted no longer than a blink of an eye, elusive, yet it remains firm in my memory to this day.

Could this strange occurrence have had anything to do with what happened a few minutes later? It would be downright spooky if it did. The other two detainees and I were ushered into one of the interrogation rooms. This time, the friendly investigator who had first questioned me upon my arrival in Quakenbrück announced to the three of us that on the coming Monday, we would be released from the verification camp, free to go wherever we wanted within the British Occupation Zone of Germany. Our papers were being prepared and we would receive them, together with our personal documents and possessions, on the day of our release. Stunned and elated at the same time, we babbled our thanks, though we wondered afterwards what we were thanking them for. After all, we'd been held against our will, threatened with being returned to the countries we had run away from, and treated like criminals, sometimes even brutally — the British-Polish intelligence services were not exactly a heavenly choir of angels!

The supernatural moment I had experienced was temporarily forgotten as we told our still-detained comrades about our freedom, assuring them that they, too, would soon be released. But now, other surprising things were beginning to happen. We were given a few Deutschmarks each, to buy ourselves a beer or two in the hotel's *Gaststätte*, the small, cozy restaurant on the main floor. Not only that, but we were told we could attend Mass the next day in Cloppenburg's Catholic church. We didn't quite know what to think of this unexpected largesse, but since the Polish people, too, have the saying about not looking a gift horse in the mouth, we decided to accept what we had been given with good grace.

The following morning, sitting on the back of a small panel truck, all seven of us were driven to Cloppenburg and deposited in front of the Catholic church. I don't remember the building or its interior decor, but I do recall that my seat was next to the centre aisle. Grouped together, we were the only ones sitting in the pews. Mass began, we remembered our responses, and the young priest, assisted by two even younger acolytes, performed the service in its liturgical order. Everything was exactly as I remembered from the now-distant past. I forget what the sermon that followed was about, but its content didn't seem to me as important as the mere sound and music of my native language. Still, it was pure, poignant oratory of a kind seldom heard in those days. I was completely engrossed in it and then suddenly became aware of tears flowing from my eyes. I wasn't really crying, but I was deeply moved, and this emotion stayed with me until the priest came to the end of his sermon. It was then that I couldn't control it anymore: I began sobbing. It was unstoppable, and I don't recall caring whether anyone witnessed what was happening to me. Even with the service over, I hardly noticed my friends quietly filing out, leaving me to my emotional outburst.

I felt someone's hand on my shoulder and looked up to find the priest standing in the aisle next to me. I don't recall his exact words, but I think he asked me if I was all right and possibly offered his help. I must have declined that offer, because I remember him walking away. Shortly after, I regained my composure and joined my comrades, who were waiting for me outside on the truck's back panel. On our way back to Quakenbrück, any tactless questions about my crying jag were avoided, and none ever came up afterwards.

On the previous pages, I've described only three typical interrogations, but in reality, there must have been at least ten instances in which I, like all the other runaways from the East, were subjected to those good cop/bad cop grillings. From one occasion to the next, hope alternated with the fear of being shipped back to the Soviet zone. The latter would have meant either incarceration in the notorious, formerly Nazi-run (and now Soviet-operated) concentration camp in Bautzen or several years of hard labour in the uranium mines of Joachimstal near the Czech border.

Small wonder, then, that I can remember two separate occasions in which fellow inmates suddenly became quite irrational, screaming, beating their heads against the wall, and behaving like caged animals, only to just as suddenly retreat into sullen silence before gradually returning to normalcy. I am firmly convinced that their breakdowns were, like mine, the result of mental stress accumulated over a long time. We had seen the war with all its horror and barbarity, had spent years filled with hate and fear, and often on the run. Was it any wonder that at some time or other our minds would demand to be rid of those burdens and, frankly, snap?

On a murky Monday morning, along with two other ex-detainees, I said farewell to our comrades-in-misery left behind in the reception camp. We'd been told to pick up our belongings where they'd been taken from us, in the small building near the railway station. Nothing had changed since I'd first reported there. The man at the door was as hostile as before, and his boss, Dr. Gawenda, appeared equally surly as he handed us our belongings. When I checked the contents of my vandalized briefcase I saw that everything was still there. Only much later did I realize that my student ID from the Academy was missing. Each of us was handed twenty Deutschmarks for train fare to a place called Remagen where, we were told, an appropriate authority would provide us with well-paid employment.

The absence of my Academy identification card didn't worry me. I was too elated about being released from the verification camp's confinement to pay attention to such a seemingly minor detail. Only later did it occur to me that, since the Cold War was being fought by two world powers with intimidation, threats, and spying, an ostensibly innocent item such as a student ID card could enable someone to cross the borders that were gradually closing between Germany's western and eastern occupied zones. After all, it had served me well as proof of identity upon my arrival in Quakenbrück. A simple change of photo would give the bearer legality in the Soviet occupation zone and a chance at some fascinating intelligence work. But now that I was in the West and relatively free, I had worries other than those left behind in workers' heaven.

We left, but on our way to the railway station my companions stopped and, laughing grimly, told me that this "well-paid Remagen employment" was in reality heavy labour in French coal mines. They had both spoken with Polish refugees who had run away from those mines and were now working on German farms instead. Of course, now a little wiser, none of us headed for Remagen. I parted ways with them at the railway station and boarded a train that, with some transfers, took me to Bünde. From there, I walked the few kilometres to Muckum and the Middings' farm where Christine was staying.

I arrived both mentally and physically exhausted from the stress of my ordeal in Quakenbrück, the ever-present uncertainty about my eventual fate, and finally, my emotional breakdown. On arriving at the farm, I thanked its owners for putting us up and then slept for the rest of that day and through the following night.

28 FAREWELL TO EUROPE

It was the first time I had been in that part of Germany. The Middings' farmhouse was built in the characteristic Westphalian style: one large U-shaped building, all of it under a common roof, including a paved inner courtyard surrounded by stalls and pens for livestock and storage, with living quarters — kitchen, bedrooms, and a living room — at the bottom part of the U. All the rooms were quite small, and the somewhat musty living room was used only when special guests, such as the local pastor, came to visit. All other social life took place in the very roomy kitchen.

It was apparent to me that the Middings, like most German farmers, were fortunate in not having had to suffer the hunger and other miseries I had seen and experienced in East Germany. They were well fed and strong, the women brisk and cheerful, the men taciturn and sometimes projecting an aura of distrust. I never learned how large the farm was, but it clearly gave its owners complete self-sufficiency and probably some good money from the sales of whatever it produced.

Right from the beginning, it was clear that Christine and I could not just stay on the Middings' farm as non-paying guests. I had to find some sort of employment and earn enough Deutschmarks to leave the refugee status behind us. I had already written to my uncle in Winnipeg to tell him about our successful flight from the Soviet zone and about our readiness to leave Europe for Canada. This was, of course, the original plan my uncle and I had agreed upon in our letters while I was still in Dresden.

The search for work was more complicated than I had anticipated. Apart from having to walk the three or four kilometres from the village of Muckum to the small town of Bünde, where I might have found some employment, I ran directly into the web of German bureaucracy. At the local labour exchange I faced not only a variety of "maybes" and "come back laters," but also the legal barrier of a ruling which stipulated that one couldn't be given work unless one was a permanent resident. On the other hand, permanent residency status could be obtained only if one were already employed. And if that absurdity wasn't enough to satisfy the bureaucracy, there was yet another obstacle in the employment-seeker's way. He or she had to produce a document from the police, signed by a local government official, a physician, or a clergyman, stating that, to the best of his knowledge, the "above-mentioned" person was of good character and had no criminal record.

Our stay at the Middings' farm was, of course, only temporary, but I persuaded the head of that family to state in writing that I was now permanently domiciled at his address. The next step involved obtaining the certificate of good character and a blameless past. I got the appropriate form for this next step at the police station when I registered as a resident. Since I didn't know any government officials or physicians who would sign a certificate attesting to my flawless character, only a clergyman could help me out. I headed for the one and only church in the almost exclusively Protestant town of Bünde. The minister, an elderly man, instantly became suspicious of this refugee from the East and practically bristled when I told him I was a Pole. He queried me at some length about my past and fell silent rather suddenly when he learned that I had been baptized in the Catholic faith. Today, as I recall watching him at that moment, I am sure he must have been struggling between his own Protestant ideology and the Christian dictum to love your fellow man. After a while the latter won out. He turned to me, saying he would sign the certificate, even though he didn't know me beyond what I had told him about myself and even though I was of a different faith. He signed; I thanked him profusely, and made a quick exit.

The next morning I returned to the labour exchange where, to my delight, I was told that a graphic artist was needed at "some British office" and that the job didn't even require any knowledge of the English language. Fortunately, I had brought with me from Dresden a few examples of my graphic work, precisely with the idea of having them on hand if such a job were offered. I ran back to Muckum, told everyone about my stroke of luck, got my work samples and returned to Bünde to present myself at my prospective employer's place of business.

However, this wasn't just any ordinary business: it was the INFORMATION CENTRES SECTION of the INFORMATION SERVICES DIVISION attached to the CONTROL COMMISSION FOR GERMANY (BRITISH ELEMENT), located at the ZONAL EXECUTIVE OFFICES, BUENDE, 62 HQ. COG. BAOR. I was understandably impressed by this whole salad of names, numbers, and abbreviations (I already knew that the BAOR acronym stood for the British Army of the Rhine). I fully anticipated encountering officious-looking men in uniform rushing around, carrying important papers, as well as lots of other people busy at typewriters. But the medium-sized, two-storey building was quiet, with only a female receptionist in the hallway and a faint murmur of voices coming from various directions. After I had stated my business, the receptionist showed me to a room on the main floor, where a civilian gentleman named Bradshaw met me. I was offered a seat, showed him the examples of my work, my identification, and the proof of my studies at the Dresden Academy: a certificate of acceptance, signed by the then pro rector, Professor Sauerstein. The whole hiring process lasted no more than ten minutes. Mr. Bradshaw informed me about my wages, which were quite good, then told me about the working hours and took me upstairs to show me my desk and drafting board and to introduce me to my colleagues.

I started work the next day, designing portable displays for a travelling exhibition showing views of various British colonial possessions. I recall designing displays presenting daily life in Nigeria and Uganda, but there were, of course others, for example, showing the rebuilding of postwar Europe and the benefits of the Marshall Plan. I selected the readily available and pertinent photo material, drew up layouts, and, if necessary, painted landscape backgrounds. Since the exhibitions were shown only in West Germany, all lettering was done in German by lettering specialists

Working for the British Army on the Rhine (BAOR).

who were part of the graphics crew. Except for me, all members of that crew were German and had served in the Wehrmacht. Like all Germans, they were glad that the war was over. I had the feeling they looked askance at me, the Pole who worked with them as an equal, but I was already well acquainted with that kind of attitude and simply ignored it.

There was, however, a difficulty involved in my getting to and from work. Every morning, rain or shine, I had to walk those three kilometres from Muckum to Bünde and cover the same distance on my way back from work. There was no bus service on that stretch of road, and when late October rains turned into early November snow, I decided we had to move closer to town. However, Christine didn't want to leave the Middings' farm, so I found a room with another farming family, only a ten-minute walk away from Bünde.

Throughout that winter of 1948–49, I was in constant correspondence with my uncle in Winnipeg, primarily about our plans to leave Europe for Canada. As time went on, these plans progressed, mainly due to my uncle's efforts. Having been for many years involved in the travel business, he was now the owner of a Winnipeg-based travel agency and knew which buttons to push in order to get us across the Atlantic. Of course, I was also in regular and frequent contact with my father in Poland and was greatly relieved to learn that, despite the death of my mother and his own personal tragedy, he was slowly regaining his peace of mind and even some of his sparkling, wry wit. He still lived in Poznań, with a family whose daughter had pianistic ambitions, and he tutored the young woman in return for room and board. He was composing again, a fact which told me that, rather than just dwelling on the past, he was now looking toward the future.

Christmas 1948 came and went. The new year arrived, and with it came the news from Canada that the immigration department in Ottawa was studying our application to immigrate and settle in that country. However, even if this were granted, not only my uncle, but also an officially recognized refugee organization had to act as our sponsor. I didn't know whether the UN's International Refugee Organization was still active — after all, the war had been over for more than three years, and the millions of refugees wandering across Europe had surely by now returned home, or dispersed and settled in many other parts of the globe. Naturally, given the politics of postwar Poland, that country's government not only frowned upon, but, by closing the borders, actively discouraged, Poles from emigrating to the West. An exception was made in the case of the elderly, whom the State regarded as no longer useful. On the other hand, the Polish government encouraged the return of Polish refugees to their homeland, but neither Christine nor I were interested in accepting that invitation. It was a moot point, since my right to return had been revoked in 1947, probably as a result of my activities in the decidedly anti-Communist Polish Resistance. Not that I didn't feel a deep longing for my native land. Had postwar Poland's new political system been one based on democratic and humanist values, I would have returned home as a matter of course. But by now Canada had been in my mind for so long that I could hardly wait to get underway.

Toward the end of February 1949, my uncle sent me a letter he had received from the Canadian Department of Immigration, accepting

Christine and me as prospective immigrants. He added a note in which he told me that we were being co-sponsored, in addition to him, by the Canadian Christian Council for the Resettlement of Refugees. Things were really beginning to move, he wrote, but two matters still remained to be looked after before we could board the ship that would take us to Canada: a medical examination and a trip to Hamburg, where we could pick up our tickets at the Cunard Line offices and receive precise information about the port of embarkation and date of departure. It was hard to believe that all this was really happening, but sure enough, in early March, a letter arrived from the Canadian immigration department, instructing us to report, with our luggage, to a transit camp in Hanover for the medical check-up. We had a few days left to write letters — Christine to her parents in Dresden and I to my father in Poznań — notifying them of our impending departure. There was also sufficient time to settle any outstanding accounts with our hosts and for me to resign from my job with the British Information Services, from whom I received a highly complimentary letter of reference. I remember all our farewells as genuinely cordial.

We checked into the Hanover transit camp around March 10. Located in one of the city's suburbs, it had served during the war as housing for forced labourers, and after the war had become a DP (Displaced Persons) camp for those who were either waiting to return to their countries of origin or expecting to immigrate to various other countries in Europe or overseas. There were still a few such camps throughout Germany, all of them resembling, more or less, those with which I was familiar from my time in Dresden. However, this collection of dilapidated wooden sheds on the outskirts of Hanover was particularly grim. I counted five or six sheds standing close together, one of them given over to the Canadian administration and a medical examination room, and the others divided by thin plywood walls into small rooms, each containing two sets of double bunks and a puny wood stove. A little window let some daylight into the room assigned to us, but half of its glass was missing and had been replaced by a piece of heavy cardboard. In a corner of the camp stood a hut containing a kitchen which provided the inmates with food that was plentiful, monotonous, and mostly devoid of any discernible taste. But we didn't mind all that. Our thoughts were on the future.

Nor did we mind the presence of another couple in the room we occupied. I never learned their names, but that was not uncommon at a time when circumstances sometimes threw people together only briefly, huddling in a bomb shelter, for instance, or sitting in a railway station waiting room. This couple had originally come from Bukovina, an area located partly in Romania and partly in Ukraine. They were of German origin, descended from families who had emigrated from Germany to that area several generations back. The language they spoke was a strange mixture of Romanian, with some Slavic traces, a few words of odd-sounding German, and perhaps a bit of what sounded to me like Hungarian thrown in for good measure. Just the same, with the help of gestures, we managed to understand one another reasonably well. Their story closely resembled others I'd already heard, sometimes directly from people of German descent. Right after the 1939 invasion of Poland, many of them had been persuaded by the Nazi government to abandon their old domiciles in Latvia, Estonia, Hungary, Ukraine, Russia, and other East European countries, and move to the western Polish territories now annexed by Nazi Germany. Once there, they had received fully furnished homesteads and residences from which the Polish owners had been evicted, as well as all kinds of formerly Polish businesses and agricultural properties, from small farms to huge tracts of fertile land and attendant forests. Replete with farm machinery, livestock, homes, barns and stables, maybe even a fine manor here and there, all this was now to belong to the new owners in perpetuity, guaranteed by the government of the Third Reich. Small wonder then that the couple we shared a room with were proud of having risen from being dirt-poor farmers in Bukovina to unexpectedly becoming *Gutsbesitzer* (estate owners). This was, in fact, what the man proudly called himself when I first asked him what he did for a living. I'm sure it didn't even occur to him that the land and the house on it — a nice two-storey building with a colonnade in front — had been obtained by plain robbery. When he showed me a picture of that house, I asked if he knew what had happened to the previous owner. "Oh," he said. "They shot him."

"Who shot him?" I asked, whereupon he shrugged and said it was maybe the police or maybe the soldiers. However, when the Russians came, he said, and then the "Polacks," too, he and his wife had to flee, in the middle of the grim winter of 1944–45; and now they were going to live in Canada. In a subsequent talk we had, he made it quite clear that he hoped to someday return to his *Gutsbesitz* (estate) and take possession of it. After all, it had been given to him by the rightful German government, hadn't it? After that, I didn't even bother to speak to him again.

Our medical examinations took no more than ten minutes each, and once they were over, we were directed to the Canadian administration office. There, a bored-looking gentleman told us, in English, to report two days hence to the Cunard Line's office in Hamburg to receive our travel documents. From there, we would proceed to the port of Cuxhaven to board the MS *Samaria*, which would take us to the Canadian port of Halifax. My English consisting at that time of three words — *yes, no,* and *hello* — I could hardly understand what the man said. But, just as in the train station in Braunschweig, Christine's knowledge of the language came in handy and she was able to translate the gist of these instructions.

Two days later, with luggage in hand, we said farewell to our room-mates with a nod and a hand wave and happily left the camp to march off to the railway station. The journey to Hamburg took only a couple of hours, and once there, we easily found our way to the Alster Quay and the nearby Cunard Lines offices. I wasn't surprised to see how modest they were, located in what must once have been a very small store that had

The Samaria, *1949.*

somehow escaped not only the fierce Allied bombings but also the terrible firestorm of 1943. The little building stood in the midst of ruins and great mounds of rubble that had not yet been removed.

Inside, a middle-aged German-speaking man, pleasant and efficient, closely inspected our identification papers and the letters we'd received from the Canadian immigration authorities. After entering all this data in a large, important-looking volume, he finally handed us our tickets. We signed the appropriate receipts, thanked the man, and left. This had to be the first time I ever said "thank you" in English.

There was no time for us to vent our emotions, even though that moment was so profoundly moving. We had to run back to the railway station to catch the train to Cuxhaven, a port at the mouth of the Elbe estuary, about a hundred kilometres northwest of Hamburg and less than two hours away by train, stops included. We got to the station with mere minutes to spare. But even once the train was underway, we could say very little to one another. We were simply overcome by the sudden, unexpected speed with which events were unfolding. I looked out the window at the landscape gliding by, some of it urban, but most of it rural, thinking how it reminded me of the plains of western Poland, which I now so badly missed.

We spent the night in a modest hotel in Cuxhaven. Next morning, boarding the *Samaria* was quick and unceremonious. Our travel documents were checked once again, and we were shown to our respective cabins. Christine was to be accommodated in an ample space given over to several women, while I was directed to a similar area for male passengers. The *Samaria*, which had previously been a passenger vessel, had been turned into a troop ship during the war and now transported thousands of refugees from war-torn Europe to their destinations in North and South America.

The ship left the dock at midmorning, with only a few passengers (among them myself) actually aware of her departure. As she slowly moved out of the port and into open water of the North Sea, I walked down the main deck and stood at the stern, looking down at the wake, watching the land diminish on the horizon and finally disappear altogether.

INDEX

ABOUT THE AUTHOR

Jan Kamieński was born in Poznań, Poland, in 1923. In 1949 he immigrated to Winnipeg, Manitoba, where he worked as a commercial artist, designer, and illustrator. From 1958 to 1980 he was an editorial cartoonist and writer, art critic, and columnist for the *Winnipeg Tribune*. Between 1980 and 1988, when he retired, he was an editorial cartoonist for the *Winnipeg Sun*. After retirement, he returned to painting and has had his work showcased in a number of exhibitions in recent years. He continues to live in Winnipeg.

OF RELATED INTEREST